CASEY DUÉ

THE CAPTIVE WOMAN'S LAMENT IN GREEK TRAGEDY

University of Texas Press

AUSTIN

This book has been supported by an endowment dedicated to classics and the ancient world and funded by the Areté Foundation; the Gladys Krieble Delmas Foundation; the Dougherty Foundation; the James R. Dougherty, Jr. Foundation; the Rachael and Ben Vaughan Foundation; and the National Endowment for the Humanities. The endowment has also benefited from gifts by Mark and Jo Ann Finley, Lucy Shoe Meritt, the late Anne Byrd Nalle, and other individual donors.

Publication of this book has been aided also by a subsidy from the Center for Hellenic Studies.

LIBRARY OF CONGRESS CATALOGING-IN-PUBLICATION DATA

Dué, Casey, 1974–
The captive woman's lament in Greek tragedy / by Casey Dué. — 1st ed.
p.   cm.
Includes bibliographical references (p.   ) and index.
ISBN 0-292-70946-3 (cl. : alk. paper)
1. Greek drama (Tragedy)—History and criticism.   2. Laments—Greece—History and criticism.   3. Women and literature—Greece.   4. Prisoners of war in literature.
5. Women prisoners in literature.   6. Slavery in literature.   7. Revenge in literature.   8. Women in literature.   I. Title.
PA3136.D84   2006
882'.01093522—dc22   2005016159

CONTENTS

ACKNOWLEDGMENTS

I have received a great deal of support during the writing of this book. A University of Houston New Faculty Research Grant and a summer grant from the University of Houston Women's Studies Program allowed me to complete the bulk of the research and writing, and a Center for Hellenic Studies fellowship supported me in the final stages.

Portions of the book began as conference papers delivered at the University of Houston International Women's Day panel entitled "Women and War" (sponsored by the Women's Studies Program); the CAMWS annual meetings held in Austin, Texas, Lexington, Kentucky, and St. Louis, Missouri; and "Ética y estética: De Grecia a la modernidad," held at the Universidad Nacional de La Plata, Argentina. I would like to thank the audience members at each of these events for their questions and comments.

Several individuals have made invaluable contributions to my thinking and to the book that has resulted. I am grateful to Michael Anderson, Richard Armstrong, Francesca Behr, Mary Ebbott, Gloria Ferrari, Douglas Frame, Ryan Hackney, Leonard Muellner, Gregory Nagy, Kirk Ormand, and Dora Pozzi for reading and commenting on various portions and drafts of the book, as well as my readers for the University of Texas Press. Their close readings and insightful criticisms greatly improved the final product, though I am of course responsible for any remaining errors. My wonderful colleagues at the University of Houston, Richard Armstrong, Francesca Behr, and Dora Pozzi, deserve special thanks for their ongoing advice and support throughout the writing process.

I would also like to thank Jim Burr and Joanna Hitchcock of the University of Texas Press for initially soliciting the book and overseeing its writing, editing, and production.

Most especially I would like to express here my gratitude and appreciation to two people without whom I could never have completed this project:

my husband, Ryan, for his constant encouragement and brilliant editing; and my friend and colleague in all things, Mary Ebbott, whose thoughts on Greek tragedy and its presentation of marginal characters have been an inspiration throughout.

THE CAPTIVE WOMAN'S LAMENT IN GREEK TRAGEDY

INTRODUCTION

*What a pitiful sorrow it would be to hurl this primordial city
down to Hades, the slave and quarry of the spear in the crumbling
ash, destroyed and losing its honor at the hands of Achaean men
and through the will of the gods, with its women overcome and
taken into slavery—oh! oh!—young and old women alike, pulled
by the locks of their hair, as if they were horses held by the mane,
their veils all ripped and torn. The city, emptied, wails in many
different voices of lament for its lost population. I am afraid in
advance of the heavy doom that is to be.*
　　　　　　　　　—AESCHYLUS, *Seven Against Thebes* 321–32[1]

Laments of captive women play a substantial role in the Greek literature
that has come down to us. In the extract from *Seven Against Thebes* that I
cite above, the chorus of Theban women lament in anticipation of disaster,
envisioning with perfect clarity the simultaneous destruction of their city
and the capture and rape of its women. That disaster is never in fact realized,
since the Thebans are in the end victorious, but the laments of the chorus
make clear what is at stake in the siege. The laments of the extant tragedies
that deal with the Trojan War are similarly preoccupied with the plight of
the captive Trojan women, who, foreign and enslaved, would in all other
circumstances be completely without a voice in Greek society.[2]

1. The translations in this book are my own except where indicated.
οἰκτρὸν γὰρ πόλιν ὧδ᾽ ὠγυγίαν / Ἀίδα προϊάψαι, δορὸς ἄγραν / δουλίαν ψαφαρᾷ
σποδῷ / ὑπ᾽ ἀνδρὸς Ἀχαιοῦ θεόθεν / περθομέναν ἀτίμως, / τὰς δὲ κεχειρωμένας ἄγε-
σθαι, / ἒ ἔ, νέας τε καὶ παλαιὰς / ἱππηδὸν πλοκάμων, περιρ-/ρηγνυμένων φαρέων. βοᾷ /
δ᾽ ἐκκενουμένα πόλις, / λαΐδος ὀλλυμένας μιξοθρόου: / βαρείας τοι τύχας προταρβῶ.
2. Cf. Weil 1945 [translation by Mary McCarthy in Miles 1986, 191–92]: "here [in Attic
tragedy] the shame of the coerced spirit is neither disguised, nor enveloped in facile pity,
nor held up to scorn; here more than one spirit bruised and degraded by misfortune is
offered for our admiration."

This appreciation for the consequences that war brings about for women has a long history. In book 8 of the *Odyssey*, Odysseus is famously compared to a lamenting woman, fallen over the body of her husband, as she is being dragged away into captivity.

ταῦτ᾽ ἄρ᾽ ἀοιδὸς ἄειδε περικλυτός· αὐτὰρ Ὀδυσεὺς
τήκετο, δάκρυ δ᾽ ἔδευεν ὑπὸ βλεφάροισι παρειάς.
ὡς δὲ γυνὴ κλαίῃσι φίλον πόσιν ἀμφιπεσοῦσα,
ὅς τε ἑῆς πρόσθεν πόλιος λαῶν τε πέσῃσιν,
ἄστεϊ καὶ τεκέεσσιν ἀμύνων νηλεὲς ἦμαρ·
ἡ μὲν τὸν θνήσκοντα καὶ ἀσπαίροντα ἰδοῦσα
ἀμφ᾽ αὐτῷ χυμένη λίγα κωκύει· οἱ δέ τ᾽ ὄπισθε
κόπτοντες δούρεσσι μετάφρενον ἠδὲ καὶ ὤμους
εἴρερον εἰσανάγουσι, πόνον τ᾽ ἐχέμεν καὶ ὀϊζύν·
τῆς δ᾽ ἐλεεινοτάτῳ ἄχεϊ φθινύθουσι παρειαί·
ὡς Ὀδυσεὺς ἐλεεινὸν ὑπ᾽ ὀφρύσι δάκρυον εἶβεν.

(*Odyssey* 8.521–31)

The renowned singer sang these things. But Odysseus
melted, and wet the cheeks below his eyelids with a tear.
As when a woman laments, falling over the body of her dear husband
who fell before his city and people,
attempting to ward off the pitiless day for his city and children,
and she, seeing him dying and gasping,
falling around him wails with piercing cries, but men from behind
beating her back and shoulders with their spears
force her to be a slave and have toil and misery,
and with the most pitiful grief her cheeks waste away,
So Odysseus shed a pitiful tear beneath his brows.

The simile is so striking because the generic woman of the simile could easily be one of Odysseus' own victims. As Gregory Nagy has demonstrated, the simile picks up the narrative of the fall of Troy precisely where Demodokos' song is interrupted, with the fight raging near the house of Deiphobus (*Odyssey* 8.516–20).[3] Although the woman of the simile does not actually speak, the language of the simile has powerful associations with the lamentation of

3. On the internalized lamentation of Odysseus and the identification of the lamenting woman see Nagy 1979, 100–101. On Odysseus as one of his own victims see also Foley 1978, 7.

captive women elsewhere in epic, with the result that the listener can easily conjure her song.[4]

An equally striking simile is applied by Achilles to his own situation in *Iliad* 9:

ὡς δ᾿ ὄρνις ἀπτῆσι νεοσσοῖσι προφέρῃσι
μάστακ᾿ ἐπεί κε λάβῃσι, κακῶς δ᾿ ἄρα οἱ πέλει αὐτῇ,
ὣς καὶ ἐγὼ πολλὰς μὲν ἀΰπνους νύκτας ἴαυον,
ἤματα δ᾿ αἱματόεντα διέπρησσον πολεμίζων
ἀνδράσι μαρνάμενος ὀάρων ἕνεκα σφετεράων.

(*Iliad* 9.323–27)

Like a bird that brings food to her fledgling young
in her bill, whenever she finds any, even if she herself fares poorly,
so I passed many sleepless nights,
and spent many bloody days in battle,
contending with men for the sake of their wives.

As we will see, Achilles too draws on the suffering of captive women in order to articulate his own sorrow, as he struggles against his mortality and the pleas of his comrades that he return to battle. By using a traditional theme of women's laments, that of the mother bird who has toiled to raise her young only to lose them, Achilles connects on a visceral level with the women that he himself has widowed, robbed of children, and enslaved.[5]

The setting of the *Iliad* is the Trojan War, a war in which Greeks besiege and ultimately destroy a foreign city. The poem is remarkable for the way that its preoccupation with mortality and the human condition extends even to the enemy. The killing of Hektor by the central figure of the *Iliad*, Achilles, is a great victory for the Greeks, and yet the camera immediately shifts, as we witness the gut-wrenching reactions of Hektor's mother, father, and wife to his death. Similarly, the *Iliad* ends not with the funeral of Achilles, who is doomed to die very soon, but instead with the funeral of Hektor. Achilles' own short life and imminent death resonate throughout the laments that are sung for his deadliest enemy. In the words of Simone Weil, who was struck by the equity of compassion with which the suffering of the Greeks and Trojans is narrated: "The whole of the *Iliad* lies under the shadow of

---

4. See Dué 2002, 5–11.

5. I will return to this well-known simile in chapter 5, where I will discuss its associations with lamentation and vengeance in the context of both epic and tragedy.

the greatest calamity the human race can experience—the destruction of a city. This calamity could not tear more at the heart had the poet been born in Troy. But the tone is not different when the Achaeans are dying, far from home."[6]

The enslavement and sexual violation of women and the death of husbands are realities of war that are neither condemned nor avoided in epic poetry.[7] As Michael Nagler has shown, the taking of Troy is explicitly compared in the *Iliad* to the tearing of a woman's veil and hence characterized as a rape.[8] In *Iliad* 11, Diomedes mocks Paris for the minor wound that he has inflicted on him:

οὐκ ἀλέγω, ὡς εἴ με γυνή βάλοι ἢ πάϊς ἄφρων·
κωφὸν γὰρ βέλος ἀνδρὸς ἀνάλκιδος οὐτιδανοῖο.
ἢ τ᾿ ἄλλως ὑπ᾿ ἐμεῖο, καὶ εἴ κ᾿ ὀλίγον περ ἐπαύρῃ,
ὀξὺ βέλος πέλεται, καὶ ἀκήριον αἶψα τίθησι.
τοῦ δὲ γυναικὸς μέν τ᾿ ἀμφίδρυφοί εἰσι παρειαί,
παῖδες δ᾿ ὀρφανικοί· ὃ δέ θ᾿ αἵματι γαῖαν ἐρεύθων
πύθεται, οἰωνοὶ δὲ περὶ πλέες ἠὲ γυναῖκες.

(*Iliad* 11.389–96)

I don't care—it's as if a woman or senseless child struck me.
The arrow of a worthless coward is blunt.
But when I wound a man it is far otherwise. Even if I just graze his
    skin,
the arrow is piercing, and quickly renders the man lifeless.
His wife tears both her cheeks in grief
and his children are fatherless, while he, reddening the earth with his
    blood,
rots, and vultures, not women, surround him.

---

6. Weil 1945 [in Miles 1986, 189]. Weil's well-known essay was written in 1940, during the occupation of France.

7. On this point, see also Scodel 1998, citing *Iliad* 2.354–55: τὼ μή τις πρὶν ἐπειγέσθω οἶκον δὲ νέεσθαι / πρίν τινα πὰρ Τρώων ἀλόχῳ κατακοιμηθῆναι ("Let no one hasten to return home before sleeping beside a wife of the Trojans"). It should be noted, however, that this is said in the context of paying the Trojans back for the theft of Helen (2.356: τίσασθαι δ᾿ Ἑλένης ὁρμήματά τε στοναχάς τε, "and getting payment for his struggles and groans in connection with Helen").

8. See Nagler 1974, 44–63 and Monsacré 1984, 68–69. See also again the extract from the *Seven Against Thebes* cited above, which likewise equates the tearing of a woman's veil with the capture of a city.

The horror that Diomedes describes, which culminates in the enemy being left an unlamented corpse that will be eaten by vultures, will in fact be the fate of countless Trojans. And yet the *Iliad* is not without lamentation. The *Iliad* ends with the haunting songs of women who are soon to be the Greeks' captive slaves—widowed, foreign, old and young, they are the antithesis of the Greek citizen ideal, the ultimate other.[9] But the grief they initiate is a communal grief, a communal song of mourning that on the surface laments Hektor, but is even more fundamentally Achilles' own song of sorrow.[10]

Although there were many Greek tragedies about the Trojan War, it happens that the three surviving plays most appropriate for this study are all by Euripides. This is mostly an accident of survival. The Trojan War with its aftermath was a popular subject for tragedy, and we know the titles of many lost tragedies that must have featured captive women—Sophocles' *Aikhmalotides* ("The Captive Women") is a particularly suggestive example.[11] Other lost plays that may have featured the laments of captive women include Aeschylus' *Myrmidons, Award of the Arms (Hoplôn Krisis), Thracian Women,* and *Salaminian Women;* Sophocles' *Polyxena, Phrygians, Eurysakês,* and *Cassandra;* and Agathon's *Fall of Troy.*

Why were the Greeks (especially the Athenians) so fascinated with the plight of the captive Trojan women, their own victims in the war that serves as the cornerstone of Greek literary and artistic traditions? Although some might read this fascination as a simple manifestation of colonial imperialism, in this book I have chosen to pursue a different point of view. By analyzing the place of the laments of captive women in the tragedies that they occupy, I hope to show that the Athenians had a particular appreciation, inherited from epic, of the universality of wartime suffering, to the extent that they could explore their own sorrows by experiencing that of their enemies. At the same time, the Athenians maintained a very complex relationship with the Trojan War, such that at various points in the history of the fifth century the Athenians could distance themselves from the Greek collective and interpret the significance of the sack of Troy from the perspective of the defeated Trojans.

Recent work by scholars coming from a variety of specialties within our field has begun to show that the opposition between Greek and barbarian,

---

9. Helen is a special case. As I argue elsewhere, Helen (the wife/stolen concubine of Paris) evokes the captive woman in a foreign land, longing for legitimate status. This is especially true when she laments Hektor. See Dué 2002, 67.

10. See "Lamentation and the Hero" in Nagy 1979, 94–117 and Dué 2002, 67–81.

11. On the Trojan War as a subject for tragedy see Aristotle, *Poetics* 1459b.

while undoubtedly an important theme of Greek artistic and poetic tradi-tions, is not as strong a motif as the belief in the shared humanity of Greeks and foreigners. This is especially true of the Athenian treatment of Trojans in epic, drama, and art, but can even be extended to the Persians, as I will discuss in detail in chapter 2.[12] This equalizing and even conflation of Greek and foreigner is central to the very artistic traditions in which one would most expect to find oppositions: a Panhellenic poem about a united Greek expedition against an Asian city, the exploration of Athenian civic identity in tragedy, and the building program that celebrates Athenian victory and continuity in the face of the Persian sack of the city.

This line of argument directly confronts the predominant view among classicists and historians of the ancient world that sees Athenian exploration of their civic identity in the oppositions that are constructed in much of the Greek artistic and intellectual tradition between man and woman, master and slave, Greek and foreigner, and, finally, the eulogy of a state funeral and the wild lamentation of women.[13] The songs of captive women that occupy so much of Greek literature conflate all of these oppositions. In her conclusion to a recent book on the representation of women in Greek tragedy, Foley articulates the traditional view and then qualifies it:

> Unquestionably, ancient Greece left a legacy to later Western culture that reinforced symbolic links between female, "nature," domestic/private, emotion/the irrational, and passivity and male, culture, public, rational/the self-controlled, and activity. Greek conceptions of the self and of models of human achievement were also structured in our documents from a male point of view, with women, barbarians, slaves, and children serving to define less fully human alternatives. . . . At the same time, tragedy offers a dialogue in which women, slaves, barbarians, and even divinities are represented in a complex and powerful public performance.[14]

As Foley perceives, the categories of male, female, Greek, barbarian, slave, and free become blurred in Greek tragedy as often as they are sharply drawn.

---

12. For tragedy, see Hall 1989, 211–23; Croally 1994, 110–15; and Saïd 2002. For Athe-nian treatment of Trojans in art, see Anderson 1997 and Ferrari 2000. For the Persians, see Ebbott 2000 and 2005. For the Homeric epics, see Mackie 1996; Erskine 2001, 51–60; and chapter 3 below.

13. These dichotomies have been powerfully analyzed over the past few decades by a variety of scholars. See, e.g., Dubois 1984, Goldhill 1986, Loraux 1986, Hall 1989 and 1996, Cartledge 1993, and Croally 1994. For a theoretical critique of the limits of this kind of binary analysis see Gellrich 1995.

14. Foley 2001, 333.

This blurring is due in part to the nature of the genre, at least part of whose function is to question and hold up for criticism by inversion and exaggeration the institutions that are central to civic life.[15]

But there is more to the captive woman's lament than that. The plight of the captive woman is not simply a recurring theme by which Athenians explore and then ultimately reinforce their collective (and superior) identity. The emotions of tragedy ensure that Athenians at times identify with and at others react with pity to those who should be least like them, uniting all oppositions for the duration of the performance and perhaps even beyond it. Aeschylus' *Persians* is a tragedy that should not be a tragedy if we are to assert a rigid distinction between Greeks and barbarians. After all, the plot consists of the defeat of the Persians at Salamis, a great Athenian victory. The lamentation of the Persians upon defeat takes up a significant portion of the play. The *Persians* is a tragedy precisely because the Athenians had the capacity to see themselves in the Persians.[16]

As with the question of Greeks and barbarians, the prominence of women's songs in a medium that is composed and performed by and for men is surprising and poses serious challenges for the modern critic. In the case of women's laments the foundational work of Margaret Alexiou, *The Ritual Lament in the Greek Tradition,* shows that for this one category of feminine speech, at least, continuities can be traced from the oral epic poetry of the *Iliad* and *Odyssey* to Archaic and Classical Greek lyric and drama all the way through to modern Greek funeral lament.[17] This is a crucial point. The representation of women in tragedy is one of the most discussed issues in classical studies, and recent work has had mixed results.[18] Little evidence survives that can inform us about women's speech or song in "real life." All we have are the *representations* of women in men's literature, and the picture that this literature provides is demonstrably distorted. Nevertheless, the work of Laura McClure and others has gone a long way toward demonstrating useful ways in which the speech of women in tragedy and other genres can be analyzed.[19]

15. On the space between polarities that tragedy opens up, see also Gellrich 1995 and Ebbott 2005.

16. My use of the term "tragedy" here of course assumes that tragedy must be sorrowful. For further discussion, see chapter 2 and the conclusion.

17. Alexiou 1974.

18. A good introduction to the topic can be found in Griffith 2001. See also Easterling 1987, Bouvrie 1990, Seidensticker 1995, and Foley 2001.

19. See, e.g., McClure 1999 and Lardinois and McClure 2001. In general McClure has a far more pessimistic view of the significance attached to women's speech in Greek drama than I employ in this book. It should be noted, however, that I am addressing

In this book I do not attempt to evaluate or prove a theory about the relationship between the historical reality of Archaic and Classical Greek funeral laments and the stylized representations of lament in Greek tragedy.[20] Rather I am more interested in the way that the captive woman's lament functions as a theme in Greek epic and then tragedy, with its own particular conventions, resonance, and emotional impact. In chapter 1, however, I will address the relationship between women's song traditions and men's representations of those song traditions in the light of new comparative evidence.

A TAXONOMY OF TRAGIC LAMENT

What are the features of lament, and how do we see them expressed or represented in Greek tragedy? The Greek lament tradition has in fact over the past several decades attracted a great deal of attention from both classicists (who focus on the laments that survive in Archaic and Classical Greek literature) and anthropologists (who trace the continuity of ancient traditions in modern Greek communities, traditions that have persisted over perhaps more than 3,500 years).[21] The seminal work of Margaret Alexiou was the first to explore the continuity of this tradition. In recent years laments have been interpreted as powerful speech-acts, capable of inciting violent action. Many scholars have pointed out that in the context of la-

---

a particular genre of women's song, the lament, which I argue was the one sanctioned genre within which women could speak out in the Classical period, both onstage and in life. I acknowledge that lament was viewed as potentially dangerous and that attempts were made to suppress it in the Archaic and Classical periods. But as Loraux has shown, even while attempts were made to suppress the mourning voice of women in the *polis,* in tragedy it took center stage, and the ritual lament of women at funerals was never successfully suppressed; see chapter 1. McClure's work does not emphasize lament as a genre of speech in Greek tragedy (see, however, Lardinois and McClure 2001, 10); if she did so, our work might have more points of contact.

20. On the stylized representation of various genres of verbal art in Greek epic see Martin 1989, especially p. 225. On the relationship between actual funerary practices and the laments of Greek tragedy see Foley 2001, 21–29.

21. For ancient Greek laments see Alexiou 1974, Vermeule 1974, Loraux 1986, Sultan 1993, McClure 1999, Murnaghan 1999, and Dué 2002; for continuity in modern communities see Alexiou 1974 and 2001, Danforth 1982, Caraveli 1986, Seremetakis 1990 and 1991, Holst-Warhaft 1992, Herzfeld 1993, and Sultan 1999. See also the recent bibliography on lament in Roilos and Yatromanolakis 2002. Tsagalis 2004 unfortunately appeared only after this book was in press. I have, however, made references to it in notes wherever possible.

ment, women can voice subversive concerns, and speak in ways that they cannot under any other circumstances.[22] It is in fact one of the central aims of this book to point out the many instances in which women in tragedy use the "language of lament" to manipulate their listeners and achieve various goals.

For classicists who study ancient Greek laments, there are a number of formal examples that survive in Homeric epic and tragedy.[23] As will become clear, however, in this book I do not restrict my analysis to formal laments for the dead. The laments of tragedy are for the most part divorced from funerary ritual, in the sense that tragedy rarely presents to the viewer an actual funeral.[24] But there is of course a great deal of calamity and death in tragedy, and the conventions of Greek funeral lament are at the heart of the poetry of tragedy. Aeschylus' *Persians,* for example, consists mainly of a series of laments for the Persian war dead and for Persia as a nation. Other tragedies have a similar structure, particularly those for which the chorus

22. For the Greek tradition (ancient and modern), see especially Alexiou 1974, 21–22 and 124–25; Caraveli 1986; Serematakis 1990 and 1991; Holst-Warhaft 1992; and Foley 2001, 19–56. For parallels in other cultures see Nenola-Kallio 1982, Raheja and Gold 1994, Abu-Lughod 1999, and Davidson 2000. On the pervasive presence of the "abandoned woman" and her subversive role in literature, see Likping 1988 and Hagedorn 2004.

23. Although most extant Archaic lyric poetry is fragmentary, it too provides a great deal of evidence. See Alexiou 1974, 103–4. Of interest to this study are not only the *thrênoi* of the lyric poets (Simonides fragments 520–31 and Pindar fragments 129–39, on which see, e.g., Derderian 2001) but also the various compositions of Stesichorus and other lyric poets who treated the fall of Troy theme in their poetry. Stesichorus composed long narrative poems on many epic themes, including a *Sack of Troy* and a *Nostoi (Homeward Voyages)*. Unfortunately, only meager amounts of this poetry survive beyond the titles. Gregory Nagy has demonstrated the way that the final lines of Sappho 44 (the Wedding of Hektor and Andromache) interact with Iliadic epic traditions about Apollo, Hektor, and Achilles. (Πάον᾽ ὀνκαλέοντες ἐκάβολον εὐλύραν / ὕμνην δ᾽ Ἕκτορα κ᾽Ανδρομάχαν θεοεικέλο[ις, "Calling upon Paon the far-darter with the beautiful lyre, to sing of Hektor and Andromache the godlike.") See Nagy 1974, 134–39 and 1999, 28–29. On wedding songs as laments, see chapter 1.

24. There are important exceptions to this formulation, of course. One of these is the burial of Astyanax in the *Trojan Women,* and another is the lamentation that takes place at the tomb of Agamemnon in the *Libation Bearers.* I would argue, however, that even where we do find funerals or any of the various funeral rituals in tragedy, they are abnormal, corrupt, or otherwise extraordinary in some way. Foley (2001) deliberately focuses her study on the laments that do take place in a ritual context, while noting that the language of lament is used in a variety of other contexts in tragedy. See also Segal 1993, 15 for a discussion of the way that tragedy incorporates and transforms various forms of song by separating them from their cultic occasion.

is a group of captive women, or those that revolve around the death of a central hero.[25] Lamentation and funeral ritual are both incorporated into and transformed by tragedy, as Charles Segal has shown:

> All of the three extant tragedians incorporate within their plays the rites of lamentation that we know from archaic poetry and from other premodern societies. All draw heavily on the function of song in an oral culture to give ritualized expression to intense emotion and to provide comfort, solace, and security amid anxiety, confusion, and loss. By absorbing the cries of grief into the lyricism of a choral lament, the tragic poet is able to identify the emotional experience of suffering with the musical and rhythmic impulse of dance and song.[26]

Segal argues that while tragedy is heavily indebted to earlier poetic forms of commemoration and expression of suffering, it is also "radically new" in that it transforms whatever it uses and synthesizes genres and rituals in new ways.[27]

Formal laments for the dead in the Greek tradition generally conform to a three-part pattern, which consists of a direct address, a narrative of the past or future, and then a renewed address accompanied by reproach and lamentation.[28] In tragedy, these three elements are both combined and isolated from one another in countless ways to express immeasurable sorrow. Any one of the three parts may evoke the genre, emotions, and rituals of lament, thereby contributing to the overall atmosphere of sorrow and evoking the pity of the audience. Just as lamentation in tragedy is generally separated from the rites of an actual funeral, so also the poetic structure, traditional themes, and language of lament can be manipulated and employed with great effect in nonritual contexts.

Alexiou's study identifies three basic categories of Greek ritual laments: those for gods and heroes, those for the fall of cities, and those for the dead. Although the protagonists of tragedy are indeed heroes in the cultural and

---

25. Of the complete plays, fragments, and titles of Greek tragedies that survive, the following are a small selection of likely examples of tragedies whose structures revolve around extended laments: Phrynichus' *Capture of Miletus* and *Phoenician Women;* Aeschylus' *Libation Bearers, Niobe, Phrygians* (or *Ransom of Hektor*), *Thracian Women,* and *Salaminian Women;* Sophocles' *Aikhmalotides* (*Captive Women*), *Andromache, Electra, Polyxena;* Euripides' *Andromache, Bacchae, Hecuba, Suppliants,* and *Trojan Women.*

26. Segal 1993, 16.

27. Segal 1993, 13–15.

28. Alexiou 1974, 133. See also Lohmann 1970, 108–12; Foley 1999, 168–74; and Tsagalis 2004, 46–47.

religious sense of that word, I would argue that the laments of tragedy are most closely related to laments for the dead.[29] This is probably because tragedy does not for the most part represent the worship of heroes onstage, but rather their prototypical suffering and death. As in epic, the laments of tragedy are sung by family members for family members, as though this were the first time that the hero was ever lamented. In this way, what is a lament for the dead onstage becomes a lament for the hero on the part of the audience.

But whereas the majority of the laments of tragedy are a special combination of lament for the dead and lament for the hero, the laments of captive women span all three categories. Captive women lament their fallen city as much as they lament their husbands, brothers, and sons. The spectacle of Troy and its sack dominates the odes that Trojan women sing. As Shirley Barlow has noted, the odes "manage to create, through a series of brilliant images, the extraordinary physicality and intimacy of that place—its houses, its acropolis, its gates, its temples, its altars, its graven images."[30] Not all words spoken by captive women in these plays are formal laments, but they are infused with the traditional imagery, metaphors, and themes of laments for fallen cities and laments for the dead.

Alexiou shows that the lament for the fall of cities, an important Byzantine poetic tradition, particularly after the fall of Constantinople in 1453, was already a traditional form of song in classical times.[31] The following passages from Aeschylus' *Persians* are adduced by Alexiou to demonstrate some of the features of this kind of lament:

Ξε. βεβᾶσι γὰρ τοίπερ ἀγρέται στρατοῦ.
Χο. βεβᾶσιν, οἴ, νώνυμοι.

(Persians 1002–3)

XERXES: Gone then, are the army's leaders.
CHORUS: Gone, alas, unnamed!

Ξε. πεπλήγμεθ᾽ οἴᾳ δι᾽ αἰῶνος τύχᾳ·
Χο. πεπλήγμεθ᾽: εὔδηλα γάρ·

(Persians 1008–9)

---

29. On this point see also Nagy's discussion of the terms *thrênos* and *goos* in tragedy (Nagy 1994–1995a and 1998). See Dué and Nagy 2003 for an introduction to Greek hero cults.
30. Barlow 1986, 35.
31. Alexiou 1974, 84.

XERXES: We are stricken with misfortune through the ages.
CHORUS: We are stricken—it is too clear.[32]

In these passages we find the use of the perfect tense, which conveys the idea that prosperity, happiness, and the city itself have vanished.[33] We may compare *Trojan Women* 582: βέβακ᾽ ὄλβος, βέβακε Τροία ("Happiness has gone, Troy has gone"). The antiphonal structure exhibited here is a fundamental feature of these laments and indeed all Greek laments.[34] In both the *Hecuba* and the *Trojan Women* there are multiple exchanges between Hecuba and the chorus, as well as between Hecuba and the other protagonists. In the *Andromache,* Andromache and her young son lament their impending deaths in a similar antiphonal exchange.

An anonymous tragic fragment about the defeat of the Persians is cited by Alexiou to demonstrate another important feature of laments for the fall of cities, and that is a series of questions, usually beginning with "where?":

Ποῦ γὰρ τὰ σεμνὰ κεῖνα; ποῦ δὲ Λυδίας
μέγας δυνάστης Κροῖσος ἢ Ξέρξης βαθὺν
ζεύξας θαλάσσης αὐχέν᾽ Ἑλλησποντίας;
ἅπαντ᾽ ἐς Ἅιδην ἦλθε καὶ Λήθης δόμους.

Where are those majestic things? Where is Kroisos,
great lord of Lydia, or Xerxes, who yoked
the deep neck of the sea of Hellespont?
All are gone to Hades' and Lethe's halls.[35]

Questions beginning with "where?", accompanied by an answer in the perfect tense, are the mark of laments for fallen cities, but questions are a common feature of laments for the dead as well.[36] The mourner asks how she can begin to express her grief, or reproaches the dead by asking why he has left her or why he has abandoned his family. The captive woman's lament combines these themes, as the city, husbands, and children are mourned together, and the mourner expresses fear and anxiety about her own future in captivity and longs for death.[37]

32. The translations here are Alexiou's (1974, 84).
33. Cf. *Persians* 249–52, discussed in chapter 2 below.
34. See Alexiou 1974, 131–60 and Tsagalis 2004, 48–50.
35. Fragment 909.372 (Nauck). Translation is Alexiou's.
36. See Alexiou 1974, 161–65 and 182–84.
37. On the mourning woman's fears for her own future see also Herzfeld 1993.

As a stunning example of the combination of themes and emotions that
converge in the captive woman's lament I cite again the antiphonal choral
passage from the *Trojan Women* mentioned above:

Αν. Ἀχαιοὶ δεσπόται μ᾽ ἄγουσιν.
Εκ. οἴμοι. Αν. τί παιᾶν᾽ ἐμὸν στενάζεις;
Εκ. αἰαῖ Αν. τῶνδ᾽ ἀλγέων
Εκ. ὦ Ζεῦ Αν. καὶ συμφορᾶς.
Εκ. τέκεα Αν. πρίν ποτ᾽ ἦμεν.

Εκ. βέβακ᾽ ὄλβος, βέβακε Τροία
Αν. τλάμων. Εκ. ἐμῶν τ᾽ εὐγένεια παίδων.
Αν. φεῦ φεῦ Εκ. φεῦ δῆτ᾽ ἐμῶν
Αν. κακῶν. Εκ. οἰκτρὰ τύχα
Αν. πόλεος Εκ. ἃ καπνοῦται.

Αν. μόλοις, ὦ πόσις μοι
Εκ. βοᾶις τὸν παρ᾽ Ἅιδαι
παῖδ᾽ ἐμόν, ὦ μελέα.
Αν. σᾶς δάμαρτος ἄλκαρ.

Αν. †σύ τ᾽†, ὦ λύμ᾽ Ἀχαιῶν
Εκ. τέκνων δή ποθ᾽ ἁμῶν
    πρεσβυγενὲς Πριάμωι.
Αν. κοιμίσαι μ᾽ ἐς Ἅιδου.

Αν. οἵδε πόθοι μεγάλοι Εκ. σχετλία, τάδε πάσχομεν ἄλγη
Αν. οἰχομένας πόλεως Εκ. ἐπὶ δ᾽ ἄλγεσιν ἄλγεα κεῖται.
                                    (*Trojan Women* 577–97)

ANDROMACHE: The Achaean masters are leading me away.
HECUBA: Woe is me! ANDROMACHE: Why do you sing my own song of
    lament?
HECUBA: Alas! ANDROMACHE: Alas for this pain—
HECUBA: Oh Zeus! ANDROMACHE: and disaster!
HECUBA: Children! ANDROMACHE: We were once your children.

HECUBA: Happiness has gone, Troy has gone!
ANDROMACHE: Miserable! HECUBA: And the nobility of my children is
    gone!
ANDROMACHE: Alas! Alas! HECUBA: Alas for my

ANDROMACHE: evils. HECUBA: Pitiful is the fortune
ANDROMACHE: of the city HECUBA: which is now smoldering.

ANDROMACHE: Please come, my husband—
HECUBA: You call for one who is in Hades,
    and my son, unhappy woman!
ANDROMACHE: please come as defender of your wife!

ANDROMACHE: You, the outrage of the Achaeans,
HECUBA: the eldest of my
    children by Priam.
ANDROMACHE: Take me to Hades.

ANDROMACHE: Great is my longing [*pothoi*]— HECUBA: Wretch, we
    suffer this pain—
ANDROMACHE: for the city that is gone. HECUBA: pain lies on top of
    pain.

Here Andromache and Hecuba lament the city of Troy, Hektor, their children, and their own suffering in a dizzying antiphonal exchange. The complex
combination of themes and emotions is signaled by the structure, in which
Andromache and Hecuba at some points complete each other's sentences,
and at others interrupt with a completely different syntax.[38]

As I will argue in chapter 2 with reference to the *Persians,* the word *pothos*
invoked by Andromache here conveys several ideas at the same time. In the
first instance, the longing might be assumed to be that of a wife for her
husband. At the same time the audience experiences or at least is reminded
of longing for the absent hero. But in the next line, Andromache completes
the thought, and the *pothos* becomes a longing for the city of Troy.[39]

Just as tragedy makes use of the initial questions of traditional laments to
express the desperation of captive women, so also do captive women narrate
the past in order to articulate the contrast between their past and present
experiences.[40] In the *Hecuba,* for example, Polyxena laments herself as she
expresses her willingness to die:

τί γάρ με δεῖ ζῆν; ἢ πατὴρ μὲν ἦν ἄναξ
Φρυγῶν ἁπάντων· τοῦτό μοι πρῶτον βίου·

38. Cf. similar exchanges at *Hecuba* 414–31 and *Andromache* 504–36.
39. See chapter 2.
40. On the contrast between past and present as a typical theme of Greek laments,
see Alexiou 1974, 165–77 and Tsagalis 2004, 44–45, and as a typical theme of Greek love
songs, see Carson 1986, 117–22.

ἔπειτ' ἐθρέφθην ἐλπίδων καλῶν ὕπο
βασιλεῦσι νύμφη, ζῆλον οὐ σμικρὸν γάμων
ἔχουσ', ὅτου δῶμ' ἑστίαν τ' ἀφίξομαι·
δέσποινα δ' ἡ δύστηνος Ἰδαίαισιν ἦ
γυναιξὶ παρθένοις τ' ἀπόβλεπτος μέτα,
ἴση θεοῖσι πλὴν τὸ κατθανεῖν μόνον·
νῦν δ' εἰμὶ δούλη.

(EURIPIDES, *Hecuba* 349–57)

Why is it necessary for me to live? I whose father was lord
of all the Phrygians? This was the most important thing in life for me.
Then was I nursed on fair hopes
to be a bride for kings, the object of considerable rivalry among suitors,
to see whose home and hearth I would make my own;
and over the women of Ida I was queen—I, the unfortunate one!—
a maiden marked amid women and girls,
equal to the gods, save for death alone.
But now I am a slave.

Polyxena's lament is striking precisely because it is not a lament for the dead. Lamenting women often describe the plight in which the dead man (be he husband or father) has left them, speculating on the miseries that await them. As Michael Herzfeld has shown in his work on modern Crete, Greek women traditionally do this in an attempt to gain sympathy and make a place for themselves in the living community, now that they no longer have the protection of the man who has died.[41] But Polyxena is here narrating her life story in anticipation of her own death; she no longer has a place in the living community.

Andromache too narrates her life experiences, combining her story with the desperate questions and longing for death that are likewise traditional components of laments for the dead:[42]

ἥτις σφαγὰς μὲν Ἕκτορος τροχηλάτους
κατεῖδον οἰκτρῶς τ' Ἴλιον πυρούμενον,
αὐτὴ δὲ δούλη ναῦς ἐπ' Ἀργείων ἔβην

41. Herzfeld 1993.
42. Cf. Andromache's rhetorical question just a few lines earlier: ὡς δεινὰ πάσχω. τί δέ με καὶ τεκεῖν ἐχρῆν / ἄχθος τ' ἐπ' ἄχθει τῷδε προσθέσθαι διπλοῦν; ("What terrible things I have suffered! Why did I have to give birth and add sorrow on top of sorrow?" *Andromache* 395–96). On the wish for death as a typical theme of Greek laments, see Alexiou 178–81 and Tsagalis 2004, 42–44.

κόμης ἐπισπασθεῖσ᾽· ἐπεὶ δ᾽ ἀφικόμην
Φθίαν, φονεῦσιν Ἕκτορος νυμφεύομαι.
τί δῆτ᾽ ἐμοὶ ζῆν ἡδύ; πρὸς τί χρὴ βλέπειν;
πρὸς τὰς παρούσας ἢ παρελθούσας τύχας;
εἷς παῖς ὅδ᾽ ἦν μοι λοιπὸς ὀφθαλμὸς βίου·
τοῦτον κτενεῖν μέλλουσιν οἷς δοκεῖ τάδε.

(EURIPIDES, *Andromache* 399–407)

I endured the sight of the Hektor's death by dragging from a chariot,
and of Ilium piteously burning.
I myself embarked on an Argive ship as a slave,
dragged by my hair. And when I arrived in
Phthia, I became the bride of Hektor's killers.
How, then, is life sweet for me? Where can I look?
To my present or my past fortunes?
I had one child left to me, the light of my life,
and those to whom these things seem best intend to kill him.

Captive women frequently lament themselves in anticipation of death
and disaster, because lament is the only medium through which women have
a sanctioned public voice, the one weapon they have with which to defend
themselves in desperate circumstances. Here, Andromache's words are
addressed to Menelaus (who is threatening to kill her and her son) and
to the chorus of Greek women of Phthia. The chorus' reaction is telling:
ᾤκτιρ᾽ ἀκούσασ᾽ ("Upon hearing [her words], I pity her," 421). Compare
the chorus' reaction to Andromache's earlier, more rational (and masculine)
arguments: ἄγαν ἔλεξας ὡς γυνὴ πρὸς ἄρσενας ("You have said too much
for a woman speaking to men," 364).[43] We can see that whereas her previous
reasoned arguments failed, the emotionally powerful and traditional form
of lament has gained for Andromache not only the approval of the Greek
chorus, but even their sympathy.

Euripides' surviving tragedies that deal most directly with the sack of
Troy theme feature captive women not only as protagonists but also as the
chorus. In the *Hecuba* and the *Trojan Women,* the suffering of Hecuba as
an individual is balanced against the suffering of the Trojan Women as a
collective in the choral odes. Thus the plays comprise a series of laments
by Hecuba, interspersed with choral odes that are themselves laments and

43. The translation here is that of Lloyd (1994).

exemplify many traditional aspects of the genre. In Euripides' *Trojan Women*, the captive women who make up the chorus of the drama call upon the Muse and propose to sing a new kind of song about Troy:

ἀμφί μοι Ἴλιον, ὦ / Μοῦσα, καινῶν ὕμνων / ἄεισον ἐν δακρύοις ᾠδὰν
ἐπικήδειον· / νῦν γὰρ μέλος ἐς Τροίαν ἰαχήσω, / τετραβάμονος ὡς ὑπ'
ἀπήνας / Ἀργείων ὀλόμαν τάλαινα δοριάλωτος, / ὅτ' ἔλιπον ἵππον
οὐράνια / βρέμοντα χρυσεοφάλαρον ἔνο-/πλον ἐν πύλαις Ἀχαιοί·

(Trojan Women 511–21)

Sing for me, O Muse, the story of Troy, a mournful song in new strains, with tears; for now I will cry out a song for Troy, telling how as a wretched captive of war I was destroyed by the four-footed beast that moved on wheels, when the Achaeans left at our gates that horse, loud rumbling to the sky, with its trappings of gold and its freight of warriors.[44]

What follows is an account of the fall of Troy, told from the perspective of the now-captive Trojan women. When the wooden horse was brought into Troy, everyone rejoiced with songs (529). At night choruses of young women danced and sang to Phrygian tunes from the Libyan pipe (544–47) and torches were lit in the houses (548–50). The chorus then goes on to recount how they were in the palace dancing and singing in honor of Artemis when they heard the "bloody shout" (551–57):

βρέφη δὲ φίλι-/α περὶ πέπλους ἔβαλλε μα-/τρὶ χεῖρας ἐπτοημένας· /
λόχου δ' ἐξέβαιν' Ἄρης, / κόρας ἔργα Παλλάδος. / σφαγαὶ δ' ἀμφιβώμιοι
/ Φρυγῶν, ἔν τε δεμνίοις / καράτομος ἐρημία / νεανίδων στέφανον ἔφερεν
/ Ἑλλάδι κουροτρόφον, / Φρυγῶν πατρίδι πένθη.

(Trojan Women 557–67)

Beloved infants threw their arms around the garments of their mothers, terrified; Ares was emerging from his place of ambush. It was the work of the maiden Pallas. Phrygians were slaughtered at the altar, and among the bed linens headless desolation offered up a crown of young

---

44. Translation after that of Coleridge (1891). For another female chorus that proposes a new kind of song to be sung, representing an alternative tradition about women, cf. *Medea* 410–45.

women to raise sons for Greece, and sorrow [*penthos*] for the land of the Phrygians.[45]

In this book I argue that in the Greek tradition women have always sung songs about wars and the deeds of heroes. But when they tell the tale of Troy, the song is one of *penthos,* not *kleos.*[46] Here the chorus recounts events that were narrated in an epic tradition now lost to us, the *Ilioupersis* ("Sack of Troy"). This song allows its Greek audience to visualize the events through the eyes of the other side. For the duration of the song the audience experiences *as a Trojan,* and even more extraordinarily, *as a woman,* first the euphoria of believing the war to be over and then the horror of the sack of the city. In men's songs about Troy, heroes kill their warrior opponents, and both men win *kleos.*[47] In women's songs, children are terrified, husbands are slain, and women are raped and taken captive. Just as the protagonists of the Trojan War plays such as Hecuba, Polyxena, and Andromache tell the tale of Troy through lament, so too do the choruses of these plays offer an alternative version, a new song about the fall of Troy, told from the point of view of the women who survived it.

In the *Hecuba,* a no less extraordinary account of the sack is sung and danced by the chorus:

μεσονύκτιος ὠλλύμαν, / ἦμος ἐκ δείπνων ὕπνος ἡδὺς ἐπ' ὄσσοις / σκίδναται, μολπᾶν δ' ἄπο καὶ χοροποιῶν / θυσιᾶν καταλύσας / πόσις ἐν θαλάμοις ἔκει-/το, ξυστὸν δ' ἐπὶ πασσάλῳ, / ναύταν οὐκέθ' ὁρῶν ὅμι-/λον Τροίαν / Ἰλιάδ' ἐμβεβῶτα.

ἐγὼ δὲ πλόκαμον ἀναδέτοις / μίτραισιν ἐρρυθμιζόμαν / χρυσέων ἐνόπτρων λεύσ-/σουσ' ἀτέρμονας εἰς αὐγάς, / ἐπιδέμνιος ὡς πέσοιμ'·

---

45. These lines are extremely difficult to translate, and I consulted many published translations in order to formulate my own. The adjective χαράτομος ("headless") in line 564 agrees with the abstract noun ἐρημία ("desolation, being left alone") and is thought to refer to the murdered husbands of the Trojan women, who are then raped in their beds. I have translated it literally in order to reproduce the Greek as accurately as possible. It is not entirely clear on which noun the genitive νεανίδων in line 565 depends, but it is most closely connected with στέφανον, and I have translated accordingly.

46. On the equivalence of *kleos* and *penthos* in Greek epic, see Nagy 1979, 94–117 and chapter 1.

47. I don't mean to suggest that the actions of the Greeks were praised or sanctioned in the *Ilioupersis* tradition. In the *Iliad* the gods express outrage at the mutilation of Hektor's corpse by Achilles, but the poem is nevertheless a song of *kleos.* Also, as I discuss in chapter 1, epic poetry often incorporates the song traditions of women, particularly laments, within the epic narrative so that in epic too lament can provide an alternative perspective on the action.

ἐς εὐνάν. / ἀνὰ δὲ κέλαδος ἔμολε πόλιν· / κέλευσμα δ᾽ ἦν κατ᾽ ἄστυ
Τροί-/ας τόδ᾽· ὦ / παῖδες Ἑλλάνων, πότε δὴ πότε τὰν / Ἰλιάδα σκοπιὰν
/ πέρσαντες ἥξετ᾽ οἴκους;

　　λέχη δὲ φίλια μονόπεπλος / λιποῦσα, Δωρὶς ὡς κόρα, / σεμνὰν
προσίζουσ᾽ οὐκ / ἤνυσ᾽ Ἄρτεμιν ἁ τλάμων· / ἄγομαι δὲ θανόντ᾽ ἰδοῦσ᾽
ἀκοίταν / τὸν ἐμὸν ἅλιον ἐπὶ πέλαγος, / πόλιν τ᾽ ἀποσκοποῦσ᾽, ἐπεὶ /
νόστιμον / ναῦς ἐκίνησεν πόδα καί μ᾽ ἀπὸ γᾶς / ὥρισεν Ἰλιάδος· / τάλαιν᾽,
ἀπεῖπον ἄλγει.　　　　　　(EURIPIDES, *Hecuba* 914–42)

It was in the middle of the night my ruin came, in the hour when sleep
steals sweetly over the eyes after the feast is done. My husband, the music
over, and the sacrifice that initiates the dance now ended, was lying in
our bridal-chamber, his spear hung on a peg, with never a thought of the
throng of sailors encamped upon the Trojan shores.

　　I meanwhile was braiding my hair in a headband before my golden
mirror's countless rays, so that I might lay down to rest in my bed; when
through the city rose a din, and a cry went ringing down the streets of
Troy, "O sons of Hellas, when, oh! when will you sack the citadel of Ilium,
and seek your homes?"

　　Up sprang I from my bed, with only a tunic about me, like a Dorian
girl, and sought in vain, ah me! to station myself at the holy hearth of
Artemis; for, after seeing my husband killed, I was hurried away over the
broad sea; with many a backward look at my city, when the ship began
her homeward voyage and parted me from Ilium's shore; until alas! I suc-
cumbed to grief.[48]

The perspective of this ode is even more intimate than that of the *Trojan
Women*. The chorus describes how they were in their bedrooms, preparing
for bed. The feast and dancing are over and the weapons have been hung up
on their pegs when the shouts begin. At this moment, the chorus, describing
their state of undress when Troy fell, makes an extraordinary comparison:
they were dressed only in their tunics (*monopeplos*, 933), "like a Dorian girl."
In describing that moment of shock and horror in which the Trojan women
spring from their marriage beds, realize what is happening, and seek refuge
with Artemis, the chorus compares themselves to a Greek girl—momentarily
collapsing the distinction between Greek and Trojan amidst the chaos of a
city under assault.

　　This choral ode from the *Hecuba* has as much in common with traditional
laments for the dead as it does with laments for the fall of cities. This kind

48. Translation after that of Coleridge (1891).

of song, common to both captive female protagonists and choruses in Greek tragedy, combines grief for the loss of one's home with the helplessness and anxiety about the future traditionally expressed in laments for individuals. In this way the captive woman's lament merges two traditions and becomes a category in its own right, with its own conventions and emotional force.

This category of lament is itself closely tied to a similar and overarching phenomenon in Greek tragedy: women who lament themselves. As Alexiou has pointed out, Cassandra, the suppliant women of Aeschylus, Jocasta, Antigone, Deianeira, Alcestis, Hecuba, Polyxena, Medea, Phaedra, Andromache, and Iphigeneia all perform laments for themselves in anticipation of death or disaster.[49] Of these, Cassandra, Hecuba, Polyxena, and Andromache are captive Trojan women. Medea, it could be argued, casts herself in the role of the captive woman in order to gain sympathy and indulgence from Jason while she formulates her revenge. Several of the remaining women on the list in fact commit suicide, the culmination of the helplessness to which their lamentation gives voice. In this way tragedy reinvents the characteristic wish for death on the part of the mourner, and turns the mourner into the lamented dead.

So far I have stressed the traditional form of Greek laments and the way that the captive woman's lament in Greek tragedy manipulates this form in order to speak out and elicit the sympathy of the other characters and the audience. As we will see in the ensuing chapters, the traditional content of laments for the dead—including traditional metaphors, imagery, and themes—is likewise incorporated into the songs of captive women. Many laments in the Greek tradition are also love songs or songs about the loss of love.[50] Erotic imagery and reflections on marriage are intertwined with grief and sorrow, thereby uniting the traditional concerns of Greek women in a single but

49. Alexiou 1974, 113. Included in Alexiou's list are also some men: Ajax, Oedipus, and Philoctetes. For Ajax, see discussion below. Although lament seems to have been the particular province of women, men do lament in Greek epic and tragedy (see, e.g., Monsacré 1984; Foley 2001, 28–29).

50. For modern Greek parallels, see Caraveli-Chavez 1978. In the modern Greek tradition many laments for the dead are also wedding songs, and, as was the ancient practice, young people who die before marriage are buried in their wedding clothes. (See Alexiou 1974, 120–22 and Danforth 1982, 74–91; for parallels in the Russian tradition, see Nagy 1994–1995b, 51.) On shared themes and metaphors, see also Alexiou and Dronke 1971 and Alexiou 2001, 399–410. The conflation of marriage and death in ancient Greek literature and art has been well studied—see, e.g., Seaford 1987; Rehm 1994; Ferrari 2002b, 190–93.

constantly shifting emotional dynamic. The tragedians develop these traditional themes of love, loss, marriage, and death in the tragedies that feature women as protagonists precisely because these are the themes particularly associated with women's song traditions. As I have argued elsewhere, captive women fulfill one of two paradigms: they are either unmarried women who have lost their fathers, or married women who have lost their husbands.[51] The first group, represented by such figures as Polyxena and Cassandra, are depicted as being on the verge of marriage or else eminently marriageable; they narrate their girlhood and lament the marriage they should have had. The second group consists of women who have been married but are often depicted as young brides, cruelly separated from their newly wed husbands. All use the language of lament to speak out about their own suffering and the consequences of war for women.

MARGINAL FIGURES AND CHORAL AUTHORITY

The central importance of the chorus for the theme and plot of any given drama is underscored by the titles assigned to these tragedies by our sources, which frequently name the play after the composition of the chorus (e.g., the *Libation Bearers* of Aeschylus or the *Trachinian Women* of Sophocles). Choruses comprising captive women are a relatively common feature of Greek tragedy. It is therefore important to consider the significance of choral identity and the function of choruses in general if we are to assess the thematic impact in tragedy of captive women and their laments.

Current scholarship on the chorus of Greek tragedy is very much divided, however, in its interpretation of the nature of the chorus itself and its relationship to the audience. Many scholars emphasize the role that the chorus plays in reacting to events onstage on behalf of the audience. They are the physical, cognitive, and emotional link between the world of the heroes in the drama and the world of the fifth-century Athenian audience; the audience therefore experiences the action and suffering of the drama by way of the chorus.[52] In recent years, however, there have been several studies that seek to undermine the authority of the chorus by emphasizing its marginality and frequent lack of knowledge or agency within the plays.

---

51. Dué 2002, 65.

52. See, e.g., Vernant and Vidal-Naquet 1990, as well as the modifications, clarifications, and further development offered in Longo 1990, Henrichs 1994–1995 and 1996, Nagy 1994–1995b, and Goldhill 1996.

John Gould writes: "[the members of the chorus] express, not the values of the *polis,* but far more often the experience of the excluded, the oppressed, and the vulnerable."[53]

The former view of the chorus must therefore account for the extraordinary disparity between the Athenian citizen audience and the marginal identity of the chorus of most dramas.[54] For choruses of captive women, we must ask how characters who are wholly opposite to the Greek citizen male could speak to the values of those in the audience or teach the young men portraying them. It is in fact the disparity between the chorus member and the character of the captive woman he becomes in performance that is one of the more extraordinary aspects of the captive woman's lament.

The most obvious category separating the Athenian audience and many tragic choruses is gender. Helene Foley points out that female choruses outnumber male ones by 2 to 1 in extant tragedy.[55] Claude Calame, moreover, has demonstrated some of the many continuities (as well as the discontinuities) involved in the incorporation of choruses of young women from Archaic and aristocratic festival contexts into the world of the City Dionysia.[56] The impersonation of the choral dancing of adolescent females by adolescent males seems to have been a crucial element in the experience of being a chorus member.

The choral singing and dancing of young men in tragic choruses is only one component of tragedy's engagement with feminine modes of discourse, however, and is part of a larger structure. The classic study in English of the feminine and the theater is Froma Zeitlin's *Playing the Other* (1996), which draws on her own earlier pathfinding work and that of other scholars such as Nicole Loraux and Jean-Pierre Vernant. In her analyses of several individual works of epic, tragedy, and comedy, Zeitlin articulates the theory that Greek tragedy uses the feminine to explore the masculine, and does so under the aegis of the god Dionysus, who is the god most clearly associated with the crossing of boundaries and the impersonation of the other. The experience of "playing the other" belongs to both the actors onstage and the spectators in the audience, and it is by no means confined to the playing of female

53. Gould 1996, 224. On this view of the chorus see also Mastronarde 1998. On the marginal identity of many Greek choruses see also Foley 2003. On marginal characters (including but not limited to choruses) in Greek tragedy, see Ebbott 2005.

54. Goldhill (1996) has in fact carefully answered the arguments of Gould (1996) and in my opinion establishes the collectivity of the chorus as one of the several authoritative voices within the *agôn* of a given tragedy.

55. Foley 2001 and 2003.

56. Foley 2001, 6 and Calame 1994–1995, who also cites the important work of Webster (1970) and Herington (1985) in this area. On choral performances by actual young women (as opposed to young men playing women), see Calame 1999a.

roles by male actors. The tragedies of Euripides offer the most complete exploration of the phenomenon:

> [T]he distinctive features of Euripidean theater . . . may lend support to my suggestion about the intimate relations between the feminine and the theater. Thus, I see the distinctive traits in Euripidean drama as various and interlocking functions of one another: his greater interest in and skill at subtly portraying the psychology of the female characters and his general emphasis on interior states of mind as well as on the private emotional life of the individual, most often located in the feminine situation. We may add to these his particular fondness for plots of complex intrigue (usually suggested by women) that use strategies of trickery, deceit, contrivance, and devising (*dolos, apatê, technê, mêchanê*) and that, with their resort to disguise and role playing, are an explicit sign of an enhanced theatricality. Finally, we may include more generally Euripides' thematic concern with metaphysical questions of reality and illusion in the world.[57]

By viewing plays with these plots the audience becomes inextricably involved in tragedy's exploration of the feminine, even if only temporarily:

> In the end tragedy arrives at closures that generally reassert male, often paternal (or civic), structures of authority, but before that the work of the drama is to open up the masculine view of the universe. It typically does so, as we have seen, through energizing the theatrical resources of the female and concomitantly enervating the male as the price of initiating actor and spectator into new and unsettling modes of feeling, seeing, and knowing.[58]

Here I am less interested in the experience of the professional first, second, and third actors who act out the plot and more interested in that of the nonprofessional chorus members. What is their connection to the feminine aspects of Greek drama, and to the experience and emotions of the audience? One well-known if not universally accepted answer has been

57. Zeitlin 1996, 364–65.

58. Zeitlin 1996, 364. Zeitlin finds a great deal of support for her arguments in the work of Plato, in which the figure of Socrates objects to tragedy because of the same built-in structures that Zeitlin articulates. The impersonation of women and social inferiors such as slaves and the enacting of feminine emotions were thought to be dangerous for the citizen and the city (see Foley 2001, 13). See also Foley, 2001, 109–21 on Plato and Aristotle's discussions of women and the feminine in Greek tragedy.

proposed by John Winkler, who emphasized the ephebic dynamic of the chorus.[59] He noted that chorus members were typically young men at the age at which they would undergo military training, and he pointed out the many similarities between what we know of the choreography of the chorus and military formations and drills.[60] Winkler argued that the focus of the City Dionysia was in fact the ephebes, and that the festival was a kind of civic initiation, or in Winkler's words, "a social event focused on those young warriors."[61] He saw the training involved in choral dancing to be rigorous and highly disciplined. The ephebes who danced in the chorus became a representative subgroup of the ephebate as a whole, making a display of the military training that they were in the process of undergoing.

Although Winkler argues that the experience of dancing in the chorus was a kind of rite of passage, he cautions that it was not exactly so, because not all ephebes danced in the chorus: "More accurately, they were *representative* of those actually undergoing social puberty: only a select group of the best ephebic singer-dancers could actually perform."[62] Winkler notes that because of this he has not emphasized in his discussion what he calls the most obvious connection to rites of passages, the fact that sometimes these ephebes played the role of women. He argues that the experience of being in the audience is as important as performing onstage, and that in any case, the chorus need not be women.[63] Here I take some exception to Winkler's argument. While it is true that not all choruses are women, the choruses of two-thirds of the surviving tragedies are. Since the same chorus danced all four plays that were entered by each playwright, the vast majority of all choruses would have danced the role of a woman.

But Winkler is right that the category of woman is only one of many interlocking categories of marginality that constitute the composition of tragic choruses. Building on Winkler's work, Gregory Nagy has shown that it is the playing of any number of marginal characters that is the crucial dynamic:

The chorus members in the seasonally recurring Athenian dramatic festivals are to be understood, at least from the ritual point of view,

59. Winkler 1985 and 1990b. Not all scholars have accepted Winkler's arguments in their entirety. I focus here on the components of Winkler's discussion that he himself considered the least speculative.

60. See also Pickard-Cambridge 1968, 232–57 and the collected primary sources in Csapo and Slater 1994, 360–68.

61. Winkler 1990b, 37. Other scholars have since built on the work of Winkler, emphasizing initiatory/rites of passage themes in the surviving Greek tragedies. See especially the collected essays in Padilla 1999.

62. Winkler 1990b, 60.

63. Winkler 1990b, 60.

as citizens-in-the-making. At the moment of their performance, the rank-and-file chorus members are marginal to society as chorus members. They are notionally precivic, not yet civic. Moreover, they act out mostly marginal members of society in the world of heroes, such as old men, young girls, prisoners of war. Their acting out such roles conforms to the ritual function of the chorus as an educational collectivization of experience. Their experience of *paideia* "education" in the chorus is like a stylized rite of passage, or initiation, which leads from the marginality of precitizenship into the eventual centrality of citizenship.[64]

Thus when ephebes sing and dance the role of the captive Trojan women, their marginal status is overdetermined. They are women *and* slaves *and* foreign: they are as marginal as they can possibly be.

In her work on marginal figures in Greek tragedy, Mary Ebbott has demonstrated that the overdetermined marginality of choruses and other dramatic characters participates in an ongoing exploration in tragedy of the self by way of the other. She points out, however, that the oppositions set up between self and other are not as strictly maintained as is often asserted:

When marginal figures such as foreigners, slaves, and bastards function as the Other through which the central Self is explored, there is an interaction between these usually separate categories. In different genres we may see the strict oppositions that I have enumerated between insiders and outsiders, but while these outsiders create, mark, and signify difference in tragedy, they also break down difference. The boundaries they define they also cross, and these seemingly contradictory actions co-exist. . . . The Self is explored through the Other, but is not subsumed by the Other. Instead, there is this interaction between the two.[65]

Ebbott's formulation applies to the tragic experience as a whole. Main characters, chorus members, and, through them, audience members participate in this crossing of boundaries as the centrality of Athens is explored by way of the margins.[66]

---

64. Nagy 1994–1995b, 49–50.
65. Ebbott 2005. On this point see also Goldhill 1996, 253.
66. See also Zeitlin 1990 and Vidal-Naquet 1997.

LEARNING LESSONS FROM THE TROJAN WAR

Nagy's equation of participation in the chorus with education is a formulation that is at least as old as Plato's *Laws* 654a: ἀπαίδευτος ἀχόρευτος, or, as Simon Goldhill paraphrases in his own discussion of the educational dynamic of choral performance, "lack of training in singing, dancing, and poetry is synonymous with lack of education." This education is much more than training in the skills of singing and dancing: "the poet and his poetry constitute a way of transmitting the cultural heritage of a society."[67] This simultaneous commemorative and didactic function is arguably the primary role of tragedy in Athenian society, even if we acknowledge, as we should, that the work and creative processes of the poet are far more complicated than that role might suggest.[68] That tragedy is in some sense didactic is perhaps not a surprising statement. But defining the nature of the lesson that tragedy seeks to teach is indeed a difficult task.

Sometimes the chorus makes specifically Athenian connections in their song that perhaps provide a clue to their function. When Hecuba's daughter Polyxena goes off to her death earlier in the *Hecuba*, this is the song of her fellow captive women:

Χο. αὔρα, ποντιὰς αὔρα, / ἅτε ποντοπόρους κομί-/ζεις θοὰς ἀκάτους
ἐπ' οἶδμα λίμνας, / ποῖ με τὰν μελέαν πορεύ-/σεις; τῶι δουλόσυνος πρὸς
οἶ-/κον κτηθεῖσ' ἀφίξομαι; ἢ / Δωρίδος ὅρμον αἴας, / ἢ Φθιάδος ἔνθα τὸν
/ καλλίστων ὑδάτων πατέρα / φασὶν Ἀπιδανὸν πεδία λιπαίνειν;

ἢ νάσων, ἁλιήρει / κώπαι πεμπομέναν τάλαι-/ναν, οἰκτρὰν βιοτὰν
ἔχουσαν οἴκοις, / ἔνθα πρωτόγονός τε φοῖ-/νιξ δάφνα θ' ἱεροὺς ἀνέ-/σχε
πτόρθους Λατοῖ φίλον ὠ-/δῖνος ἄγαλμα Δίας; / σὺν Δηλιάσιν τε κού-
/ραισιν Ἀρτέμιδος θεᾶς / χρυσέαν τ' ἄμπυκα τόξα τ' εὐλογήσω;

ἢ Παλλάδος ἐν πόλει / τὰς καλλιδίφρους Ἀθα-/ναίας ἐν κροκέωι
πέπλωι / ζεύξομαι ἆρα πώ-/λους ἐν δαιδαλέαισι ποι-/κίλλουσ'
ἀνθοκρόκοισι πή-/ναις ἢ Τιτάνων γενεάν, / τὰν Ζεὺς ἀμφιπύρωι κοιμί-
/ζει φλογμῶι Κρονίδας;

ὤ μοι τεκέων ἐμῶν, / ὤ μοι πατέρων χθονός θ', / ἃ καπνῶι κατερεί-
πεται / τυφομένα δορί-/κτητος Ἀργεῖων· ἐγὼ / δ' ἐν ξείναι χθονὶ δὴ
κέκλη-/μαι δούλα, λιποῦσ' Ἀσίαν, / Εὐρώπας θεραπνᾶν ἀλλά-/ξασ'
Ἅιδα θαλάμους.   (EURIPIDES, *Hecuba* 444–83)

---

67. Goldhill 1986, 140. See also pp. 266–74 and Calame 1999a, 221–44.
68. On the didactic aspects of Greek tragedy see, e.g., Gregory 1991; Cartledge 1997, 19–20; and Goldhill 1997, 66–67.

CHORUS: Breeze arising from out the deep, breeze that escorts swift, seafaring ships to harbors across the surging sea! Where will you take me, the child of sorrow? To whose house shall I be brought, acquired to be his slave? To some haven in the Dorian land, or in Phthia, where they say the Apidanus river, father of fairest streams, makes the land fat and rich?

Or to an island home, sent on a voyage of misery by oars that sweep the sea, leading a piteous life in halls where the first-created palm and the laurel tree put forth their sacred shoots for dear Latona, as a memorial of her divine birth-pains? And there with the maidens of Delos shall I hymn the golden headband and bow of Artemis their goddess?

Or in the city of Pallas, the home of Athena of the beautiful chariot, shall I upon her saffron robe yoke horses to the car, weaving them on my web in brilliant varied shades, or [shall I weave] the race of Titans, whom Zeus the son of Kronos lays to their unending sleep with his bolt of flashing flame?

Woe is me for my children! Woe for my ancestors, and my country, which is falling in smoldering ruin amid the smoke, sacked by the Argive spear! While I upon a foreign shore am called a slave, leaving Asia, Europe's handmaid, and receiving in its place the chambers of Hades.[69]

Here the chorus members wonder where they will be taken and what their lives will be like. The ode is remarkable in that it combines the questions and traditional themes of sorrow typical of the captive woman's laments with the far away locations of an escape song. But equally striking are the references to Athenian institutions and song traditions. The Ionian festival in honor of Apollo on Delos had special significance for the Athenians.[70] And in the second strophe the chorus alludes to the festival of the Panathenaia in Athens, imagining that they might be weavers of the Panathenaic *peplos*. This is an unrealistic speculation, of course—only the most highborn of Athenian citizen women and girls were chosen for this task. In the *Trojan Women*, the chorus goes even further: they hope that of all places in Greece they will be taken to Athens, "the famous and blessed land of Theseus."[71]

Such passages, which praise Athenian institutions and religious traditions, do not necessarily blur the distinction between Athenian and Trojan—a phenomenon that I explore throughout this book—but may in fact have

69. Translation after Coleridge (1891).
70. On the Ionian festival on Delos see Thucydides 3.104.
71. τὰν κλεινὰν εἴθ' ἔλθοιμεν Θησέως εὐδαίμονα χώραν (*Trojan Women* 208–9). See also chapter 5. Choral odes in other tragedies also single out Athens for praise. See, e.g., *Medea* 824–49 and *Oedipus at Colonus* 668–719.

the opposite effect. In chapters 4 and 5 I argue that these passages highlight Athenian participation in the Trojan War on the side of the Achaeans, and thus ask the Athenian audience to contemplate the plight of their historical victims, as well as those of the current war. That the actions of the Athenians are not outright condemned is clear from these very same passages, which portray Athens as holy and famous and powerful. This is how Athens imagines that it is seen in the eyes of others, including those of its enemies and victims in war. The passages then are a testament to the complexity of tragedy as a civic institution, in that they combine an awareness of Athens' prominence and power with a respect for the helpless victims of war.

Euripides' *Hecuba* and *Trojan Women* were produced within a relatively brief period of history, however, and I have understood them to be reflective of a particular time period, the height of the hostilities known collectively as the Peloponnesian War. It is appropriate that the mixture I have outlined in this book of pride and self-reflection, pity for the victims of war, and fear for their own potential losses be experienced and transmitted to the audience by a group of young men who in their dancing and singing as a chorus represent the Athenian ephebate. These young men will be the very ones soon fighting for Athens, and they will be in a position to either sack cities in victory or lose their lives defending their wives, mothers, and children. In this way the educational, initiatory, civic, and personal aspects of the choral experience come together most acutely in the role of captive women during this time period.

If we step back and look at the fifth century B.C. as a whole, we see that Athens moved gradually from several decades of defensive hostilities against the Persians to increasingly aggressive control over an empire and finally to war with rival Greek powers. As I argue throughout this book, the plight of the captive women of Troy as a theme must likewise have evolved in its significance over the course of the century even as tragedy itself evolved as a civic institution. Earlier in the century, a chorus of captive women of Troy was employed by Aeschylus as the incarnation of vengeance. The captive Trojan women who lament at the tomb of Agamemnon in the *Libation Bearers* become the terrifying, vengeful Erinyes of the *Eumenides*.[72] When the *Oresteia* was produced in 458 B.C., Athens was gaining strength but still recovering from the Persian sack; much of the Acropolis would have still been in ruins or awaiting rebuilding.

---

72. This particular chorus of captive women and their role as lamenters and initiators of revenge has been well studied. See especially Alexiou 1974, Holst-Warhaft 1992, Seaford 1994, Ferrari 1997, and Foley 2001.

In chapter 3 I argue in support of the thesis of Gloria Ferrari that the Athenians of the mid-fifth century B.C. could identify easily with the Trojans as a people whose homes and temples had been destroyed by an invading army. The vengeful laments of the chorus of Trojan women in the *Libation Bearers* may well have resonated with the Athenian audience on that level. For the chorus of young men playing the role, the lamentation and anger of the Trojan women within the already Atheno-centric construct of the *Oresteia* could have instructed them in the history of their city, inspired in them a determination to make Athens a world power, and initiated them into manhood through the experience of playing the ultimate other.

A generation after the *Oresteia,* the Trojan War had not lost its programmatic centrality in Athenian myth, literature, and art, but the lessons to be learned from that war had changed. Whereas once the Athenians could distance themselves from the sackers of Troy and the atrocities they committed, by the third quarter of the fifth century B.C. Athens had become a major sea power and had acquired an empire.[73] The fact that now Athens had become the sacker of cities and a world power makes the deployment of the captive woman's lament on the tragic stage all the more remarkable. Nevertheless, as I investigate the place of the captive woman's lament in Athenian tragedy, I hope to show that the exploration of sorrow through the eyes of the enemy is at the heart of ancient Greek literary, performative, and artistic expression. In doing so I rely on the work of a number of scholars who in the past decade have examined Greek lament, women's speech and the representation of women in Greek tragedy, the Greek construction of the barbarian, and the fall of Troy in Greek poetry and art, as well as those who have produced critical editions of the plays that I discuss. It is my hope that in assembling these manifold and illuminating resources for an exploration of the captive woman's lament I not only demonstrate the importance of this group of songs for our understanding of tragedy, but also offer new insight into the Athenian conception of their own identity and their relationship with the Trojan past.

73. On this point see the readings of the *Hecuba* and *Trojan Women* in Gregory 1991.

CHAPTER ONE

MEN'S SONGS AND WOMEN'S SONGS

Are the voices of women in men's poetry representative of women's independent song traditions? What role, if any, did women's song traditions play in the shaping of men's epic traditions (and, later, tragedy)? In recent years scholars have begun to suggest that women's lament traditions may have played a crucial role in the development of epic and tragedy, which were traditionally performed by men.[1] Sheila Murnaghan has noted, for example, that the majority of women's speech in the *Iliad* and the *Odyssey* is closely related to lament in both language and theme.[2] Epic poetry narrates the glory of heroes, the *klea andrôn,* but it also laments their untimely deaths and the suffering they cause by means of the mournful songs performed by the women left behind.

Turning to the Classical period, we find that Greek tragedy is similarly infused with feminine voices and indeed femininity, as the work of such scholars as Helene Foley, Nicole Loraux, and Froma Zeitlin has shown over the course of the past two decades.[3] While a definitive and comprehensive answer to the vexed question of the prominent roles women play in drama and their relationship to "real life" is yet to be found (and may never be), it seems clear at least that Greek drama employed the feminine to confront

1. Murnaghan 1999, Nagy 1999, and Sultan 1999. In the arguments that follow, I am heavily indebted to the work of these three scholars.

2. Murnaghan 1999, 206. See also Monsacré 1984, 137–96 and Dué 2002. Richard Martin (1989) has studied the many genres of stylized speech that have been incorporated into the genre of epic poetry, and he has shown that the *Iliad* and the *Odyssey* include within the overall epic frame the conventions and allusive power of a number of other preexisting verbal art forms, including prayer, supplication, boasting, and insulting, as well as lament (on lament, see especially Martin 1989, 86–88).

3. See especially Foley 2001, Loraux 1995 and 1998, and Zeitlin 1996, with references to earlier work therein. For the feminine aspects of the heroes of Greek epic, see Monsacré 1984.

questions of masculinity. In the words of Zeitlin, "the final paradox may be that theater uses the feminine for the purposes of imagining a fuller model for the masculine self, and 'playing the other' opens that self to those often banned emotions of fear and pity."[4]

Most recently in *The Mourning Voice,* Nicole Loraux examines the function of lamentation in Greek tragedy in order to explore the personal involvement of the audience in the emotional force of tragedy. Arguing against overly political interpretations of the function of tragedy, Loraux emphasizes the outlet that tragedy provides for grief in a city-state where lamentation and elaborate funerals for individuals had become restricted by law.[5] During the Peloponnesian War, women's rituals of mourning were supplanted by the grandeur of a state funeral for the citizens who gave their lives for the city, but in tragedy, women's wailing takes center stage.[6]

In this chapter I propose to give an overview of the place of the captive woman's lament in epic and tragedy within the history of Greek song traditions in general. I argue that the captive woman's lament in Greek tragedy draws on a number of song traditions, and in doing so becomes a song tradition in its own right. To what extent the stylized laments of the captive women on the Greek stage echo the laments of actual slave women and prisoners of war residing in Athens is itself an extremely interesting but probably unanswerable question.[7] Instead, in this book I seek to trace the development of the captive woman's lament as a powerful theme within the poetic conventions of Greek tragedy, while also paying special attention to the instances where these conventions and their emotional dynamic can be shown to intersect with the documented songs and experiences of actual women.

4. Zeitlin 1996, 363. Loraux agrees with this formulation (Loraux 1995, 9).

5. Loraux 2002. On the legislation of lament in the Archaic period see, e.g., Alexiou 1974, 14–23; Loraux 1986, 45–49; Holst-Warhaft 1992, 114–19; McClure 1999, 45; Murnaghan 1999, 204–5; and further below.

6. On the displacement of women's laments by the state funeral oration see especially Loraux 1986 and further below.

7. For a recent look at women and slavery in antiquity, see the collection edited by Joshel and Murnaghan (1998), which necessarily relies on male-authored and primarily literary sources (see pp. 19–20 of the introduction to that volume). On the institution of slavery in ancient Greece in general, see Finley 1960, 1980, 1981, and 1987; Sainte Croix 1981; Wiedemann 1981 and 1987; Vidal-Naquet 1986, 159–223; Garlan 1988; and Fisher 1993. For transcripts of modern Greek laments recorded by anthropologists, see Lardas 1992 (which contains translations of modern Greek laments) and the collections cited in the bibliography of Roilos and Yatromanolakis 2002, 270.

GENDER, GENRE, AND THE DEVELOPMENT OF EPIC

As I noted in the introduction to this book, the seminal work of Margaret Alexiou, *The Ritual Lament in the Greek Tradition,* was the first to explore the continuity of the Greek lament tradition from ancient times to the present day.[8] Alexiou studied the surviving laments of epic and tragedy, and traced their metaphors, themes, and diction in the laments of late antiquity, Byzantine literature, and modern Greek funerals. Since the publication of Alexiou's work, many scholars have undertaken the study of lament, but *Ritual Lament* remains a basic guidebook to this incredibly rich and enduring tradition of women's song.[9]

What Alexiou and other scholars of the Greek tradition have found is that Greek women's laments have maintained a continuous tradition of song-making that is both independent of and parallel to the stylized versions that have been preserved in epic, drama, and later Greek literature. Moreover, there is a great deal of comparative evidence from other cultures to show that the Greek tradition is by no means an isolated phenomenon, and that women all over the world have been singers of lament since ancient times and continue to be so today.[10] It is very likely then, if not provable, that the laments of Greek epic, although performed by a male *aoidos,* would nevertheless have evoked for ancient audiences the songs their mothers and grandmothers performed at funerals upon the death of family members and extended relatives. In this way epic subsumes a distinctly feminine mode of singing within its own mode of expression, the dactylic hexameter, no doubt transforming it, but also maintaining many of its essential features.

A ground-breaking book by Aida Vidan can shed light on the dynamics of the process by which women's song-making becomes incorporated into heroic narratives. Vidan's book, *Embroidered with Gold, Strung with Pearls: The Traditional Ballads of Bosnian Women,* publishes and analyzes for the first time women's songs of the South Slavic tradition that were collected by Milman Parry and Albert Lord and which are now housed in the Milman Parry Collection of Oral Literature. With few exceptions, to date only the

8. For continuation and application of Alexiou's work, see Caraveli-Chavez 1978 and Caraveli 1986, Danforth 1982, Seremetakis 1990 and 1991, Holst-Warhaft 1992, Herzfeld 1993, Sultan 1993 and 1999, Murnaghan 1999, Derderian 2001, and Dué 2002.

9. See also Alexiou 2001.

10. See Bowers 1993 for a brief survey, as well as Rosenblatt, Walsh, and Jackson 1976; Holst-Warhaft 1992, 20–27; and the bibliography in Roilos and Yatromanolakis 2002, under the heading "Ethnographic and Comparative Material."

men's heroic songs collected by Parry and Lord have been published and discussed.[11] It was the study of the South Slavic epic tradition that prompted Parry and Lord to formulate their thesis that the *Iliad* and the *Odyssey* were composed within a flourishing culture of oral epic song by means of centuries-old traditional techniques for composition-in-performance; this thesis revolutionized the field of Homeric studies.[12] Vidan's book continues the work of Parry and Lord by introducing and publishing several of the women's songs collected in the very same areas in the former Yugoslavia in which Parry and Lord had collected the heroic songs that they compared to Homeric poetry.

Vidan shows that the women's songs share traditional language and many themes with the men's heroic songs, but differ from them in important ways. The women's songs, as one might expect, offer a uniquely female point of view on the action, and are performed in vastly different contexts, such as weddings or intimate gatherings of female friends and relatives. This performance context in turn affects the content and length of the songs. Moreover, whereas the men's songs that Parry and Lord collected are generally described as epic or heroic poetry, the women's songs of this region can be divided into three basic (though often overlapping) groups: lyric songs, humorous songs, and narrative ballads.[13] Nevertheless, Vidan points out, formulas, blocks of lines, and themes travel with ease across genre boundaries.[14]

The women's songs of the former Yugoslavia were at one time so pervasive in the culture that it has been argued by at least one researcher that the men's heroic song tradition evolved out of that of the women's songs.[15] The vast majority of the songs in the Milman Parry Collection of Oral Litera-

11. See Bartók and Lord 1951, as well as the songs and translations published by the Milman Parry Collection in the series *Serbocroatian Heroic Songs* (Serbian Academy of Sciences and Harvard University Press, 1953–). Women's songs are included in Bartók and Lord 1951, and Coote 1977 and 1992 also discuss the women's songs in the Parry Collection. For a brief overview of the collections and publications of South Slavic oral traditional songs, see Vidan 2003, 2–3, with citations there.

12. The findings of Parry and Lord are best studied in the work of Parry and Lord themselves, as published in Parry 1971 and Lord 1960, 1991, and 1995. For an introduction to and overview of the significance of this work see the introduction by Stephen Mitchell and Gregory Nagy to the fortieth-anniversary edition of Lord's 1960 book, *The Singer of Tales.*

13. Vidan 2003, 12. See Vidan 2003, 12–31 for a discussion of the problems of terminology in the study of the South Slavic song tradition.

14. Vidan 2003, 22.

15. Vidan 2003, 15, quoting Nikola Andric.

ture are in fact women's songs.[16] These so-called women's songs, however, could also be performed by men. Of the three hundred singers of women's songs in the collection, fifty are men. Similarly, it is not unheard of to find a woman singer of heroic songs in the South Slavic tradition, particularly if the woman's father was a singer.[17]

The distinction between women's songs and men's songs in this tradition seems to be the musical accompaniment (men's/heroic songs were accompanied by a musical instrument, the *gusle*, while women's were not) and the setting (men's songs were meant for public performance; women's songs were sung in intimate settings) rather than the content or plot of the songs themselves:

> The customary division of South Slavic folk poetry into men's (epic or heroic) songs and women's songs (lyric songs, ballads, and humorous narrative songs) has caused perhaps even greater misunderstanding. As early as 1824 Vuk Karadžić recognized that the boundaries are far from clear: "All our folk songs are divided into heroic songs which people sing with the gusle, and women's songs which are sung not only by women or girls, but also by men, especially young men, most often in unison. Women's songs are sung by one or two people for their own entertainment, while heroic songs are sung mostly for others to listen to; for that reason, in the performance of women's songs more attention is given to singing than to the song, while in the performance of heroic ones the attention is turned mostly to the song." [quoted from Karadžić, coll. & ed., *Srpske narodne pjesme*, vol. 1 (1969 edition), 529. Translation is Vidan's.] He mentions further on in the same text that heroic songs were mostly sung in Bosnia and Herzegovina, Montenegro, and the southern mountainous regions of Serbia, and that in those areas most households had a gusle. Moreover, he claims, most men knew how to perform with the gusle, and that many women and girls were endowed with this skill as well. It is hardly surprising, then, that Karadžić faced a dilemma when it came to grouping some of the materials he had collected, or that he thought that many of them appeared to be on the borderline between women's and heroic songs."[18]

It appears then that there was a great deal of fluidity of genre and transfer between the women's and men's song traditions in the region surveyed by

16. Of the 12,544 texts contained in the Milman Parry Collection of Oral Literature, approximately 11,250 are women's songs. See Vidan 2003, 4.

17. Vidan 2003, 3–4.

18. Vidan 2003, 14.

Parry and Lord. Women were able to sing songs for each other that were sometimes nearly indistinguishable from men's heroic poetry,[19] and men could learn and perform the song traditions of women. Vidan argues that such mixing of gender and genre in the composition and performance of these songs was most common in areas where division between the sexes was not strict.[20]

I have chosen to emphasize Vidan's work on the women's songs of the South Slavic tradition both because of its recent publication and because it extends the applicability of the fieldwork of Parry and Lord to Greek epic traditions. Moreover, much of Vidan's work accords well with the wealth of comparative evidence available from the study of modern Greek women's laments for the dead, even though the content and ritual function of modern Greek laments make them very different from the women's songs of the South Slavic tradition.[21] In the modern Greek tradition, laments are a distinctly feminine mode of song. Because of its powerful and even subversive force this type of song is to some extent disapproved of by men, but it is nevertheless appreciated for its beauty.[22] Anna Caraveli has pointed out that while only women perform ritual laments for the dead at modern Greek funerals, men may sing laments in other contexts, and that professional male musicians actively admire the laments of women.[23]

Caraveli argues that there are four registers of lament, "in ascending order of efficacy and importance":

1. Laments that are simply recited as poetry.
2. Laments that are sung, but not on a ritual occasion or in an extraordinary emotional context.
3. Laments that are sung in an extraordinary, heightened emotional context but in an ordinary setting, such as one's home or the fields.

19. For examples of women who knew heroic songs or claimed to know them, see Vidan 2003, 15–16 and 19, with further citations there. There seem to have been on the one hand women who could sing narrative poetry that very closely resembled heroic/epic poetry, but was distinctly feminine in its outlook and plot, and on the other women who had been exposed to performances of men's/heroic poetry and therefore could recite the plot of certain songs and even reproduce them to a certain extent. See, in addition to Vidan 2003, Murko 1990.

20. Vidan 2003, 17–19.

21. For a study of South Slavic funeral laments (not addressed in Vidan's work), see Kerewsky-Halpern 1981 as well as Foley 2002, 195–99.

22. Caraveli 1986. On the subversive power of lament, see, in addition to Caraveli, Alexiou 1974, 21–22 and 124–25; Serematakis 1990 and 1991; Holst-Warhaft 1992; and Foley 2001, 19–56.

23. Caraveli 1986, 179.

4. Laments that are performed both in a heightened emotional context and
on a ritual occasion (for example, during tending of the grave, memorial
services, funerals).[24]

These four registers are indicative of the wide range of meaning and functions women's laments can have within a given society. In her fieldwork
Caraveli found that women sang laments in relatively unemotional and
ordinary contexts—even as an accompaniment to everyday tasks—as well
as in ritual settings.[25] Independently of their initial emotional and compo-
sitional context, many sung laments are appreciated as poetry, at the same
time maintaining a great deal of their emotional force. Laments are most
often sung in the company of other women, in intimate settings, much
like the women's songs of the South Slavic tradition: "The existence of a
muted, separate women's world creates the opportunities for strong friend-
ships among women. Rituals of shared grieving reinforce, intensify, and
negotiate a great variety of relationships that often pass into daily narrative
as metaphors of and codes for female experiences."[26]

We may compare Caraveli's analysis with the words of Ibrahim Hrusta-
novic, the son of one of the female singers whose songs are included in the
Parry Collection:

> [My mother] told me songs very well. This time she told me about three
> hundred songs. And earlier she had told me some. I have wondered where
> she learned all these songs. She said to me: "When I was a girl," she said,
> "my father was wealthy, perhaps the wealthiest in this area. I," she said,
> "never had to do anything, but I would invite other girls, neighbors and
> they would come for a meal or drink with me. And what would we do?
> We would embroider, sing and be merry, entertain and court."[27]

Very often the female singers whose songs are included in the Parry Collection told Parry and Lord that they had learned their songs from their
mothers, grandmothers, or other older women in their villages and towns.
In this way stories, formulas, and themes were passed down over genera-

24. Caraveli 1986, 177.
25. So also in the South Slavic tradition; see Vidan 2003, 9.
26. Caraveli, 1986, 177. Abu-Lughod 1999 documents a similar women's world (and
lament and love song tradition) among the Bedouin Awlad 'Ali. Such a world is frequently
evoked in the surviving fragments of the poetry of Sappho.
27. Vidan 2003, 80.

tions, and each generation learned the techniques of composition from the generation before. This process resembles the more formal process by which men in the South Slavic tradition learned to become composers and singers of heroic poetry. In *The Singer of Tales,* Lord describes the three-step training process that oral traditional poets go through as they learn to sing tales before an audience and eventually become accomplished artists.[28] According to Lord, the first stage is one of listening and absorbing. In the second stage the singer begins to sing and has to learn to fit his thoughts and their expression into a fairly rigid form. The second stage ends when the singer can sing one entire song before an audience. In the third stage an increase in repertoire and a growth in competency takes place; it ends when the singer becomes an accomplished practitioner of the art, and can provide entertainment for several nights.

One of the most important metaphors that Lord uses for describing the learning process is that of learning a language. In his chapter on the formula Lord writes:

In studying the patterns and systems of oral narrative verse we are in reality observing the "grammar" of the poetry, a grammar superimposed, as it were, on the grammar of the language concerned. Or, to alter the image, we find a special grammar within the grammar of the language, necessitated by the versification. The formulas are phrases and clauses and sentences of this specialized poetic grammar. The speaker of this language, once he has mastered it, does not move any more mechanically within it than we do in ordinary speech.

When we speak a language, our native language, we do not repeat words and phrases that we have memorized consciously, but the words and sentences emerge from habitual usage. This is true of the singer of tales working in his specialized grammar. He does not "memorize" formulas, any more than we as children "memorize" language. He learns them by hearing them in other singers' songs, and by habitual usage they become part of his singing as well. Memorization is a conscious act of making one's own, and repeating, something that one regards as fixed and not one's own. The learning of an oral poetic language follows the same principles as the learning of language itself, not by the conscious schematization of elementary grammars but by the natural oral method.[29]

28. Lord 1960, 21–26.
29. Lord 1960, 35–36.

The process that Lord describes here, I would argue, is true of women's songs as well.[30] Moreover, because women sing their songs both in formal rituals at which men are present, and informally in the presence of their children and family members, it is possible for the "language" of lament to be appreciated and assimilated by members of both sexes—even if the singing of those laments is the particular province of women.[31]

Lord's comparison of traditional singing to a language is particularly appropriate when we consider that in the Greek tradition the language of lament is used to express a variety of emotions and experiences, including those of a bride as she leaves home, the joy of new love, the sorrow of lost love, the anxieties of a mother, and the anger of a widow.[32] Because ritual lamentation gives Greek women a public voice that they are not allowed in any other context, women can use lament to protest their position in life and the status quo.[33] This special mode of speech and song can then be manipulated and employed by women in even nonritual contexts to comment on their lives and situations.[34] Framed within the poetic and social conventions of lament, women's songs have the power to explore the full range of women's experiences and to voice their concerns and emotions before the community.

This brief survey of the social context of women's songs in the South Slavic and modern Greek traditions suggests that the laments of Archaic and Classical Greece and their counterparts in epic and tragedy at least

30. The multiformity and fluidity of the oral system within which laments are generated varies considerably from culture to culture, of course. Danforth describes one such system (1982, 71–72): "[Modern] Greek funeral laments are part of a longstanding oral tradition in which the literary concept of one authentic or correct version of a song does not exist. . . . In Potamia, although several women have the ability to compose very original laments, the vast majority of laments sung are well known to most women. In such cases the variation that exists involves the complexity and the degree of elaboration with which traditional themes are presented." On the oral formulaic qualities of modern Greek laments and love songs see also Alexiou 1974 and 2001 and Caraveli-Chavez 1978.

31. On lamentation as a language, cf. Danforth 1982, 73: "laments constitute a public language, a cultural code, for the expression of grief."

32. On this point see especially Caraveli-Chavez 1978; Danforth 1982, 74–95; and Caraveli 1986, 178–92. For application of this principle to Homeric poetry see Dué 2002.

33. See Caraveli 1986 and Holst-Warhaft 1992. Danforth (1982) gives the following quote as an epigraph to his *Death Rituals of Rural Greece:* "Songs are just words. Those who are bitter sing them. / They sing them to get rid of their bitterness, but the bitterness doesn't go away" (translation is Danforth's).

34. See Ebbott 1999 for a discussion of this phenomenon in the *Iliad.* For a striking parallel in Bedouin Awlad 'Ali society, see Abu-Lughod 1999, 238–40.

potentially served a similar function, namely, to speak about, comment upon, share, and even protest the experiences of Greek women, by way of a mode of speech and song that is the particular province of women. That women's song traditions could be assimilated and incorporated into men's poetry has been postulated by Richard Martin and others, who argue that the conventions and even emotional force of such songs is preserved within the overarching medium of ancient Greek epic.[35] Other scholars have gone so far as to suggest that women's lament traditions are not merely incorporated into Greek epic, but indeed are the very foundation of epic.[36] The comparative evidence discussed here offers many points of contact and support for the work of these scholars, and argues for a primacy of women's song traditions within the poetics of a song culture such as that of the ancient Greeks.

THE POETRY OF PRAISE AND LAMENT

Turning now to ancient Greek epic, we find that the *Iliad* and the *Odyssey* are infused with voices of lament at every point, and that those voices are primarily the voices of women.[37] Although the poems of the Epic Cycle are now lost to us, it is clear from what we know of them that in these poems, too, laments for heroes played an important role.[38] When epic poetry is performed by characters within the *Iliad* and the *Odyssey*, there it has the effect of inspiring mourning in those who are most connected to the ac-

35. See note 2 above. See also Foley 2002, 188–218 for a discussion of the "ecology" of genres within Serbian oral poetry, which, like ancient Greek epic, includes magical charms, lyric songs, and funeral laments, among others. For women's laments preserved in Persian epic see Davidson 2000.

36. See note 1 above.

37. Important exceptions to this rule are Achilles and Odysseus, each the star of his own epic. Achilles, as Monsacré (1984) has shown, is a master of both men's and women's song traditions; Odysseus is famously compared to a lamenting captive woman, one of his own victims, when he hears his own *kleos* performed by Demodokos in the court of the Phaeacians (see the introduction to this volume). Men frequently cry and sometimes lament in the Homeric epics, but more formal songs of lament in funeral contexts seem to be the province of women (see van Wees 1998).

38. To cite just a few examples, there are likely to have been laments for Antilokhos, Memnon, and Achilles in the *Aethiopis* ("Song of the Ethiopians"), laments for Astyanax and other Trojans in the *Ilioupersis* ("Sack of Troy") and *Little Iliad*, and laments for various Greek heroes in the *Nostoi* (*Homecomings*).

tion.[39] In other words, what is epic *kleos*—the latest entertainment—for the generic audience of epic is at the same time a song of lament for those with a stake in the tale, with the result that the only distinction between a song of lament and epic poetry becomes the listener. So closely tied are *penthos* and *kleos* that in many instances within the poems themselves they are the same thing.[40]

Thomas Greene has suggested that lamentation in epic collapses the boundaries between the audience and the heroic past, producing "a hallowed communion between the two."[41] He argues that in fact the *telos* of most of the European poetry known as epic is tears, and that through tears the communion between past and present is most accessible. One way that this "hallowed communion" is achieved is through the rituals and lament traditions of hero cult.[42] The heroes of epic are characters in a traditional narrative, but they are also religious entities who were regularly worshiped in countless rituals and festivals throughout the Greek world.[43] The songs of lament for such figures as Achilles and Odysseus within epic are an important part of ritual lamentation for the hero on the part of the communities for whom the epics are performed.[44] We know, for example,

---

39. The *Iliad* and the *Odyssey* refer in several places to the various epic traditions that came to be known as the Epic Cycle. These songs, epic in nature, are represented either as entertainment (for an audience that is disconnected from the events narrated [see, e.g., *Odyssey* 1.153–55 and 325–27, *Odyssey* 8.73–82 and 499–520]) or as a source of tears (see, e.g., *Odyssey* 1.328–44, 4.113–16, and 8.83–86 and 521–32). In the *Iliad* there are no representations of the performance of epic poetry by a professional bard, but epic poetry is nevertheless performed by the heroes themselves when they narrate the past (by way of the medium of epic poetry, the dactylic hexameter). In these cases the purpose of narrating epic poetry is didactic (if the story is about the remote past or a previous generation of heroes—see, e.g., *Iliad* 9.527–99 and 11.669–761), or else it is a subject of lament (as in *Iliad* 6.414–28, 19.291–94, and 22.60–71). For more on the function of these narratives within the *Iliad* and the *Odyssey* see the work of Martin (1989), Alden (2000), and Dué (2002).

40. For *kleos* as the "latest form of entertainment," see *Odyssey* 1.351–52. On the relationship between *kleos* and *penthos* in the *Iliad* and the *Odyssey* see Nagy 1979, 94–117. On the mixture of lament and praise see also Martin 1989, 144.

41. Greene 1999, 195.

42. On this point, see also the related arguments of Seaford (1994, chapter 5). Seaford's approach to the Homeric texts is ultimately very different from my own, but I agree with his emphasis on the importance of the laments and funeral rituals in the final books of the *Iliad* and their meaning for the audiences of the emerging city-state in the Archaic period.

43. For these two dimensions of the Greek hero see Dué and Nagy 2003.

44. See Nagy 1979, 94–117 and Dué 2002, 80–81.

that Achilles was ritually lamented by the women of Elis at sunset on the evening preceding the Olympic games.[45]

The lamentation of women in epic poetry, as in rituals of hero cult, emphasizes the mortality of the hero. At the same time, the overarching medium of epic poetry, which includes these laments, conveys upon the hero the immortality of *kleos*.[46] Epic *kleos,* as has been demonstrated by Nagy and others, has its origins in praise poetry. Epic narrates the *klea andrôn,* the famous deeds of heroes. The women's songs of Greek epic and tragedy, on the other hand, narrate the loss of loved ones, the loss of homeland, and the loss of freedom experienced by captives of war. As Sheila Murnaghan has shown, "lament is at once constitutive of epic and antithetical to it, one of epic's probable sources and a subversive element within epic that can work against what epic is trying to achieve." Helene Foley argues similarly: "Women historically played the role not only of physically lamenting the dead but of expressing and even acting on views that from Homer on challenged public ideology about death and glory."[47]

How then do we explain the relationship between the sorrow and anger of lament and the glory of epic? Nancy Sultan has recently argued that women's laments function as the inception point for a hero's *kleos:*

> In Homeric poetry and modern Greek songs, the story of the hero's hard-won fame and reputation should be told in a performative context, once he returns to his wife and family. The wife (or mother) listens, internalizes his life story and, in effect, takes possession of it, weaving the story into her future laments. The traditional place in which this transfer of tale occurs is the death/marriage bed.[48]

The widow's lament traditionally expresses sorrow and anger while detailing the miserable plight of those left behind, but these same features are also

45. Pausanias 6.23.3. See Nagy 1979, 114. For this and other examples of cult practices in honor of Achilles, see Nilsson 1906, 457 as well as Hedreen 1991.

46. *Kleos* is fame or glory, especially the fame or glory that comes from being glorified by poetry or song. It is also the word that epic poetry uses to refer to itself. The *Iliad* is the *kleos* of Achilles, his immortality in song. See Nagy 1979, 16–18. For more on the mortality of the hero as contrasted with the immortality of song, see chapter 2 below.

47. Murnaghan 1999, 203; Foley 2001, 14. See also Foley 2001, 14 for lament as a "voice of dissent" in Greek epic and tragedy. Finally, on the seeming oxymoron of the "glorious *thrênos,*" see Loraux 2002, 56–65.

48. Sultan 1999, 91. Cf. *Odyssey* 11.223–24, in which Odysseus' mother directs him to tell his wife about everything that he has seen and heard in Hades.

the first articulation of a hero's deeds and his importance to the community. Andromache's lament for Hektor in *Iliad* 24 illustrates this combination of sorrow and celebration:

ἆνερ, ἀπ᾽ αἰῶνος νέος ὤλεο, κὰδ δέ με χήρην
λείπεις ἐν μεγάροισι· πάϊς δ᾽ ἔτι νήπιος αὔτως
ὃν τέκομεν σύ τ᾽ ἐγώ τε δυσάμμοροι, οὐδέ μιν οἴω
ἥβην ἵξεσθαι· πρὶν γὰρ πόλις ἥδε κατ᾽ ἄκρης
πέρσεται· ἦ γὰρ ὄλωλας ἐπίσκοπος, ὅς τέ μιν αὐτὴν
ῥύσκευ, ἔχες δ᾽ ἀλόχους κεδνὰς καὶ νήπια τέκνα,
αἳ δή τοι τάχα νηυσὶν ὀχήσονται γλαφυρῇσι,
καὶ μὲν ἐγὼ μετὰ τῇσι· σὺ δ᾽ αὖ τέκος ἢ ἐμοὶ αὐτῇ
ἕψεαι, ἔνθά κεν ἔργα ἀεικέα ἐργάζοιο
ἀθλεύων πρὸ ἄνακτος ἀμειλίχου, ἤ τις Ἀχαιῶν
ῥίψει χειρὸς ἑλὼν ἀπὸ πύργου λυγρὸν ὄλεθρον
χωόμενος, ᾧ δή που ἀδελφεὸν ἔκτανεν Ἕκτωρ
ἢ πατέρ᾽ ἠὲ καὶ υἱόν, ἐπεὶ μάλα πολλοὶ Ἀχαιῶν
Ἕκτορος ἐν παλάμῃσιν ὀδὰξ ἕλον ἄσπετον οὖδας.
οὐ γάρ μείλιχος ἔσκε πατὴρ τεὸς ἐν δαῒ λυγρῇ·
τὼ καί μιν λαοὶ μὲν ὀδύρονται κατὰ ἄστυ,
ἀρητὸν δὲ τοκεῦσι γόον καὶ πένθος ἔθηκας
Ἕκτορ· ἐμοὶ δὲ μάλιστα λελείψεται ἄλγεα λυγρά.
οὐ γάρ μοι θνήσκων λεχέων ἐκ χεῖρας ὄρεξας,
οὐδέ τί μοι εἶπες πυκινὸν ἔπος, οὗ τέ κεν αἰεὶ
μεμνήμην νύκτάς τε καὶ ἤματα δάκρυ χέουσα.

(*Iliad* 24.725–45)

Husband, you have perished, cut off from your life-force, and you leave
    me a widow
in the halls. And our son is still very much a child,
the one whom you and I, ill-fated, bore, nor do I think that he
will reach manhood. For sooner will this city be utterly
sacked. You, its guardian, have died, you who
protected it, you who shielded its cherished wives and helpless children,
those who will soon be carried off in the hollow ships,
and I among them. And you, my child, will either
follow me and perform unseemly tasks,
toiling for a cruel master, or else one of the Achaeans
will hurl you from a tower, taking you by the hand—a miserable
    death—
angry because Hektor killed his brother
or father or maybe even his son, since very many of the Achaeans

bit the dust with their teeth at the hands of Hektor.
For your father was not gentle in the midst of sorrow-bringing battle.
Therefore the people grieve for him throughout the city,
and you, Hektor, have brought unspeakable lamentation and sorrow
    upon your parents.
But for me especially you have left behind grievous pain.
For when you died you did not stretch out your arms to me from our
    marriage bed,
nor did you speak to me an intimate phrase, which I could always
    remember when I weep for you day and night.

Andromache's words are reproachful, as is typical of Greek laments for the dead, and tell Hektor of the suffering that she and their son will have to endure, now that Hektor has abandoned them in death.[49] But at the same time her lament establishes the memory of Hektor as the guardian and sole protector of Troy for all time. His death means the city's destruction, the death of its men, and the enslavement of the women and children. But these same words initiate his *kleos*. Her grief, and the city's grief, are Hektor's glory.[50]

The laments of such figures as Andromache and Briseis therefore have a dual function. On the level of narrative they are laments for the dead, the warrior husbands and sons who inevitably fall in battle. They protest the cruel fate of the women left behind, and narrate the bitter consequences of war. The grief expressed by the women left behind is raw and real. But for the audience of ancient epic the laments for these husbands and sons are also the prototypical laments for heroes, who for them continue to be lamented and mourned on a seasonally recurring basis. The poetry of epic, as Thomas Greene observes, collapses the boundaries between the two forms of song.

In the *Iliad*, grief spreads quickly from individual to community. As each lament comes to a close, the immediately surrounding community of mourners antiphonally responds with their own cries and tears:[51]

ὣς ἔφατο κλαίουσ᾽, ἐπὶ δὲ στενάχοντο γυναῖκες
Πάτροκλον πρόφασιν, σφῶν δ᾽ αὐτῶν κήδε᾽ ἑκάστη.

(*Iliad* 19.301–2)

49. On the element of reproach and the traditional accusation of abandonment see Alexiou 1974, 182–84. On this passage in particular see also Holst-Warhaft 1992, 112–13.

50. See also Sultan 1999, 80–81. Cf. as well pp. 92–93, in which Sultan discusses the final lines of this lament, and notes that the fact that Hektor did not die in their marriage bed is a source of particular grief for Andromache. It is there that the hero's story is transferred from husband to wife.

51. On the antiphonal refrain of Greek laments, see Alexiou 1974, 131–60 and Caraveli-Chavez 1978.

So [Briseis] spoke lamenting, and the women wailed in response,
with Patroklos as their pretext, but each woman for her own cares.

As I have argued elsewhere, Briseis' lament for Patroklos in *Iliad* 19 and the
corresponding wailing it initiates exemplify the process by which personal
grief is transformed into collective sorrow.[52] Briseis' song extends not only to
the collective experience of the women around her who lament their fallen
husbands, but to the audience of the epic as well. It is not insignificant then
that the final lament of the *Iliad*, sung by Helen (who is the cause of the
war), ends with the antiphonal wailing not of the women (as at *Iliad* 6.499,
19.301, 22.515, and 24.746), but of the *dêmos*: ὡς ἔφατο κλαίουσ', ἐπὶ δ'
ἔστενε δῆμος ἀπείρων, "So she spoke lamenting, and the people wailed in
response" (*Iliad* 24.776).

Ancient sources attest that the grief within epic poetry did indeed manifest
itself in the audience. In the Classical period, for example, Plato provides us
with the following exchange between Socrates and a rhapsode:

Σωκράτης. ἔχε δή μοι τόδε εἰπέ, ὦ Ἴων, καὶ μὴ ἀποκρύψῃ ὅτι ἄν σε
ἔρωμαι· ὅταν εὖ εἴπῃς ἔπη καὶ ἐκπλήξῃς μάλιστα τοὺς θεωμένους, ἢ τὸν
Ὀδυσσέα ὅταν ἐπὶ τὸν οὐδὸν ἐφαλλόμενον ᾄδῃς, ἐκφανῆ γιγνόμενον
τοῖς μνηστῆρσι καὶ ἐκχέοντα τοὺς ὀιστοὺς πρὸ τῶν ποδῶν, ἢ Ἀχιλλέα
ἐπὶ τὸν Ἕκτορα ὁρμῶντα, ἢ καὶ τῶν περὶ Ἀνδρομάχην ἐλεινῶν τι ἢ περὶ
Ἑκάβην ἢ περὶ Πρίαμον, τότε πότερον ἔμφρων εἶ ἢ ἔξω σαυτοῦ γίγνῃ καὶ
παρὰ τοῖς πράγμασιν οἴεταί σου εἶναι ἡ ψυχὴ οἷς λέγεις ἐνθουσιάζουσα,
ἢ ἐν Ἰθάκῃ οὖσιν ἢ ἐν Τροίᾳ ἢ ὅπως ἂν καὶ τὰ ἔπη ἔχῃ;
Ἴων. ὡς ἐναργές μοι τοῦτο, ὦ Σώκρατες, τὸ τεκμήριον εἶπες· οὐ γάρ
σε ἀποκρυψάμενος ἐρῶ. ἐγὼ γὰρ ὅταν ἐλεινόν τι λέγω, δακρύων
ἐμπίμπλανταί μου οἱ ὀφθαλμοί· ὅταν τε φοβερὸν ἢ δεινόν, ὀρθαὶ αἱ
τρίχες ἵστανται ὑπὸ φόβου καὶ ἡ καρδία πηδᾷ.
. . .
Σωκράτης. οἶσθα οὖν ὅτι καὶ τῶν θεατῶν τοὺς πολλοὺς ταὐτὰ ταῦτα
ὑμεῖς ἐργάζεσθε;
Ἴων. καὶ μάλα καλῶς οἶδα· καθορῶ γὰρ ἑκάστοτε αὐτοὺς ἄνωθεν ἀπὸ
τοῦ βήματος κλάοντάς τε καὶ δεινὸν ἐμβλέποντας καὶ συνθαμβοῦντας
τοῖς λεγομένοις. δεῖ γάρ με καὶ σφόδρ' αὐτοῖς τὸν νοῦν προσέχειν·
ὡς ἐὰν μὲν κλάοντας αὐτοὺς καθίσω, αὐτὸς γελάσομαι ἀργύριον
λαμβάνων, ἐὰν δὲ γελῶντας, αὐτὸς κλαύσομαι ἀργύριον ἀπολλύς.

(PLATO, *Ion* 535B–E)

---

52. See Dué 2002, 80–81. For a similar transformation of the laments of women into a
collective, civic sorrow, see Segal's discussion of Euripides' *Hippolytus* 1462–66 (Segal 1993,
121) and McClure 1999, 41 and 156.

Socrates: Stop and tell me this, and don't conceal what I am going to ask of you: When you perform epic poetry well and produce the greatest effect upon the audience, such as when you sing of Odysseus leaping forth on the floor, revealed to the suitors and casting his arrows at his feet, or the description of Achilles rushing at Hector, or the piteous sorrows of Andromache, Hecuba, or Priam, are you in your right mind? Are you not carried out of yourself, and does not your soul in its enthusiasm seem to be among the persons or places of which you are speaking, whether they are in Ithaca or in Troy or whatever may be the scene of the poem?

Ion: How vivid is the evidence you have adduced, Socrates. For I will not conceal it and will tell you. Whenever I relate a tale of pity, my eyes are filled with tears, and when I speak of horrors, my hair stands on end from fear and my heart throbs.

. . .

Socrates: And are you aware that you rhapsodes produce similar effects on most spectators?

Ion: Only too well; for I look down upon them from the stage, and see them every time weeping, casting terrible glances, and being astonished at the things being recounted. And I am obliged to give my very best attention to them; for if I make them cry I myself shall laugh when I get my money, but if I make them laugh I myself shall cry for losing it.[53]

Plato's depiction of the effect of lamentation in epic has its own purpose within the dialogue and in the corpus of Plato's writings as a whole, but if we can trust this passage even as an exaggerated approximation of the truth, it is clear that the laments of such figures as Briseis, Andromache, and Hecuba inspired a very tearful and emotional reaction in ancient Athenian audiences of the Classical period, and probably throughout the history of epic performance. The passage suggests that the emotions that Aristotle posited as central to the experience of viewing tragedy, namely pity and fear, were elicited by epic as well if it was performed successfully.

These tears for the plight of the captive Trojan women and the fallen Trojan warriors are remarkable, and, as I noted in my introduction to this book, point to an appreciation for the plight of the defeated, regardless of

53. Translation after Jowett (1895). On this passage, see also Greene 1999, who adduces further passages from the work of Plato that characterize epic poetry as a medium that elicits tears and uncontrolled emotion in both the performer and the audience. On the disapproving stance taken by Plato toward the *mimesis* of lament (especially in tragedy), see Seaford 1994, 140–41; Nagy 1998; Loraux 1998, 10–11; and van Wees 1998. See also the discussion in Segal 1993, 62–67, on the "unmanliness" of male tears in the Classical sources.

nationality or ethnicity. The extent to which the Trojans can be considered "barbarians" is a question that will have to be reserved for later chapters, but I submit now that the emotional dynamics of lamentation in epic allowed an identification with the Trojan suffering that superceded national and ethnic loyalties. Because the laments of the captive women of epic formed a continuum with—and in fact evoked for the audience—the rituals and song traditions of Greek women, their emotional impact was potentially as powerful as that of the laments sung at actual funerals by the wives, mothers, and grandmothers of the community of listeners.

Caraveli notes that in some instances in the modern Greek tradition the first few notes of a melody associated with lament were enough to cause a family of mourners to burst into tears. She writes: "Such reactions on the part of diverse audiences suggest that responses to specific styles of lament performances are, to some extent, learned. Not only are the texts of laments symbolic languages unto themselves, but performance components also carry symbolic associations, thus triggering 'pain' in the participants and facilitating the creation of an extraordinary emotional context."[54] Nicole Loraux has made similar suggestions about the triggering effects of the music that would have accompanied the laments of Greek tragedy.[55]

LAMENTING WOMEN ON THE TRAGIC STAGE

I now propose to turn from Greek epic to Greek tragedy, where women's laments play an equally important role in a medium that, like epic, belongs to men. In Greek tragedy, female characters are famously outspoken: they debate, praise, blame, make plans, pray, scheme, sympathize, narrate the past, and make speech-acts. But one thing that female characters do in tragedy above all else is to lament. Both epic and tragedy then are infused with the grief of women, despite the fact that these are male-oriented performance traditions. Epic poetry was composed and performed by men; tragedy was composed by men and all roles were performed by male actors. Women *may* have been in the audience, but the scholarly consensus seems to be that the dramas were intended not for the benefit of women, but rather for the benefit of the male citizen body.[56]

54. Caraveli 1986, 175–76.
55. See Loraux 2002, 54–65.
56. On the much-discussed question of whether women were in the audience of the Athenian dramatic festivals, see, among others, Podlecki 1990; Winkler 1990b; Henderson 1991; Goldhill 1997; Katz 1998; McClure 1999, 4–6; Foley 2001, 3.

Helene Foley's well-known article entitled "The Politics of Tragic Lamentation" explores in detail the representation of women's laments in tragedy
and their relationship to the laws, customs, and attitudes of fifth-century
Athens.[57] Foley shows that the laments enacted in tragedy, particularly those
that are closely tied to funeral ritual, have a complex relationship with societal
practices. Whereas in tragedy women perform elaborate public laments, tear
their cheeks, and rip their clothing, laws enacted from the Archaic period
onward expressly prohibited these actions.[58] Other elements of the funeral
ritual that take place in tragedy were likewise restricted by laws intended to
curb the power and prestige of the aristocracy, while at the same time shifting loyalties from the *oikos* to the *polis*.[59] Building on the work of Alexiou as
well as the fieldwork of scholars of modern Greek laments, Foley argues that
the intent of these laws was to suppress the incendiary power of laments to
initiate revenge. In order for the *polis* to be successful, aristocratic cycles of
vendetta, in which the laments of women played a crucial motivating role,
had to be put to an end.[60]

As women's control over funeral rituals was weakened and their voices
of lament muted, new forms of public mourning began to supplant the
aristocratic funeral. First, as Alexiou has shown, in the incipient democracy
of Athens there was a gradual transfer of mourning rituals and their associated emotions "from the ancestor of the clan cult to the hero of the state
cult."[61] Similarly, as Athenians were increasingly called to serve the state as
sailors and soldiers over the course of the fifth century B.C., the *epitaphios*

57. This article is republished in a revised and expanded form in Foley 2001, 21–55.

58. See Alexiou 1974, 14–23; Loraux 1986, 45–49 and 1998, 9–28; Holst-Warhaft 1992,
114–19; Seaford 1994, 74–105; and most recently, Frisone 2000 (with note 59 below).

59. See the very similar arguments of Alexiou (1974, 21–23) and Seaford (1994, 106) as
well as Foley (2001, 22–25, with references there). Loraux (1998) only partially agrees with
this formulation. She argues that mourning is by nature feminine (in Archaic and Classical
Greek thought) and that by regulating lamentation the Greek city-states were in actuality
regulating women. These laws also had the function of monitoring femininity in male
citizens, who were thought to be feminized by public grief and the emotions inspired by
women's laments.

60. See especially—in addition to Foley 2001—Seaford 1994, chapter 3. On the connection between lament and vendetta see also Holst-Warhaft 1992. The most recent survey of
Greek funerary legislation (not restricted to the Archaic period) is Frisone 2000, although
her approach is quite different from that of the studies I have highlighted here, in that her
focus is more on community (as opposed to the *polis*) and the religious motives for such
legislation as well as the concern for miasma. Hawke's 2004 review of this book outlines
the differences between the two approaches, and provides in notes 1 and 2 a very useful
bibliography for each.

61. Alexiou 1974, 19.

logos, or state funeral oration, effectively replaced the private funeral for the honored war dead. The grandeur and solemnity of public funerals for the war dead became an important forum for the expression of Athenian state ideology.[62]

As Foley and others have noted, however, the laws restricting lamentation were never entirely successful: some laws apparently lapsed and were later repassed, and some customs known to have been prohibited by law are alluded to as still being in practice throughout the Classical period.[63] Lament continued to be the essential medium for the articulation of grief, as is evidenced by its unbroken continuity of form and function in Greek literary and artistic traditions and in popular culture, up to the present day.

Nicole Loraux, who has discussed most fully the displacement of women's laments by the state funeral oration, has written several works that illuminate the role of lament in Athenian tragedy.[64] In *The Mourning Voice* (2002), Loraux argues for a renewed appreciation of the emotional dynamic of Greek tragedy, which she stresses in contrast to its didactic and political aspects, which have been the focus of discussion in recent decades.[65] She shows how tragedy came to be a legitimate outlet for lamentation and tears for the citizen body at the same time that women's laments were being curbed by laws and the public funeral oration was beginning to supplant private mourning rituals. As Segal notes, building on the work of Loraux, "what is repressed in the austere official ceremony of the funeral oration, as we see it in Pericles' funeral speech or in the *epitaphios* ascribed to Lysias, can appear in the unrestrained, though formalized and mythicized, laments in the tragedies."[66] Noting that tragedy was not situated either in the Agora, the political heart of the city, or on the Pnyx, where assemblies were held, but rather in the theater of Dionysus, Loraux argues that in the process of viewing tragedy the spectator learns that he is a mortal first and a citizen second. She concludes: "through the evocation of mourning . . . the spectator will be overcome, and purgation will arouse him to transcend his membership in the civic community and to comprehend his even more essential membership in

---

62. Foley 2001, 25. On this point see also Alexiou 1974, 21–23 and Loraux 1986.

63. See especially Alexiou 1974, 23 and *passim;* Blok 2001, 104–7; and Foley 2001, 25–26.

64. See especially Loraux 1998 and 2002.

65. For a fuller discussion of recent trends in the criticism and interpretation of Greek tragedy, see the foreword to Loraux 2002 by Pietro Pucci. Loraux does not deny the didactic and political functions of Greek tragedy, but rather sees tragedy as a "genre in conflict," in which multiple kinds of speech, song, and dance compete with one another.

66. Segal 1993, 20.

the race of mortals. This has always been the final word sung, not so much to the citizen as to the spectator, by the mourning voice of tragedy."[67]

Lament, therefore, seems to be as essential to Greek tragedy as it is to Greek epic, and perhaps more so. The mourning voices of women on the tragic stage are both reenactments of prototypical laments for heroes and also a vehicle for the exploration and release of contemporary sorrows. As Segal writes, "This weeping within the play also provides a cue for the desired and appropriate response of the audience, their participation in the emotional release of the theater."[68] The weeping is crucial, and as we examine the captive woman's lament in the ensuing chapters, we will have to address the question of just what the citizen spectators are weeping for. Does each audience member weep for his own sorrows, as in the response of the surrounding women to Briseis' lament of *Iliad* 19? Or is there a larger, civic sorrow that can be released by the viewing of tragedy together as a citizen body?

THE CAPTIVE WOMAN'S LAMENT

I now turn to the captive woman's lament, and its place in Greek tragedy. As we began to see in the introduction to this book, the lamentation of the captive Trojan women in the tragedies of Euripides exemplifies features of Greek lament that Alexiou has traced from antiquity to the present day.[69] I have suggested, moreover, that the captive woman's lament combines at least two of Alexiou's categories of lament, thereby forming a category in its own right that is the particular province of captive women.

I first became interested in women's lament traditions, and more specifically the captive woman's lament, while studying the speech in Euripides' *Medea* in which Medea details the plight in which Jason has left her.[70] Here is the climax of the speech:

νῦν ποῖ τράπωμαι; πότερα πρὸς πατρὸς δόμους,
οὓς σοὶ προδοῦσα καὶ πάτραν ἀφικόμην;
ἢ πρὸς ταλαίνας Πελιάδας; καλῶς γ᾽ ἂν οὖν
δέξαιντό μ᾽ οἴκοις ὧν πατέρα κατέκτανον.
ἔχει γὰρ οὕτω· τοῖς μὲν οἴκοθεν φίλοις

67. Loraux 2002, 93.
68. Segal 1993, 29, 64.
69. Because of the vast scope of Alexiou's study, the tragedies of Euripides are discussed only sporadically in that work.
70. Dué 2000.

ἐχθρὰ καθέστηχ᾽, οὓς δέ μ᾽ οὐκ ἐχρῆν κακῶς
δρᾶν, σοὶ χάριν φέρουσα πολεμίους ἔχω.

(*Medea* 502–8)

Now where can I turn? Can I go to my father's house,
the house which I betrayed along with my fatherland when I came
    here?
Or to the wretched daughters of Pelias? Indeed they will certainly
welcome me in their home after I killed their father.
For it stands thus: to my friends at home
I have made myself an enemy, and the people whom I need never have
treated badly are now my foes, thanks to you.

Medea's speech has been cited by R. L. Fowler as a prime example of
what he calls the "desperation speech" in Greek literature. In an exhaustive
study Fowler argues that the desperation speech was a literary device with
its ultimate origins in Homer that reached its full form in tragedy.[71] He
describes the speech as a series of questions that are rhetorically posed and
rejected:

> The options are rejected one after the other, until the speaker lapses
> into a state of helplessness (usually evident from an expressed wish for a
> speedy death); or, if he or she is of a more heroic bent, a decision follows
> that something truly dramatic is in order, suicide or murder being the
> commonest choices.[72]

The classic examples he cites from tragedy are Sophocles' *Ajax* 430–80 (spoken by Ajax) and Euripides' *Medea* 502–19 (cited above, spoken by Medea).
I will quote just a few lines of Ajax's lengthy speech here:

καὶ νῦν τί χρὴ δρᾶν; ὅστις ἐμφανῶς θεοῖς
ἐχθαίρομαι, μισεῖ δέ μ᾽ Ἑλλήνων στρατός,
ἔχθει δὲ Τροία πᾶσα καὶ πεδία τάδε.
πότερα πρὸς οἴκους, ναυλόχους λιπὼν ἕδρας
μόνους τ᾽ Ἀτρείδας, πέλαγος Αἰγαῖον περῶ;
καὶ ποῖον ὄμμα πατρὶ δηλώσω φανεὶς
Τελαμῶνι; πῶς με τλήσεταί ποτ᾽ εἰσιδεῖν
γυμνὸν φανέντα τῶν ἀριστείων ἄτερ,

71. Fowler 1987.
72. Fowler 1987, 6.

ὧν αὐτὸς ἔσχε στέφανον εὐκλείας μέγαν;
οὐκ ἔστι τοὖργον τλητόν.

(*Ajax* 457–66)

And now what shall I do, when I am plainly hated by the gods,
abhorred by the Greek forces
and detested by all Troy and all these plains?
Shall I leave my station at the ships
and the Atreidae to their own devices in order to go home across the
    Aegean?
And how shall I face my father Telamon, when I arrive?
How will he bear to look on me,
when I stand before him stripped, without that supreme prize of valor
for which he himself won a great crown of fame?
No, I could not bear to do it![73]

Fowler's study leads him to conclude that the desperation speech is a feature
of tragedy and the mark of the tragic figure.

In his investigation of the origin of the desperation speech Fowler naturally
looks to the Homeric heroes, who often face comparable critical moments
in the course of their trials that call for decisive action. I submit, however,
that there is another kind of speech in the *Iliad*, one that is far more likely to
be the true prototype of the desperation speech as used by Medea and Ajax.
The laments of Andromache, Briseis, and Helen have a remarkably similar
form to what Fowler calls the desperation speech. What is the relationship
between Fowler's "desperation speech," and what I have called the language
of lament?[74]

To begin to answer this question, let us look at the words of Tecmessa,
Ajax's captive concubine, who replies to Ajax's so-called desperation speech
with one of her own. She describes how she was once the daughter of a
wealthy father and then became a slave when Ajax sacked her town. Worried
that Ajax will kill himself, she begs him not to leave her to become a Greek
captive (for a second time) and an object of abuse, and pleads with him not
to abandon their son to become a helpless orphan. Then in words that echo
Andromache's in the *Iliad* she exclaims:

Ἐμοὶ γὰρ οὐκέτ᾽ ἔστιν εἰς ὅ τι βλέπω
πλὴν σοῦ· σὺ γάρ μοι πατρίδ᾽ ἤστωσας δορί·

73. Translation after Jebb (1893).
74. On "the language of lament," see the introduction to this volume.

καὶ μητέρ' ἄλλη μοῖρα τὸν φύσαντά τε
καθεῖλεν Ἅιδου θανασίμους οἰκήτορας·
τίς δῆτ' ἐμοὶ γένοιτ' ἂν ἀντὶ σοῦ πατρίς;
τίς πλοῦτος; ἐν σοὶ πᾶσ' ἔγωγε σῴζομαι.

(*Ajax* 514–20)

I have nothing left to which I can look,
save you. Your spear ravaged my country to nothingness,
and another fate has brought down my mother and father,
giving them a home in Hades in their death.
What homeland, then, could I have without you?
What wealth? My welfare is entirely in your hands.

Tecmessa's speech combines both the account of the resources she has lost and the rhetorical questions of the desperation speech proper. But these same features are typical of Greek laments.[75] And they are also, of course, particularly appropriately spoken by the captive woman in a foreign land, who has literally no place else to turn. Tecmessa here employs the language of lament even in advance of Ajax's death in an attempt to save him and protect herself and her son.

We may compare, as a number of scholars have done, Tecmessa's speech with Andromache's speech/lament to Hektor in *Iliad* 6.[76] The content of Andromache's speech in *Iliad* 6 resonates with other traditional laments in the *Iliad*, including her own laments in *Iliad* 22 and 24. Andromache is, from the standpoint of epic traditions, the quintessential lamenting and soon-to-be captive wife, even though her captive status is only foreshadowed and never actually realized in the *Iliad*. She says:

δαιμόνιε φθίσει σε τὸ σὸν μένος, οὐδ' ἐλεαίρεις
παῖδά τε νηπίαχον καὶ ἔμ' ἄμμορον, ἣ τάχα χήρη
σεῦ ἔσομαι· τάχα γάρ σε κατακτανέουσιν Ἀχαιοὶ
πάντες ἐφορμηθέντες· ἐμοὶ δέ κε κέρδιον εἴη
σεῦ ἀφαμαρτούσῃ χθόνα δύμεναι· οὐ γὰρ ἔτ' ἄλλη
ἔσται θαλπωρὴ ἐπεὶ ἂν σύ γε πότμον ἐπίσπῃς
ἀλλ' ἄχε'· οὐδέ μοι ἔστι πατὴρ καὶ πότνια μήτηρ.

75. For the questions that are a common feature of laments, see especially Alexiou 1974, 161–65. See also the introduction and chapter 4.

76. Much of my analysis of the speeches of Andromache, Tecmessa, and Briseis here is adapted from my previous discussion of this same topic in Dué 2002 (see especially pages 67–81).

ἤτοι γὰρ πατέρ᾽ ἁμὸν ἀπέκτανε δῖος Ἀχιλλεύς,
ἐκ δὲ πόλιν πέρσεν Κιλίκων εὖ ναιετάουσαν
Θήβην ὑψίπυλον . . .

Ἕκτορ ἀτὰρ σύ μοί ἐσσι πατὴρ καὶ πότνια μήτηρ
ἠδὲ κασίγνητος, σὺ δέ μοι θαλερὸς παρακοίτης·
ἀλλ᾽ ἄγε νῦν ἐλέαιρε καὶ αὐτοῦ μίμν᾽ ἐπὶ πύργῳ,
μὴ παῖδ᾽ ὀρφανικὸν θήῃς χήρην τε γυναῖκα·

(*Iliad* 6.407–32)

Daimonios one, your own spirit will destroy you, neither do you pity
your infant son nor me, ill-fated, I who will soon be
your widow. For soon the Achaeans will kill you,
making an attack all together. It would be better for me
to plunge into the earth if I lost you. For no longer will there be any
comfort once you have met your fate,
but grief. Nor are my father and mistress mother still alive.
For indeed brilliant Achilles killed my father,
and he utterly sacked the well-inhabited city of the Cilicians,
high-gated Thebe . . .

Hektor, *you* are my father and mistress mother,
you are my brother, and you are my flourishing husband.
I beg you, pity me and stay here on the tower,
don't make your child an orphan and your wife a widow.

The element of reproach, which has been noted as characteristic of laments, often takes the form of an accusation of abandonment.[77] Andromache does not reproach Hektor directly in this speech, as she does in *Iliad* 22 and 24, but she does warn him not to leave her a widow and their son an orphan.[78] Hektor admits he would rather die than see Andromache led off into captivity (6.464–65). Andromache herself expresses a wish to die if she loses Hektor (6.410–11), and this wish too is a common feature of laments.[79] The accusation of abandonment in both ancient and modern Greek

77. Alexiou 2002, 182–84. For an intertextual reading of the laments of Andromache and Briseis in the *Iliad,* see now also Tsagalis, chapter 5.

78. See *Iliad* 22.482–86, 24.726–27, 24.742–45.

79. Alexiou 2002, 178–81 and citations at note 46. Cf. *Iliad* 22.481, where Andromache wishes she had never been born, and Helen's similar wish at 24.764.

laments is typically accompanied by a description of the lamenting woman's endangered position in the community.[80] Andromache here relates how she has lost the protection of all of her family members, and sets up Hektor as her last resource.

On this last point we may compare the way that Briseis too relates the deaths of her husband and brothers:

ἄνδρα μέν ᾧ ἔδοσάν με πατὴρ καὶ πότνια μήτηρ
εἶδον πρὸ πτόλιος δεδαϊγμένον ὀξέϊ χαλκῷ,
τρεῖς τε κασιγνήτους, τούς μοι μία γείνατο μήτηρ,
κηδείους, οἳ πάντες ὀλέθριον ἦμαρ ἐπέσπον.

(*Iliad* 19.291–94)

The husband to whom my father and mistress mother gave me
I saw torn by the sharp bronze before the city,
and my three brothers, whom one mother bore together with me,
beloved ones, all of whom met their day of destruction.[81]

Tecmessa's speech in the Ajax makes use of many of the traditional lament techniques that Andromache's includes. Her speech is traditional, but I do not deny that a great deal of its power lies in its intertextual relationship with the *Iliad*. This connection is not limited to Andromache's proleptic lament for Hektor in *Iliad* 6, however; it is equally reminiscent of Briseis' lament for Patroklos.[82] And when we understand that the speeches of Andromache and Tecmessa are in fact the laments of soon-to-be captive women, we can appreciate the connections between Andromache, Briseis, and Tecmessa on another level: all three are well-born women who become captive concubines. Andromache and Tecmessa *once were and will again be* social equals, and that symmetry is part of the power of Tecmessa's speech. In fact Greek laments traditionally articulate a woman's life history while they at the same time define a woman's particular relationship with her community.

Tecmessa's speech is therefore remarkable both for its traditional content as well as for the literary bridge that it creates between epic and tragic interpretations of captive women's lament traditions. Like Andromache's in

80. Alexiou 1974, 165–84; Caraveli 1986; and Herzfeld 1993.
81. Cf. as well Electra to Orestes in the *Libation Bearers* 235–44.
82. See Rose 1995, 64 and Ormand 1999, 112–13. Both note in passing the connection with Briseis. For Tecmessa and Andromache see also Brown 1965–1966 and Kirkwood 1965.

Iliad 6, the speech is not a formal lament for the dead. Ajax is still alive, and Tecmessa's speech is in fact a speech and not a song (as will be many of the laments of Euripidean tragedy discussed in subsequent chapters). Nevertheless, Tecmessa makes use of the language of lament to give herself a voice and the opportunity to try to dissuade Ajax from killing himself.

In the introduction, I adduced a lament speech from Euripides' *Andromache* in which Andromache earns the pity of the Greek chorus when she couches her words within the traditional language of lament. Here too, the chorus pities and even praises Tecmessa: Αἴας, ἔχειν σ᾽ ἂν οἶκτον ὡς κἀγὼ φρενὶ / θέλοιμ᾽ ἄν· αἰνοίης γὰρ ἂν τὰ τῆσδ᾽ ἔπη ("Ajax, I would wish you to have pity for her even as I do; for then you would praise her words"). As in the *Andromache*, lament earns approval and pity for Tecmessa where previous attempts to speak failed. Tecmessa recalls that when she attempted to dissuade Ajax from leaving in the middle of the night on his mission to kill the Greek captains, he dismissed her harshly:

> Ὁ δ᾽ εἶπε πρός με βαί᾽, ἀεὶ δ᾽ ὑμνούμενα·
> "Γύναι, γυναιξὶ κόσμον ἡ σιγὴ φέρει."
> Κἀγὼ μαθοῦσ᾽ ἔληξ᾽, ὁ δ᾽ ἐσσύθη μόνος·
>
> > (*Ajax* 292–94)

And he said to me the familiar saying:
"Woman, silence is the adornment of women."
I learned my lesson and held my tongue, while he rushed out alone.

I submit that the "desperation speech" of Tecmessa is better understood as a manipulation of the genre of lament by a woman who needs to speak out in a desperate situation.

Recognition of the specialized speech in the laments of captive women in the *Iliad* calls for a reexamination of other desperation speeches in tragedy. The speech of Ajax in Sophocles' play of that name is likely to be, as Fowler suggests, the model for many desperate deliberations in subsequent tragedy. I argue, however, that it is also through the laments of figures like Briseis and Andromache that we should read Tecmessa's and perhaps even Ajax's rhetoric of desperation.[83] Just as Odysseus laments like a captive woman, one of his own victims, when he hears the *kleos* of his deeds at Troy in *Odyssey* 8, Ajax experiences the helplessness of the woman he will leave behind, and voices it

---

83. On Medea as a captive woman, see the introduction.

in a speech of desperation that employs the rhetoric and traditional themes of lamentation. In this way, like the *Iliad* and *Odyssey,* the *Ajax* allows an Athenian audience, however briefly, to explore the agony and consequences of war by way of the sorrow of women, as it is expressed in the captive woman's lament.

As noted above, Tecmessa's lament provides us with a perfect bridge between the captive women's laments of epic and those of later tragedy. In the next chapter, I will look at another such intermediary, Aeschylus' *Persians.* That play places the suffering of the defeated enemy before the eyes of the victorious Athenians a mere eight years after the Battle of Salamis, amid ongoing hostilities with Persia. Because the battle itself takes place in Greece, no Persian women are taken captive. But the youth of a nation is cut down, and the women left behind lament their husbands and sons. Aeschylus' play features a chorus of Persian elders who lament Persia's lost youth, and by extension, Persia itself. As we will see, the laments of the Persian elders are often directly concerned with the plight of the Persian wives who have lost their husbands. Throughout the play the audience is invited to imagine the lamentation of the Persian women and to contemplate the battle from the perspective of the widowed women. Thus in 472 B.C. the Athenians were capable of sympathizing with and even weeping for their worst enemy. The Trojan War tragedies, removed as they are by time and tradition, are not as extraordinary in their sympathy for the defeated as is *Persians,* but they too are part of a meaningful pattern that extends back as far as the *Iliad*.

CHAPTER TWO

IDENTIFYING WITH THE ENEMY

LOVE, LOSS, AND LONGING IN
THE *Persians* OF AESCHYLUS

In the first two decades of the fifth century B.C., the century in which Greek tragedy as we know it flourished, the Greeks were attacked twice by the vastly larger army and navy of the Persian Empire. Against all odds, both times they ultimately succeeded in fending them off. But the cost was high. In 480 B.C. the people of Athens abandoned their city to the Persians and retreated with their families and possessions to the nearby island of Salamis. Athens was thoroughly sacked and the acropolis largely destroyed, but the combined forces of the Greeks at Salamis managed to defeat the Persians in a decisive victory. Aeschylus' *Persians* is a tragedy that narrates and laments the Battle of Salamis from the perspective of the defeated Persians.

Aeschylus' play is an extraordinary testament to the Athenians' ability to explore the suffering of war through the eyes of their greatest enemy. In this chapter I argue that the laments of the Persian elders that make up the majority of the play are intensely Greek in their content and emotional force, thereby transcending distinctions between Greek and barbarian and in fact merging the two in the emotional experience of the audience.[1]

I propose to look specifically at the erotic imagery in the play, in order to show that, though put in the mouths of Persians, these hauntingly beautiful evocations of loss exemplify Greek women's laments and love songs. It has been argued that Aeschylus deliberately feminizes the Persian elders in order to construct them as the antithesis of the Greek male ideal.[2] I agree with this formulation only to a certain extent. Aeschylus attributes actions and speech normally associated with Greek women to the Persian elders in order to characterize them as Persian—that is, foreign, Eastern, and not Greek.[3] But the play does not demonize them. The laments of the Persians

1. For a similar reading of the overall effect of the *Persians* as a tragedy see Loraux 2002, 42–53.

2. Hall 1989 and 1996. See discussion below.

3. A particularly striking example can be found at lines 465–68, where Xerxes, upon witnessing the defeat of his army, ritually tears his clothing and laments in the manner of Greek women.

not only highlight the differences between Greeks and Persians, but also uncover their shared experiences and commonalities.[4]

The *Persians* is set in Persia, and all of the speakers are Persians. The play was produced and was part of a group that won first place in 472 B.C., just eight years after the events it depicts. It is the only surviving Greek tragedy that has an historical subject, although this is an accident of survival.[5] Aeschylus himself fought against the Persians at the Battle of Marathon in 490, and Herodotus tells us that Aeschylus' brother died in that battle.[6]

According to the play's hypothesis, Aeschylus' *Persians* was in fact indebted to a certain extent to the playwright Phrynichus' *Phoenician Women,* which was produced four years earlier and also won first place. The chorus of Phrynichus' tragedy was evidently composed of the wives of the Phoenician sailors who formed a substantial part of the Persian navy. These women were widowed by the defeat at Salamis and were no doubt the chief mourners in the play. For reasons that I will propose in this chapter, the composition of the chorus suggests to me that the play treated the Persians sympathetically and would have inspired a great deal of pity in the Greek audience.[7] In this

4. Cf. Loraux 1995, 4, in considering the oppositions between male and female that operate in Greek tragedy: "It is likely that more than one discriminating factor differentiates the citizen from his other, or others. But if one does not regard the opposition between likeness and difference—even if it is 'radical'—as the last word in Greek thinking (after all, Plato knew better than anyone else that the Same participates in the Other), one is forced to admit that the richest of discriminating factors is the feminine, the operator par excellence that makes it possible to conceive of identity as fashioned, in practical terms, by otherness. This means that a Greek man, or anyone who wishes to read the Greeks, must perform mental operations that are more complex than merely verifying a table of antithetical categories again and again."

Recent work on Herodotus likewise has a more subtle view of the Greek construction of the other than is generally found in modern interpretations of the *Persians.* See especially Pelling 1997c and Munson 2001, 3–5 and 132–33, building on the work of Fornara (1971a and 1971b), Corcella (1984), Raaflaub (1987), Hartog (1988), and Moles (1996). These scholars interpret Herodotus' narrative about the Persian Wars in the light of its composition during the Peloponnesian War. Munson (2001) notes the many similarities that Herodotus draws between the Greeks and foreign peoples in communicating to the Greeks, in the words of Munson, "things they should learn about themselves" (Munson 2001, 4).

5. The distinction between historical and mythical tragedies is somewhat misleading, because what we call myth was believed to be history by the Greeks themselves. On the other hand, the Persian Wars achieved a kind of legendary status almost as soon as they occurred. See Herington 1985, 129.

6. Herodotus 6.114.

7. In 409 B.C. Phoenician women could still be emblematic of the suffering caused by war. In Euripides' *Phoenician Women,* which takes as its plot the Seven Against Thebes

sense Phrynichus' play is even more remarkable than Aeschylus', since it was produced a mere four years after Salamis.

How is it possible that Phrynichus and later Aeschylus were able to produce tragedies on the Athenian stage about Salamis, an event that by all rights was a great victory against a superior aggressor? In other words, how can the *Persians* be a tragedy? Is not tragedy a genre that depends on the ability of the audience to feel pity for the events depicted onstage?[8] If so, how could the Persians evoke pity and sorrow from the Athenians in 476 and 472 B.C.?

Before I explore this question further, it should be noted that the playwright Phrynichus, whose tragedies do not survive, is also known to us because of an incident related by Herodotus. In the 490s B.C. the Ionian Greek cities on the coast of Asia Minor revolted against Persian rule with help from the Athenians and others; the Persians systematically subjugated them. In 494 the Persians defeated the combined Ionian navy in a sea battle near the Greek city of Miletus, and Miletus itself was destroyed by siege. All of its inhabitants were killed or enslaved.[9] Phrynichus produced a tragedy sometime thereafter entitled the *Capture of Miletus* (Μιλήτου Ἅλωσις). Herodotus relates that the Athenians wept so profusely during the performance that Phrynichus was fined 1000 drachmas for "reminding them of their own misfortunes" (ὡς ἀναμνήσαντα οἰκήια κακά), and the play was banned from ever being performed again.[10]

What is significant about this story for our purposes is that in the *Capture of Miletus* the Persians are clearly the "bad guys" of the tragedy. Presumably

---

tradition, the chorus of captive Phoenician women, whose presence in Thebes is otherwise tangential to the plot of the play, laments the horrors that war brings upon a city.

8. This definition of tragedy derives ultimately from Aristotle, who argues in his *Poetics* that the essential emotions of tragedy are pity and fear (see Aristotle, *Poetics* 1449b24–28). For more on the emotions of tragedy and pity in particular see the edition of Janko 1987 *ad* 1453a4, Konstan 2001, and the conclusion to this volume. On this passage from the *Poetics* and the emotional dynamic of *katharsis,* see Janko 1987, xvi–xx and Segal 1993, 25–29. The bibliography on *katharsis* is of course very large indeed. See the bibliography published by Schrier (1998) and the continuation by M. Heath (2004) at http://www.leeds.ac.uk/classics/resources/poetics/poetbib.htm.

9. Herodotus 6.18.

10. Herodotus 6.21. On the *Capture of Miletus* and this anecdote's relationship to the central emotions of tragedy see Rosenbloom 1995, 101–2. Loraux (2002) notes that in Herodotus the weeping of the Athenians upon viewing the tragedy is a substitute for an authentic funeral rite, and is linked directly with the evolution of tragedy as a vehicle for lamentation, which was otherwise restricted by law in the Athenian state beginning in the sixth century B.C. Loraux argues that after Phrynichus' play, lamentation in tragedy came to be restricted to heroes of the distant past, and thus distanced from the spectators. See also Alexiou 1974, 14–23; Loraux 1998, 9–28; and discussion below.

the Athenians weep upon hearing the lamentation of the captive Milesians and witnessing their downfall onstage (or hearing of it via messenger). The Athenians, moreover, had contributed a number of ships to the Ionian revolt, and so were directly affected by the outcome. Their emotional reaction is predictable: they weep for themselves and their fellow Greeks, as the Greek word *oikeia* implies. This anecdote from Herodotus makes Phrynichus' *Phoenician Women* (and Aeschylus' *Persians*) all the more surprising then as a subject for Greek tragedy. Could Phrynichus write tragedy just as easily from the point of view of the Persians as from that of the Greeks?[11] Could the Athenian audience have possibly reacted with weeping to a play like the *Phoenician Women,* in which the lamentation is Persian and not Greek?

It would be too simple to interpret the emotional force of the *Phoenician Women* or the *Persians* as *Schadenfreude*—delight in the misfortunes of the enemy.[12] Nicole Loraux has recently challenged interpretations of the *Persians* that liken it to a victory song of sorts:

> Can we say, then, that Aeschylus' tragedy follows the same logic of self-celebration as a funeral oration? . . . Was it joy they heard in the representations of the Persians' grief, where they saw a hymn of praise to Athens? I myself, hastily and somewhat imprudently, have said as much in the past. However, I have since become convinced that the interpretation of the tragic effect can never stem from such simple, or simply ideological reasons—not to mention the proposition that a tragedy might produce jubilation in an audience.[13]

There is no gloating to be found in Aeschylus' play. And while the Persians are certainly constructed as an other, as clearly demonstrated by Edith Hall's work on the play,[14] the very fact that the *Persians* is a prize-winning tragedy

11. Loraux (2002, 42–44) argues that Phrynichus "learned his lesson" from the experience of the *Capture of Miletus,* and thus presented the more acceptable sufferings of the Persians in his *Phoenician Women.* On this point see also Meier 1993, 63.

12. See also Goldhill 1988, 193 and Meier 1993, 71.

13. Loraux 2002, 45. Loraux is of course not the first to interpret the *Persians* as sympathetic to the defeated enemy. See, e.g., Murray 1940, 127–28; Goldhill 1988; and Segal 1996, 165. See also Rosenbloom 1995 and Pelling 1997 for subtle and cautious discussions of several of the issues raised here. For anti-Persian readings, see especially Hall 1989, 56–100. In her 1996 edition of the play Hall notes the extreme example of Ridgeway 1910: "[The *Persians*] is no true drama; it is rather a glorious epinician poem infinitely superior to those . . . [of] Pindar" (Hall 1996, 17, note 104). The *Persians* has been interpreted even more recently by Harrison (2000 and 2002) as a celebration of Athenian superiority over Persia.

14. Hall 1989.

should encourage us to look for more than Athenian self-congratulation in the laments of the Persian elders.

Edith Hall's *Inventing the Barbarian* (1989) explores how the Greek literary imagination constructed the idea of the Persians as a barbarian—that is, non-Greek—people with non-Greek, inferior customs in the wake of the Persian Wars:

> [*Inventing the Barbarian*] argues that Greek writing about barbarians is usually an exercise in self-definition, for the barbarian is often portrayed as the opposite of the ideal Greek. It suggests that the polarization of Hellene and barbarian was invented in specific historical circumstances during the early years of the fifth century B.C., partly as a result of military efforts against the Persians.[15]

Hall goes on to discuss the way in which a common external enemy helped to foster a Panhellenic sense of community among the Greeks who allied together to fight the Persians in the decades following Salamis.

Hall's analysis forcefully shows that the Greek imagination of the barbarian Persians in the fifth century B.C. had little to do with the actual character or customs of the Persians themselves. Whatever was opposed to Greek ideals became Persian, and portrayal of the Persians onstage or in literature was a caricature of Persian ways at best. The Persians therefore became in the Greek mind effeminate, luxurious, and excessive—the antithesis of the ideal masculine, frugal, and moderate Greek. Political differences were also an important preoccupation: to the democratic Athenian mind the Persians embodied tyranny.[16] The Persians in Aeschylus are clearly an other, and that characterization is achieved by setting up such oppositions as between male and female, frugality and luxury, moderation and excess. There is a patent desire on the part of Aeschylus to portray the Persians as exotic and foreign, and many scholars have commented on such elements as the costuming, musical elements, and even movements of the actors and chorus, which would have served to create an exotic and distinctly Persian atmosphere onstage.[17]

The influence of Hall's study has been justifiably pervasive. And yet, as I will argue, it does not provide a complete picture of the Athenian conception of the barbarian in the fifth century B.C. For one thing, Hall insists that a

15. Hall 1989, 1–2. On the relationship of Hall's work to the analogous work of Hartog (1988) on Herodotus, see Pelling 1997c and note 4 above.

16. See Goldhill 1988; Hall 1989, 56–100; and Harrison 2000 and 2002.

17. See, e.g, Pickard-Cambridge 1968, 201–2; Taplin 1977, 61–128; Meier 1993, 70–71; and Hall 1996, 19–25.

radical new treatment of barbarians in literature and art began to take place
after the Persian Wars. For Hall, there is no continuum that can be traced
from the *Iliad* through the Archaic period and into the Classical.[18] Aeschylus'
Persians is for Hall one of the first and foremost examples of a new trend.[19]
But the poetry of Aeschylus is steeped in the Homeric tradition, and there
are many points of continuity between the treatment of the Trojans in epic
and that of the Persians in Aeschylus' tragedy.[20]

The laments of the Persian elders draw on ancient themes that portray
the fallen warriors as flowers cut down before maturity. This imagery is itself
fundamentally linked to Greek hero-cult traditions, in which the beautiful
youths of myth are ritually lamented by the community. The Persian dead
are heroized and lamented in terms that are thoroughly Greek, with the
result that there can be little distinction drawn between the Greek and the
Persian soldiers. The *Persians* laments both equally.

Anthos AND *Kleos*

The *Persians* begins with the entrance song of the Persian elders, in which
the warriors of the Persian army are listed by name and described in terms
that evoke an epic catalogue, as in the following excerpt.

18. See especially Hall 1989, 1, where it is stated that there was a great difference in the
portrayal of Trojans in epic and tragedy. In support of Hall's line of argument, I note that
the use of the term "barbarian" in the plural as a reference to the non-Greek collective
does not appear until the fifth century (Hall 1989, 9). I question, however, the inclusion
of the Trojans of Athenian tragedy in the term "barbarian": the Trojans are a special case.
Moreover, I do not find the Trojans of tragedy to be radically different from those of epic.
See further discussion below in chapter 3.

19. See, e.g., Hall 1989, 57: "Aeschylus' *Persae,* which celebrates the victories over Persia,
is the earliest testimony to the absolute polarization in Greek thought of Hellene and
barbarian."

20. On Homeric diction in Aeschylus see especially Judet de la Combe 1995 as well
as Sideras 1971, 198–200 and 212–15. To be fair, Hall's 1996 commentary on the *Persians*
notes most of the points of continuity that I discuss here, and I cite her work wherever
our citations and/or ideas converge. The question is one of emphasis and interpretation.
While Hall is careful to note Homeric reminiscences wherever they occur, the significance
of the whole is not discussed. Hall's analysis of the themes of the *Persians* as a play instead
focuses on the way that the Persians are portrayed (for the first time in Greek literature)
as foreign, feminine, and inferior. Nevertheless, Hall (1996, 24) does suggest that there is
still a great deal of work to be done on the transformation of epic diction by Aeschylus.
She notes, "the point is usually not what he has borrowed, but the way in which he has
adapted or altered it."

οἷος Ἀμίστρης ἠδ' Ἀρταφρένης
καὶ Μεγαβάτης ἠδ' Ἀστάσπης,
ταγοὶ Περσῶν,
βασιλῆς βασιλέως ὕποχοι μεγάλου,
σοῦνται, στρατιᾶς πολλῆς ἔφοροι,
τοξοδάμαντές τ' ἠδ' ἱπποβάται,
φοβεροὶ μὲν ἰδεῖν, δεινοὶ δὲ μάχην
ψυχῆς εὐτλήμονι δόξῃ·

(*Persians* 21–28)

[Men] like Amistres and Artaphrenes
and Megabates and Astaspes,
commanders of the Persians,
kings and subjects of the Great King,
are set in motion, overseers of the multitude of the army,
men who subdue with the bow and drive horses,
frightening to look upon and terrible to fight against,
with steadfast determination of spirit.

The catalogue is focalized through the eyes of the Persian elders, who last saw the army departing in all of its glory. The list of fighting warriors and their attributes casts the Persian leaders as epic heroes, who are described as setting out for battle.

As many have noted, this catalogue of Persian warriors is reminiscent of Greek epic conventions. But it also contains details that are distinctly Persian in the Greek imagination. The army is *polukhrusos*—"full of gold" or "gold-bedecked."[21] The names of the warriors themselves are foreign and contain many authentic Persian elements.[22] In this way Aeschylus presents the Persian warriors as exotic and luxuriant from the very beginning of the play. As we will see, the imagery and vocabulary of luxuriousness are perhaps the most important characterizing elements in the *Persians*. But at the same time the catalogue casts the warriors in a role that is larger than life. By situating the Persians in the realm of tradition and myth in these opening lines Aeschylus

21. Hall's translation "gold-bedecked" I think captures the meaning well. Many editors prefer the emendation πολυάνδρου, but I agree with Hall that πολυχρύσου requires no emendation, given the persistent imagery of luxury applied to the Persians throughout the play. Euphorbus (discussed below) is a Trojan ally in the *Iliad* who wears gold and silver in his hair.

22. See Hall 1996 *ad loc.*

links the Persians with Greek song traditions and in particular the metaphor world of epic poetry.

This metaphor world is evoked with particular resonance when the Persian elders bring their catalogue to a close:

τοιόνδ᾽ ἄνθος Περσίδος αἴας
οἴχεται ἀνδρῶν
οὓς πέρι πᾶσα χθὼν Ἀσιῆτις
ρέψασα πόθῳ στένεται μαλερῷ,
τοκέης τ᾽ ἀλοχοί θ᾽ ἡμερολεγδὸν
τείνοντα χρόνον τρομέονται.

(*Persians* 59–64)

Such is the flower [*anthos*] of the Persian land,
such is the flower of men that has disappeared.
The entire land of Asia
laments the men she nourished with fierce longing [*pothos*].
Parents and wives, counting the days,
tremble at the increasing length of time.

The depiction of the Persian army here and elsewhere as the flower of the land is reminiscent of Athenian traditions in which soldiers who have died fighting for their city are consistently imagined to be at the peak of youth or beauty, or *hêbê*.[23] The theme of *hêbê* as a flower or blossom (*anthos*) is an important and common one in Greek poetry,[24] but the metaphor of the *anthos* is especially connected with the death of heroes in war, as glorified

---

23. For the lamented *hêbê* of the Persians, see *Persians* 512 and 926. On this point I benefited greatly from the presentation of Vincent Rosivach at the 2003 American Philological Association annual meeting, entitled "'Military' Lekythoi: Private vs. Public Mourning of Athenian War Dead." Cf. Meiggs-Lewis 48, an Athenian casualty list from ca. 447 B.C.: οἵδε παρ᾽ ἑλλέσποντον ἀπόλεσαν ἀγλαὸν ἔβεν / βαρνάμενοι, σφετέραν δ᾽ εὐκλέϊσαμ πατρίδα / ὅστ᾽ ἐχθρὸς στενάχεμ πολέμο θέρος ἐκκομίσαντας, / αὐτοῖς δ᾽ ἀθάνατον μνεμ᾽ ἀρετες ἔθεσαν ("These beside the Hellespont lost their splendid youth / fighting, but bestowed fame on their fatherland, / so that their enemies groan, having carried away the harvest of war, / but for themselves they set a deathless reminder of excellence"; translation is Rosivach's, used by permission). See next note for discussion of the meaning of *hêbê*.

24. See, e.g., *Iliad* 13.484, where Idomeneus fears Aeneas, who is in the bloom of youth (ἥβης ἄνθος). The Greek word *hêbê*, "youth," does not connote childhood, as the English word "youth" might imply, but rather the peak of young adulthood, which for the Greeks meant approximately age 16–18. Below I translate *hêbê* as "manhood," where it refers to the time when a young man reaches the age of marriage. See also Borthwick 1976 for the full range of meaning for *anthos* in Greek literature.

by epic poetry (*kleos*).²⁵ One of the primary metaphors for epic poetry in the *Iliad* is that of a flower that will never wilt:

μήτηρ γάρ τέ μέ φησι θεὰ Θέτις ἀργυρόπεζα
διχθαδίας κῆρας φερέμεν θανάτοιο τέλος δέ.
εἰ μέν κ᾽ αὖθι μένων Τρώων πόλιν ἀμφιμάχωμαι,
λετο μέν μοι νόστος, ἀτὰρ κλέος ἄφθιτον ἔσται·
εἰ δέ κεν οἴκαδ᾽ ἵκωμι φίλην ἐς πατρίδα γαῖαν,
λετό μοι κλέος ἐσθλόν, ἐπὶ δηρὸν δέ μοι αἰὼν
ἔσσεται, οὐδέ κέ μ᾽ ὦκα τέλος θανάτοιο κιχείη.

(*Iliad* 9.410–16)

My mother the goddess Thetis of the shining feet tells me
that there are two ways in which I may meet my end.
If I stay here and fight around the city of Troy,
my homecoming is lost, but my glory in song [*kleos*] will be
    unwilting [*aphthiton*]:
whereas if I reach home my *kleos* is lost, but my life will be
    long,
and the outcome of death will not soon take me.

Here Achilles reveals not only the crux of his choice but also the driving principle of Greek epic song. The unwilting flower of epic poetry is contrasted with the necessarily mortal hero, whose death comes all too quickly.²⁶

The theme of the hero as a plant that blossoms beautifully and dies quickly is also an important theme in Greek lament traditions,²⁷ including the laments for Achilles within the *Iliad,* such as the following by Thetis:

ὤ μοι ἐγὼ δειλή, ὤ μοι δυσαριστοτόκεια,
ἥ τ᾽ ἐπεὶ ἂρ τέκον υἱὸν ἀμύμονά τε κρατερόν τε

25. See, e.g., *Iliad* 4.473–89, 8.306–8, 17.53–58 (discussed below), 18.56–57 and 436–40, and 22.86–87 and 423. For *kleos* as the glory conveyed by epic song see Nagy 1979, 16–18. On the vegetal imagery that describes the deaths of warriors in the *Iliad* see also Schein 1984, 69–76 and 96–97.

26. See especially Nagy 1979, 174–84. Nagy shows that the root *phthi-* is inherently connected with vegetal imagery, and means "wilt."

27. For plant imagery in ancient, Byzantine, and modern Greek laments see Alexiou 1974, 195–97. In Longus' novel *Daphnis and Chloe* there is a stunning passage in which this central metaphor of Greek laments becomes literal. Flowers that have been cut down by an enemy (who is in this case a rival suitor for the hand of Chloe) are themselves ritually lamented; see Longus 4.7–8. On the erotic associations of meadows and gardens see Calame 1999, 151–74.

ἔξοχον ἡρώων· ὃ δ' ἀνέδραμεν ἔρνεϊ ἶσος·
τὸν μὲν ἐγὼ θρέψασα φυτὸν ὡς γουνῷ ἀλωῆς
νηυσὶν ἐπιπροέηκα κορωνίσιν Ἴλιον εἴσω
Τρωσὶ μαχησόμενον· τὸν δ' οὐχ ὑποδέξομαι αὖτις
οἴκαδε νοστήσαντα δόμον Πηλήϊον εἴσω.

(*Iliad* 18.54–60)

Alas how wretched I am, alas how unluckily I was the best child bearer
since I bore a son both faultless and powerful,
outstanding among heroes. He shot up like a sapling.
I nourished him like a plant on the hill of an orchard
and I sent him forth in the hollow ships to Ilion
to fight with the Trojans. But I will not receive him again
returning home to the house of Peleus.

The *Iliad* quotes within its narration of Achilles' *kleos* many songs of lamentation that serve to highlight the mortality of the central hero as well as underscore the immortality of song. The traditional imagery of these quoted laments, as sung primarily by Thetis, spill over into epic diction itself, with the result that similes, metaphors, and other traditional descriptions of heroes are infused with themes drawn from the natural world.

The depiction of the death of the Trojan Euphorbus in the *Iliad* is one such place where epic diction draws on the plant imagery that pervades Greek laments for heroes. Euphorbus, like Achilles, is compared to a young tree: Euphorbus topples like a tree that is overcome by a storm.[28]

ἀντικρὺ δ' ἁπαλοῖο δι' αὐχένος ἤλυθ' ἀκωκή,
δούπησεν δὲ πεσών, ἀράβησε δὲ τεύχε' ἐπ' αὐτῷ.
αἵματί οἱ δεύοντο κόμαι Χαρίτεσσιν ὁμοῖαι
πλοχμοί θ', οἳ χρυσῷ τε καὶ ἀργύρῳ ἐσφήκωντο.
οἷον δὲ τρέφει ἔρνος ἀνὴρ ἐριθηλὲς ἐλαίης
χώρῳ ἐν οἰοπόλῳ, ὅθ' ἅλις ἀναβέβροχεν ὕδωρ,
καλὸν τηλεθάον· τὸ δέ τε πνοιαὶ δονέουσι
παντοίων ἀνέμων, καί τε βρύει ἄνθεϊ λευκῷ·
ἐλθὼν δ' ἐξαπίνης ἄνεμος σὺν λαίλαπι πολλῇ
βόθρου τ' ἐξέστρεψε καὶ ἐξετάνυσσ' ἐπὶ γαίῃ·

28. Comparison of the dead to a tree is one of the most common and ancient themes in the Greek lament tradition. See Alexiou 1974, 198–201; Danforth 1982, 96–99; and Sultan 1999, 70–71.

τοῖον Πάνθου υἱὸν ἐϋμμελίην Εὔφορβον
Ἀτρεΐδης Μενέλαος ἐπεὶ κτάνε τεύχε' ἐσύλα.

(*Iliad* 17.49–60)

The point went straight through his soft neck.
He fell with a thud, and the armor clattered on top of him.
His hair was soaked with blood, and it was like the Graces [*Kharites*],
as were his braids, which were tightly bound with gold and silver.
Just like a flourishing sapling of an olive tree that a man nourishes
in a solitary place where water gushes up in abundance,
a beautiful sapling growing luxuriantly—blasts
of every kind of wind shake it and it is full of white blossoms [*anthos*],
but suddenly a wind comes together with a furious storm
and uproots the tree so that it is stretched out on the ground—
even so did the son of Atreus Menelaus strip
the son of Panthos, Euphorbus with the ash spear, of his armor after
    he had slain him.

The plant imagery in this passage is intensified by two references to blossoms.
In the simile, the tree to which Euphorbus is compared blossoms with white
flowers. Moreover, the D scholia to the *Iliad* reveal that this comparison
between Euphorbus and the tree with its blossoms is even closer than might
appear at first glance. According to the scholia, *kharites*, translated here as
"the Graces," means in the Cypriote dialect of Greek "myrtle blossoms."[29]
The flecks of blood in Euphorbus' hair look like myrtle blossoms. Since
the Arcado-Cypriote dialect layer of Homeric diction contains some of the
oldest elements of the poetic system in which the *Iliad* and *Odyssey* were
composed, it is likely that in the most ancient phases of the *Iliad* tradition
Euphorbus' hair was understood to look like myrtle blossoms.[30] Thus we
find that the comparison of a dying warrior to a flower is an ancient theme
at the core of the Greek epic tradition.

This theme is not confined to the literary tradition, however. It is fundamentally connected with communal laments for and the religious worship of
heroes. A particularly good example of such worship is the popular women's

29. Μακεδόνες δὲ καὶ Κύπριοι χάριτας λέγουσιν τὰς συνεστραμμένας καὶ οὔλας
μυρσίνας, ἅς φαμέν στεφανίτιδας. See the forthcoming publication of the 2002 Sather
Lectures by Gregory Nagy.

30. For the best account of the dialectic layers that form the Homeric system see Parry
1971, 325–64 [= Parry 1932]. See also Householder and Nagy 1972, 58–70.

festival of Adonis, the Adonia, in which the untimely death of Aphrodite's young and beautiful mortal lover was lamented by means of "gardens of Adonis." Women would plant seeds during midsummer in pots on their roofs, so that they would grow very quickly and then immediately wither in the intense summer sun.[31]

An important part of the Adonia was the singing of laments, traces of which survive in literature ranging from Sappho to late antiquity. The *Epitaph for Adonis* (Ἀδώνιδος ἐπιτάφιος) by the Hellenistic poet Bion—possibly composed for performance at the Adonia[32]—is a lament and a love song for the beautiful youth, who died in a hunting accident.[33] The poem brings together a variety of traditions concerning Adonis and his transformation after death into a species of flower.[34] A common version of the myth has Adonis transformed into the anemone. In Bion's poem, Adonis' blood brings forth the rose, and Aphrodite's tears produce the anemone:

"αἰαῖ τὰν Κυθέρειαν, ἀπώλετο καλὸς Ἄδωνις."
δάκρυον ἁ Παφία τόσσον χέει ὅσσον Ἄδωνις
αἷμα χέει, τὰ δὲ πάντα ποτὶ χθονὶ γίνεται ἄνθη·
αἷμα ῥόδον τίκτει, τὰ δὲ δάκρυα τὰν ἀνεμώναν.

(*Epitaph for Adonis* 63–66)

"Alas, Cytherean goddess, beautiful Adonis is dead."
The Paphian pours forth as many tears as Adonis
does blood. All become blossoms on the earth.
The blood produces a rose, the tears the anemone.

The narrator of the poem (a female mourner) then instructs Aphrodite to lay Adonis on her own bed, strewn with flowers and garlands, for the prothesis.[35]

31. See Plato, *Phaedrus* 276B. On the festival of Adonis, celebrated throughout the Greek world in antiquity, see Atallah 1966; Alexiou 1974, 55–57; Nagy 1984, 60–63; Winkler 1990a, 188–93; Detienne 1994; and Reed 1995. See also note 34 below.

32. See Alexiou 1974, 56 and Reed 1997, 21.

33. On the combination of lament and love song in Bion's poem see Alexiou 1974, 56 as well as Reed 1997 *ad* 42–61.

34. For the testimonia regarding Adonis' transformation see Reed 1997 *ad* 66. Reed sees flower metamorphoses as a Hellenistic literary device. Although our sources are late, I submit that the theme is extremely old (see discussion of the death of Euphorbus, above), and that Bion's poem taps into a rich tradition of laments for heroes in which the central metaphor is that of a flower or young tree.

35. For the ritual elements of a Greek funeral see Alexiou 1974, 4–10.

παγχρυσέῳ κλιντῆρι πόθες καὶ στυγνὸν Ἄδωνιν,
βάλλε δέ νιν στεφάνοισι καὶ ἄνθεσι· πάντα σὺν αὐτῷ·
ὡς τῆνος τέθνακε καὶ ἄνθεα πάντ᾽ ἐμαράνθη.

(*Epitaph for Adonis* 74–81)

On the all-golden couch lay out Adonis, even though he is repellent in
    death,
and heap him with garlands and flowers. Since he died,
everything died with him, and all the flowers have wilted.

In this poem, which reenacts the very moment of Aphrodite's discovery of
Adonis' death and her lament over his body, the wilted flower is already
the symbol of Adonis. It is even said that the fact of Adonis' death *causes*
all flowers to wilt, as if by metonymy with his own dead corpse. Thus the
death of Adonis is connected with both the creation and the premature
death of plant life.

Bion's poem was composed centuries after the *Persians* (and Aeschylus' play
was itself composed centuries after the *Iliad*), but I have chosen to focus on it
because it extends in a beautiful way an important constellation of traditional
themes and imagery connected with the heroes of Archaic Greek epic and
cult. The Persians are described as the flower (*anthos*) of the Persian land as
they march in glory toward battle—the very battle in which they will meet
their deaths: τοιόνδ᾽ ἄνθος Περσίδος αἴας / οἴχεται ἀνδρῶν (*Persians* 59–60,
cited above). The phrase is invoked a second time when the messenger ar-
rives to announce the devastating defeat: τὸ Περσῶν δ᾽ ἄνθος οἴχεται πεσόν
("the flower of the Persians has fallen and disappeared," *Persians* 252). The
Persians are in this way fundamentally linked with the warrior heroes of
Greek epic traditions, in which Greek and non-Greek alike are singled out
at the moment of death by similes and metaphors drawn from the world
of plants and flowers.

A third time the warriors are called the *anthos* of Persia, again in conjunction with death in battle: πολλοὶ φῶτες, χώρας ἄνθος, / τοξοδάμαντες,
πάνυ ταρφύς τις / μυριὰς ἀνδρῶν, ἐξέφθινται ("many men, the flower of
the land, archers, a densely crowded myriad of men has perished," *Persians*
925–27). The preceding lines (922–24) too pick up on an epic theme:

γᾶ δ᾽ αἰάζει τὰν ἐγγαίαν
ἥβαν Ξέρξᾳ κταμέναν Ἅιδου
σάκτορι Περσᾶν

Earth cries "aiai" for the youth [*hêbê*]
born of her, cut down by Xerxes,
the one who has crammed Hades full with Persians.

Here the young Persian warriors are imagined to have filled Hades—the *Greek* underworld—to the point of overflowing. Such an image recalls the opening lines of the *Iliad*, in which Achilles' anger is said to have sent many steadfast lives of heroes down to Hades (πολλὰς δ' ἰφθίμους ψυχὰς Ἄϊδι προΐαψεν / ἡρώων, *Iliad* 1.3–4).

Just as striking in these lines is the association of the Persians with the earth, here personified as lamenting the Persian dead.[36] Athenians believed that they themselves were autochthonous, born from the earth, according to the Athenian charter myth.[37] The distinction between Athenian and Persian is here so nonexistent that the Persians themselves can be described as native to the earth (ἐγγαίαν, 922).[38] Their connection to the earth reinforces the imagery of the wilted *anthos*, which is born from the earth and soon returns to it.[39]

Habros AND Hubris

The image of the *anthos*, however, is only one of a cluster of related themes of Greek lament that Aeschylus applies to the Persian warriors. Let us return briefly to Bion's lament for Adonis, and the lines immediately following the passage just discussed.

ῥαῖνε δέ νιν Συρίοισιν ἀλείφασι, ῥαῖνε μύροισιν·
ὀλλύσθω μύρα πάντα· τὸ σὸν μύρον λετ' Ἄδωνις.

36. For the personification of mother earth in the *Persians* see also Hall 1996 *ad* 61–62.

37. See, e.g., Euripides, *Ion* 29; Isocrates 4.24 and 12.124; and Pausanias 2.14 with Loraux 2000.

38. In fact the Persians and Athenians become related, albeit distantly. Cf. 185–86, in which Persia and Greece are said to be "sisters of the same race" (κασιγνήτα γένους ταὐτοῦ).

39. As Alexiou has shown, the idea of the earth as the giver of life is fundamentally connected with the offering of fruit, grain, and flowers when burying the dead. (Cf. *Persians* 611–18, where spring water, honey, wine, oil, and garlands of flowers are offered to the tomb of Darius.) Alexiou cites two funerary inscriptions that illustrate this theme (Alexiou 1974, 9; translations are Alexiou's): θρεφθὲς δ' ἐν χθονὶ τῆιδε θάνεν (Peek 697.5), "He died in the earth where he was nourished"; ἐκ γαίας βλαστὼν γαῖα πάλιν γέγονα (Peek 1702.2), "Having sprung from the earth, earth I have become once more."

κέκλιται ἁβρὸς ῎Αδωνις ἐν εἵμασι πορφυρέοισιν,
ἀμφὶ δέ νιν κλαίοντες ἀναστενάχουσιν ῎Ερωτες
κειράμενοι χαίτας ἐπ᾽ ᾽Αδώνιδι·

(*Epitaph for Adonis* 77–81)

Sprinkle him with Syrian oils, sprinkle him with perfume.
All perfumes have perished. Your perfume has perished, Adonis.
Luxuriant [*habros*] Adonis lies on crimson cloths,
and around him the *Erotes* wail in lamentation,
cutting off their hair for Adonis.

Just as Adonis' death has caused all flowers to wilt, so now all perfumes have perished, as if perfume too were a living thing. In this context, his dead body lying on crimson fabric on a golden couch, Adonis is described as *habros* (ἁβρός)—"luxuriant." And as with the image of the *anthos,* we will see that a theme rooted in the lament traditions of heroes links the Persian warriors with both the death of heroes and the *kleos* of Greek song.

Gregory Nagy has shown that the word *habros* is fundamentally connected with sensuality.[40] Adonis is *habros* in one of the two fragments of Sappho that lament his death:[41]

κατθνα‹ί›σκει, Κυθέρη᾽, ἄβρος ῎Αδωνις· τί κε θεῖμεν;
καττύπτεσθε, κόραι, καὶ κατερείκεσθε κίθωνας.

(FRAGMENT 140V)

40. I am heavily indebted in the discussion that follows to Nagy's analysis of *hubris* and *habros* in Nagy 1990a, 263–90, as well as Nagy 1985, 60–63. See also the thorough and illuminating discussion of Kurke (1992), who focuses on the political dimension of the word and its associations with an aristocratic lifestyle. Most recently, see Reed 1995, 343, noting that poets describe Adonis as *habros* "to celebrate his ephebic gorgeousness." Although I have disagreements with Reed's 1995 article that are too extensive to be synthesized in a single footnote, in general I concur with Reed's interpretation of Adonis' *habrosunê* as both sexual in nature and connected with the excesses of lamentation. Reed argues that the festival of the Adonia allowed women to express themselves sexually and to lament. These two kinds of expression (which are intricately connected on the level of formula and theme) were normally forbidden to Greek women, except in certain ritualized circumstances. My disagreements with Reed's study are mainly concerned with the interpretation of the so-called gardens of Adonis, which I (along with many other scholars) see as symbolic of Adonis' extraordinary beauty and all-too-sudden death before reaching maturity. The theme of accelerated growth and premature death is also dominant in Thetis' lament for Achilles discussed above.

41. The other is Sappho 168: ὦ τὸν ῎Αδωνιν. For other erotic/sensual contexts of the word *habros* in Sappho (applied to Aphrodite and her attendants, the *Kharites*), see also frr. 2.13–16; 58.25–26; 128.

Luxuriant Adonis is dying, Cythera. What should we do?
Beat your breasts, maidens, and tear your clothing.[42]

Already in Sappho the sensuality and eroticism of the word *habros* evokes
Asian—and specifically Lydian—luxury, as other fragments of Sappho
make clear.[43] Herodotus tells us that it was only after the austere Persians
conquered the wealthy and sensual Lydians that the Persians too learned
luxurious ways (*habrosunê*).[44] After that point in history the Persians were
always associated in the Greek mind with a soft and sensuous lifestyle, and
thus it is no surprise that the word *habros* and its compounds characterize
the Persians throughout Aeschylus' play.

But before we examine the *habrosunê* that characterizes the Persians in
Aeschylus, it is important to explore further the range of meaning that the
word *habros* encompasses. As Nagy's work on the word shows, *habros* has
both positive and negative connotations that are fundamentally intertwined
in early Greek poetry. In the victory odes of Pindar, *habros* can be applied
to both athletic victory and the glory of song:[45]

ὃς δ' ἀμφ' ἀέθλοις ἢ πολεμίζων ἄρηται κῦδος ἁβρόν
(PINDAR, *Isthmian* 1.50)

He who strives to win luxuriant [*habros*] glory in athletic competition
or in battle . . .

τιμὰ δὲ γίνεται ὧν θεὸς ἁβρὸν αὔξει λόγον τεθνακότων
(*Nemean* 7.31–32)

Honor comes to those whose reputation the god increases when they
have died, so that it is luxuriant [*habros*].

Just as the figure of Adonis combines the theme of luxuriance with the
metaphor of the *anthos* that blooms brightly only to wither very quickly,

42. The beating of the breast and tearing of clothing are two aspects of ritual lamentation. See Alexiou 1974, 6.

43. Nagy 1990a, 285.

44. Herodotus 1.71: Πέρσῃσι γάρ, πρὶν Λυδοὺς καταστρέψασθαι, ἦν οὔτε ἁβρὸν οὔτε
ἀγαθὸν οὐδέν ("For the Persians had nothing either luxurious or good before the Lydians
conquered them").

45. See Nagy 1990a, 283: "In epinician song the word *habros* and its derivatives can in
fact be so positive as to characterize the luxuriance that a victor earns and deserves as the
fruit of his struggles, either in athletics or in war." For the negative associations of *habros*,
see discussion below.

a third example of the use of *habros* in Pindar reveals how interconnected the two ideas are:

τις ἁβρὸν ἀμφὶ παγκρατίου Κλεάνδρῳ πλεκέτω μυρσίνας στέφανον
(PINDAR, *Isthmian* 8.65–66)

Let someone weave for Kleandros a luxuriant [*habros*] crown of myrtle for his victory in the pankration.

Kleandros' crown is luxuriant both because of its metonymical and metaphorical connections with victory and because of the delicate myrtle blossoms that form its substance. In Pindar's ode, the man whose crown is *habros* has achieved a place in song because of his victory in athletics; this moment of victory becomes parallel to the moment of death in battle (or in Adonis' case, hunting), where the heroes of the past achieved their place in the *kleos* of song. It is particularly appropriate then that the subject of Pindar's song is named Kleandros—the man of *kleos*. As we have seen, this name already carries with it a host of associations, including the mortality of the hero—symbolized by the *anthos*—and the unwilting immortality of song. Pindar takes the implicit associations already built into the name of Kleandros and visualizes them as a concrete object, the *habros* crown of myrtle blossoms.[46]

As Nagy has shown, the word *habros* is not in itself a necessarily negative idea, but it does inherently allude to a related concept in Greek thought, and that is *hubris*. *Hubris* is in fact a botanical term referring to excessive leaf and wood production.[47] It is unregulated growth, which can ultimately result in sterility. In Theognis and other early Greek poets, *hubris* comes to connote excessive luxury combined with savagery.[48] In Herodotus and elsewhere, the *habrosunê* of the Lydians (and later the Persians) is directly related to the *hubris* of tyranny.[49] The luxuriance of a *habros* lifestyle runs the risk of fostering an environment in which tyranny can arise.

I now propose to apply Nagy's work on *habros* and *hubris* in the poetry of Theognis and in Herodotus to an analysis of *habros* and *hubris* in Aeschylus'

46. On the connections between *habrosunê*, flowers, headbands, and athletic victory in the poetry of Pindar, see also Kurke 1992.

47. Michelini 1978. In the remainder of this chapter I will be focusing on this aspect of *hubris*. On *hubris* as a legal term denoting violence and aggressive behavior (which I submit is fundamentally connected to the botanical aspect of *hubris*), see, e.g., Fisher 1990 and Cohen 1995.

48. Nagy 1990a, 267.

49. See especially Nagy 1990a, 266 and 286–87. The Greek word *turannos*, "tyrant," is apparently borrowed from Lydian.

Persians. The *Persians* has in fact been interpreted by several critics as a trag-edy that is essentially about the *hubris* of Xerxes and its consequences.[50] As we shall see, the Persians of Aeschylus display the full range of meaning for *habros,* exemplifying both the luxuriance of the myrtle blossom of victory and the savage overgrowth of *hubris.* I argue that use of *habros* in Aeschylus' *Persians* evokes primarily the sensual and erotic aspects of this word, as it is applied to such figures as Adonis in Sappho and both earlier and later Greek laments for heroes. Secondarily, however, the word *habros* prepares us for an explanation of the Persians' downfall that centers around the *hubris* of Xerxes, the Persian king.

Although the laments of the *Persians* are sung by a chorus of male Per-sian elders, the dominant themes of the laments are characteristic of Greek women's songs. Many of the Persian laments focalize the deaths of the Persian warriors from the point of view of Persian wives. The erotically charged imagery combines themes of love, loss, and longing:

λέκτρα δ' ἀνδρῶν πόθῳ
πίμπλαται δακρύμασιν·
Περσίδες δ' ἁβροπενθεῖς ἑκά-
στα πόθῳ φιλάνορι
τὸν αἰχμήεντα θοῦρον εὐνα-
τῆρ' ἀποπεμψαμένα
λείπεται μονόζυξ.

(*Persians* 133–39)

Beds are filled with tears
in longing [*pothos*] for husbands;
each of the Persian women with their luxuriant laments
    [*habropenthês*]
is left alone under the yoke of marriage,
longing [*pothos*] for her beloved husband,
the bedmate she sent away,
a spearman eager for battle.

Here the Persian elders describe as part of their entrance song the situation in Persia since the departure of the warriors. Their concern is for the Persian

50. See, e.g., Adams 1952; Kitto 1961, 33–45; Jones 1962; Conacher 1974, 163–68; Gaga-rin 1976, 46–50; Michelini 1982, 86–98; Winnington-Ingram 1983, 1–15; and Fisher 1992, 256–63.

women, the wives who are left behind. Here again we see a close relationship between tears of grief and luxuriance, as manifested in the compound *habropenthês*.[51]

As with the figure of Adonis, the luxuriance of lament is erotic. The word *pothos*, "longing," is now yet another theme closely associated with and evoked by the word *habros*. In Bion's *Epitaph for Adonis,* Aphrodite laments that as a consequence of Adonis' death, "*pothos* has flown away like a dream": πόθος δέ μοι ὡς ὄναρ ἔπτα (58). Earlier in the Persian entrance song, the themes of lamentation and sexual desire were similarly juxtaposed:

οὓς πέρι πᾶσα χθὼν Ἀσιῆτις
ῥέψασα πόθῳ στένεται μαλερῷ

(*Persians* 61–62)

The entire land of Asia
laments the men she nourished with fierce longing [*pothos*].

Pothos is another charged word that, like *habros,* can have both sensual and religious overtones when applied to heroes. Perhaps the earliest manifestation of this combination of meaning can be found in Achilles' declaration of *Iliad* 1, in which he officially withdraws from fighting and foretells the disastrous consequences of this act:

ἦ ποτ᾽ Ἀχιλλῆος ποθὴ ἵξεται υἷας Ἀχαιῶν
σύμπαντας· τότε δ᾽ οὔ τι δυνήσεαι ἀχνύμενός περ
χραισμεῖν, εὖτ᾽ ἂν πολλοὶ ὑφ᾽ Ἕκτορος ἀνδροφόνοιο
θνήσκοντες πίπτωσι· σὺ δ᾽ ἔνδοθι θυμὸν ἀμύξεις
χωόμενος ὅ τ᾽ ἄριστον Ἀχαιῶν οὐδὲν ἔτισας.

(*Iliad* 1.240–44)

Some day a longing [*pothê*] for Achilles will come upon the sons of the
    Achaeans,
all of them together. But at that point you will not be able, even though
    in great sorrow,
to help it, when many men at the hand of man-slaying Hektor
fall dying. And you will tear your heart out inside,
angry because you did not honor the best of the Achaeans.

51. *Penthos,* "grief," is also an essential epic theme; it suffuses both the *Iliad* and the *Odyssey* at every point. See Nagy 1979, 94–117; Greene 1999; and Dué 2002, 78–81.

The surface narrative speaks of the Greek army and the longing that they will have for the absent Achilles, who is the best fighter of all the Greeks at Troy. But on the level of cult, which is always an important dimension of Homeric poetry, this longing for the absent hero is symbolic of the longing expressed in ritual laments on the part of the community. In the second-century A.D. *Heroikos* of Philostratus, a fictional dialogue in which a vine-dresser in the sanctuary of Protesilaos teaches a Phoenician visitor about Greek hero cult, the longing of the community for the absent hero translates into a longing on the part of a Phoenician to learn about the Greek heroes. On two occasions in this dialogue the Phoenician longs (*potheô*) to hear more about such figures from Troy as Protesilaos and Achilles.[52]

In the *Persians,* the longing is, on the surface, the sexual desire of the Persian wives.[53] But especially in lines 61–62, where the subject is actually the land of Asia, we can see that the Persian warriors are being set up as absent heroes on the level of community and perhaps even cult. The theme recurs several times. We may compare 511–12: ὡς στένειν πόλιν / Περσῶν, ποθοῦσαν φιλτάτην ἥβην χθονός ("Thus the city of the Persians laments, longing [*pothousan*] for the beloved youth [*hêbê*] of the land").[54]

Throughout the laments of the Persians the Greek concepts of *habros, pothos,* and *penthos* are constantly combined to express the grief of the Persian women for the absent warriors:

πολλαὶ δ᾽ ἁπαλαῖς χερσὶ καλύπτρας
κατερεικόμεναι
διαμυδαλέους δάκρυσι κόλπους
τέγγουσ᾽, ἄλγους μετέχουσαι.
αἱ δ᾽ ἁβρόγοοι Περσίδες ἀνδρῶν
ποθέουσαι ἰδεῖν ἀρτιζυγίαν,
λέκτρων [τ᾽] εὐνὰς ἁβροχίτωνας,
χλιδανῆς ἥβης τέρψιν, ἀφεῖσαι,
πενθοῦσι γόοις ἀκορεστοτάτοις.
κἀγὼ δὲ μόρον τῶν οἰχομένων
αἴρω δοκίμως πολυπενθῆ.

52. *Heroikos* 7.1 and 23.2. For more on the hero cults of antiquity and Philostratus' *Heroikos,* see Dué and Nagy 2003.

53. For the word *pothos* in Greek literature as the longing of a widow for her husband, as well as the importance of the word in Greek lament traditions, see Vermeule 1979, 154–55, 165, and 177.

54. See also lines 547–48 and 730.

νῦν γὰρ δὴ πρόπασα μὲν στένει
γαῖ᾽ Ἀσὶς ἐκκενουμένα.

(Persians 537–49)

Many are the women who, tearing their veils
with delicate hands,
soak their bosoms so that they are drenched with tears,
as they take their share of pain.
The luxuriantly lamenting [*habrogooi*] Persian women,
longing [*potheousai*] to gaze upon the husbands to whom they were
    recently joined,
and abandoning their marriage beds with their luxurious linens
    [*habrokhitonas*],
the pleasure of sensuous youth [*hêbê*],[55]
grieve with insatiable lamentation.
And I too assume as a burden the fate
of those who have disappeared, a fate that is truly full of grief.
For now the whole land of Asia wails in lament,
emptied of men.

The laments of the Persian women are once again *habros* (*habrogooi*, 541; cf. *habropenthês*, 135), as they long (*potheousai*) for their absent husbands.[56] The Greek word *goos* is in fact the usual term for a lament by a female relative.[57] That the women's longing and songs of lamentation are erotic in nature is made clear by the following lines, in which the marriage beds with their luxurious linens are imagined, the beds that were the delight of *hêbê*. Here the word *eunê* is literally a bed, as the reference to linens demonstrates, but it is also the word in Greek used more often than not for sex (as is *lekhos* or *lektron*, a word that is coupled with *eunê* in this very passage). This then is yet another remarkable passage in the *Persians* that uses the terminology, themes, and imagery of Greek women's love songs and laments to depict the loss that Persia as a nation has suffered.

---

55. See note 24 on *hêbê* above.

56. Cf. a similar juxtaposition at *Persians* 1073, one of the final lines of the play: γοᾶσθ᾽ ἁβροβάται ("lament, you who walk in a *habros* manner").

57. γόος is usually applied to the laments of nonprofessional female relatives, while θρῆνος is used of lament "especially composed and performed at the funeral by nonkinsmen" (Alexiou 1974, 12). In tragedy, however, there is little distinction between the two terms. See Dué 2002, 69, with citations there.

But here again the realm of women's laments is fused with that of epic *kleos,* as I will now go on to show. The work of Richard Martin has explored Homeric poetry as an overarching system that incorporates within its own formal conventions many other genres of speech and song.[58] Elsewhere I have suggested that the most pervasive of these genres is lament, as voiced primarily by such women as Andromache, Briseis, Hecuba, and Penelope.[59] The laments of Aeschylus' *Persians* are infused with traditional themes of women's song-making, but they are also highly allusive and inseparable from the epic traditions that showcase women's song-making. In the passage cited immediately above, for example, the Persian women are said to tear their veils in a traditional gesture of grief. For Aeschylus' audience such a gesture may well have called to mind the actions of a paradigmatic epic figure like Andromache, when she learns of Hektor's death:

τῆλε δ᾽ ἀπὸ κρατὸς βάλε δέσματα σιγαλόεντα,
ἄμπυκα κεκρύφαλόν τε ἰδὲ πλεκτὴν ἀναδέσμην
κρήδεμνόν θ᾽, ὅ ῥά οἱ δῶκε χρυσῆ Ἀφροδίτη
ἤματι τῷ ὅτε μιν κορυθαίολος ἠγάγεθ᾽ Ἕκτωρ
ἐκ δόμου Ἠετίωνος.

(*Iliad* 22.468–72)

She threw down far from her head the shining headband,
the head-piece and the net and the woven headband
and the veil, which golden Aphrodite gave to her,
on the day when Hektor with his patterned helmet led her in marriage
from the house of Eëtion.[60]

Even if Andromache is not imagined to be the paradigm for the Persian wives, other aspects of Aeschylus' passage resonate with the laments of the *Iliad.* In addition to tearing their clothing, the Persian women "soak their bosoms so that they are drenched with tears" (διαμυδαλέους δάκρυσι κόλπους τέγγουσ᾽, 539–40). This too is a traditional depiction of grief, but

58. Martin 1989.
59. Dué 2002, 78.
60. Hektor's mother Hecuba likewise tears off her veil when she learns of her son's death at the hands of Achilles (*Iliad* 22.405–7): ἣ δέ νυ μήτηρ / τίλλε κόμην, ἀπὸ δὲ λιπαρὴν ἔρριψε καλύπτρην / τηλόσε, κώκυσεν δὲ μάλα μέγα παῖδ᾽ ἐσιδοῦσα· ("But now Hektor's mother / tore her hair out, and threw off her shining veil / far away from her, and she wailed especially loudly when she looked upon her son").

the traditional diction is particularly evocative of epic. Compare the following two passages from the *Iliad* with the verses of Aeschylus:[61]

δεύοντο δὲ δάκρυσι κόλποι

(*Iliad* 9.570)

Her bosom was soaked with tears.

δάκρυσιν εἵματ᾽ ἔφυρον

(*Iliad* 24.162)

They stained their clothes with tears.

In this case the allusive power of Aeschylus' depiction of grief for the Persian warriors is almost certainly not in a specific reference, but rather in the force of tradition.[62]

Perhaps the most striking aspect of the *Persians* passage (and the play as a whole) is the way that it eroticizes the death of young warriors by means of constant reference to the marriages (and sexual unions) that have been left behind:

ὡς πολλὰς Περσίδων μάταν
ἔκτισαν εὐνῖδας ἠδ᾽ ἀνάνδρους.

(*Persians* 288–89)

how many of the Persian women in vain
Athens has made bereft and husbandless.[63]

But this too is a crucial epic theme. The *Odyssey* is at its core the story of a marriage bed left behind; the *Iliad* narrates the death of countless bride-

---

61. I am indebted to the commentary of Hall (1996 *ad* 539–40) for these references.

62. In the case of *Iliad* 9.570, the woman referred to is Althaea, who actually prays for the death of her son Meleager.

63. This is how the passage is usually translated. Given the themes I have been tracing, however, I am very much inclined (as is Hall) to translate the word εὐνῖδας as something like "bedmate," taking it as cognate with εὐνή ("marriage bed"). The translation would then read: "how many of the Persian women Athens has made bedmates in vain and husbandless." The idea is that the sexual unions were rendered fruitless, since there was no opportunity for a proper marriage or children to result from it.

grooms—most notably Hektor's. The Panhellenic poetry of the *Iliad* generally avoids sex and romance of any kind, but there is an erotic subtext in
many passages of lamentation.[64] Andromache is metonymically connected
to Aphrodite as she begins her lament for Hektor in *Iliad* 22.470; when she
realizes that Hektor is dead, she throws down from her head the adornments
that "golden Aphrodite" had given her on her wedding day. Likewise Briseis
is compared to golden Aphrodite when she begins her lament for Patroklos
in *Iliad* 19.[65] In Andromache's lament of *Iliad* 24, she complains that Hektor did not leave her with an "intimate phrase" or embrace her one last
time:

ἐμοὶ δὲ μάλιστα λελείψεται ἄλγεα λυγρά.
οὐ γάρ μοι θνήσκων λεχέων ἐκ χεῖρας ὄρεξας,
οὐδέ τί μοι εἶπες πυκινὸν ἔπος, οὖ τέ κεν αἰεὶ
μεμνήμην νύκτάς τε καὶ ἤματα δάκρυ χέουσα.

(*Iliad* 24.742–45)

But for me especially you have left behind grievous pain.
For when you died you did not stretch out your arms to me from our
     marriage bed,
nor did you speak to me an intimate phrase, which I could always
remember when I weep for you day and night.

I submit that the laments of women in Greek poetry more often than
not merge with the love song, and that the death of young warriors is an
inherently erotic theme, because of the implicit loss of love and sexual union
that such a death carries with it.[66] Epic poetry, which is essentially a man's
genre, narrates the deaths of warriors with a view to another warrior's heroic
exploits—his *kleos*. Thus the death of Hektor becomes the *kleos* of Achilles.

---

64. Nagy has shown that the *Iliad* and the *Odyssey*, as Panhellenic poetry that must
appeal to all Greeks, screen out distinctly local features—particularly elements of romance
and fantasy; see especially Nagy 1990a, 70–73 and note 99, as well as Dué 2002, 21–26
and 57–64. On the general avoidance of fantasy and elements of folktale in the *Iliad* and
Odyssey (in contrast with the Epic Cycle) see Griffin 1977; Davies 1989, 9–10; and Burgess
2001, 157–71.
65. *Iliad* 19.282. See Dué 2002, 74.
66. See also the work of Loraux and Vernant on the "beautiful death" in Loraux 1975
and 1986 and Vernant 1991, 50–74 (with further references there). Also very relevant to this
discussion is the work of Monsacré (1984, especially pp. 69–72), in which she discusses the
way that hand-to-hand combat is portrayed or referred to as a wedding at several points
in the *Iliad*.

But women's songs of love and loss, songs of which the *Iliad* occasionally provides a glimpse, narrate the deaths of warriors from the perspective of the bride left behind.

The *pothos* of the Persian women depicted in the passage under discussion is specifically that of "newlyweds" (ἀρτιζυγίαν, 542). As I have already begun to suggest, the *Iliad* too is full of the deaths of bridegrooms, some barely mentioned, others with elaborate death scenes.[67] The Trojan ally Iphidamas is one such bridegroom:

> ἔσπετε νῦν μοι Μοῦσαι Ὀλύμπια δώματ' ἔχουσαι
> ὅς τις δὴ πρῶτος Ἀγαμέμνονος ἀντίον ἦλθεν
> ἢ αὐτῶν Τρώων ἠὲ κλειτῶν ἐπικούρων.
> Ἰφιδάμας Ἀντηνορίδης ἠΰς τε μέγας τε
> ὃς τράφη ἐν Θρήκῃ ἐριβώλακι μητέρι μήλων·
> Κισσῆς τόν γ' ἔθρεψε δόμοις ἔνι τυτθὸν ἐόντα
> μητροπάτωρ, ὃς τίκτε Θεανὼ καλλιπάρῃον·
> αὐτὰρ ἐπεί ῥ' ἥβης ἐρικυδέος ἵκετο μέτρον,
> αὐτοῦ μιν κατέρυκε, δίδου δ' ὅ γε θυγατέρα ἥν·
> γήμας δ' ἐκ θαλάμοιο μετὰ κλέος ἵκετ' Ἀχαιῶν
> σὺν δυοκαίδεκα νηυσὶ κορωνίσιν, αἵ οἱ ἕποντο.
>
> (*Iliad* 11.218–28)

Tell me now, you Muses that have homes on Olympus,
who was first to face Agamemnon,
whether of the Trojans themselves or of their renowned allies?
It was Iphidamas son of Antenor, a man both brave and of great
    stature,
who was raised in fertile Thrace, the mother of sheep.
Cisses brought him up in his own house when he was a child—
Cisses, his mother's father, the man who begot beautiful-cheeked
    Theano.
When he reached the full measure of glorious manhood [*hêbê*],
Cisses would have kept him there, and wanted to give him his daughter
    in marriage.
But as soon as he had married he left the bridal chamber and went off
    to seek the *kleos* of the Achaeans
with twelve ships that followed him.

---

67. Compare Odysseus' words at *Hecuba* 322–25: εἰσὶν παρ' ἡμῖν οὐδὲν ἧσσον . . . νύμφαι τ' ἀρίστων νυμφίων τητώμεναι, / ὧν ἥδε κεύθει σώματ' Ἰδαία κόνις ("Among us are . . . brides bereft of excellent bridegrooms, whose bodies this Trojan dust has covered").

These lines serve to mark the first death in Agamemnon's *aristeia*. The importance of "getting it right" is signaled by the invocation of the Muses at the beginning of the catalogue. Iphidamas' prominence as the first to be killed earns him a relatively expanded life history before the narrator depicts the death itself. The narrator focuses on the fact that Iphidamas is a newlywed, who gave it all up to become part of the *kleos* of another man. Iphidamas is not lamented by his bride in our *Iliad*. Instead his compressed life history, with its account of his recent marriage, serves as the lament for this doomed bridegroom.[68]

Iphidamas is by no means the only bridegroom of the *Iliad*, or the most memorable. In *Iliad* 2.700, for example, we learn of the bride of Protesilaos, Laodameia:[69]

τοῦ δὲ καὶ ἀμφιδρυφὴς ἄλοχος Φυλάκη ἐλέλειπτο
καὶ δόμος ἡμιτελής· τὸν δ᾽ ἔκτανε Δάρδανος ἀνὴρ
νηὸς ἀποθρῴσκοντα πολὺ πρώτιστον Ἀχαιῶν.

(*Iliad* 2.700–702)

His wife was left behind in Phulakê, tearing both cheeks in
    lamentation,
his house left half built. A Dardanian man killed him
as he leapt out of the ship, by far the first of the Achaeans.

Protesilaos' story is nearly identical to that of Iphidamas, but even more compressed. In just three lines we learn of his marriage, his immediate departure for Troy (before his house was even built), his famous death—the first of the Trojan War—and the lamentation of the bride he left behind. Protesilaos and Iphidamas are part of a pattern that pervades the *Iliad,* a pattern which alludes to women's song traditions but also constitutes *kleos*.

But the greatest and most lamented bridegroom of them all is of course Achilles. In an earlier work I have explored the way the figure of Briseis,

---

68. Cf. as well the lines that mark Iphidamas' death, shortly thereafter (*Iliad* 11.241–43): ὡς ὃ μὲν αὖθι πεσὼν κοιμήσατο χάλκεον ὕπνον / οἰκτρὸς ἀπὸ μνηστῆς ἀλόχου, ἀστοῖσιν ἀρήγων, / κουριδίης, ἧς οὔ τι χάριν ἴδε, πολλὰ δ᾽ ἔδωκε· ("Thus he fell and slept a bronze sleep [of death], pitiful, since he had just come as a helper for his people straight from the wooing of his wife, the bride of his youth, of whom he did not have any pleasure, although he had given much for her"). On the death of the Trojan warrior Simoeisios, who is described as a blooming unmarried youth (ἠίθεον θαλερόν, 4.474), see Schein 1984, 73–76.

69. For more on Protesilaos and Laodameia see Dué and Nagy 2003, with reference to the myths about the couple narrated in Philostratus' *Heroikos*.

Achilles' concubine, casts him as a bridegroom in her lament for Patroklos in *Iliad* 19.[70] Achilles himself speculates about marriage in *Iliad* 9, as he contemplates returning home to Phthia:

ἢν γὰρ δή με σαῶσι θεοὶ καὶ οἴκαδ' ἵκωμαι,
Πηλεύς θήν μοι ἔπειτα γυναῖκά γε μάσσεται αὐτός

(Iliad 9.393–94)

For if the gods save me and I return home,
then Peleus will get me a wife himself.

Of course we know that Achilles will not return home and get married, and in this sense he is the ultimate and eternal bridegroom.[71] The allure of the doomed young man manifests itself in a variety of local myths and traditions about Achilles' romantic exploits in and around the Troad and even in the afterlife, where he is linked with such figures as Polyxena, Helen, Iphigeneia, and Medea.[72]

These more local traditions about Achilles are also likely to have been the subject of women's laments and love songs. The poetry of Sappho is an indication of this. As the fourth-century A.D. rhetorician Himerius tells us, in her wedding songs "[Sappho] compared the bridegroom to Achilles, and likened

---

70. Dué 2002. See especially pp. 14, 39, and 67–81.

71. For the phrase "eternal bridegroom" I am again indebted to Greg Nagy, who uses the term in teaching to explain the appeal of Achilles for the Greek song-culture; see also Aitken and Maclean 2001, lvii. Achilles did of course have a son, Neoptolemus/Pyrrhus, by Deidameia, whom he impregnated while posing as a girl on the island of Scyros; for sources, see Gantz 1993, 580–82. In the *Cypria* tradition, according to the summary of Proclus, Achilles marries Deidameia and begets Neoptolemus after landing on Scyros on the way to Troy, following the Achaeans' attack on the Mysians; see Anderson 1997, 43. Despite this episode in what is apparently imagined to be Achilles' childhood, in the *Iliad* and elsewhere Achilles is portrayed as a youthful and eligible bachelor; see Dué 2002, 14 and 74–76, with note 27. Cf. Pausanias 10.26.4: τοῦ δὲ Ἀχιλλέως τῷ παιδὶ Ὅμηρος μὲν Νεοπτόλεμον ὄνομα ἐν ἁπάσῃ οἱ τίθεται τῇ ποιήσει· τὰ δὲ Κύπρια ἔπη φησὶν ὑπὸ Λυκομήδους μὲν Πύρρον, Νεοπτόλεμον δὲ ὄνομα ὑπὸ Φοίνικος αὐτῷ τεθῆναι, ὅτι Ἀχιλλεὺς ἡλικίᾳ ἔτι νέος πολεμεῖν ἤρξατο ("Homer gives the name Neoptolemus to the son of Achilles in all of his poetry, but the *Cypria* says that Lykomedes named him Pyrrhus, while Phoenix gave him the name of Neoptolemus—young warrior—because Achilles was young when he first went to war"). It is common in epic for the names of children to reflect the attributes of their parents.

72. For local myths about Achilles' romantic encounters in the Troad see Dué 2002, 33–34 and 60–64. For Archaic vase paintings that suggest a romance between Achilles and Polyxena in Cyclic traditions see Scaife 1995. For Achilles in the afterlife see Nagy 1979, chapters 9–10; Hedreen 1991; Gantz 1993, 133–35; and Dué 2002, 41–42.

the young man's deeds to the hero's" (τὸν νυμφίον τε Ἀχιλλεῖ παρομοιῶσαι καὶ εἰς ταὐτὸν ἀγαγεῖν τῷ ἥρωι τὸν νεανίσκον ταῖς πράξεσι).[73] One such bridegroom is Achilles' worst enemy, Hektor, who, together with his bride Andromache, is given Achilles' epithet *theoeikelos* ("godlike") in Sappho fragment 44.[74]

Epic knows Achilles as a killing machine; Sappho knows Achilles as a bridegroom. But as we have seen, the dichotomy between men's and women's songs about Achilles is not cut and dried. Homeric poetry alludes to traditions in which Achilles is above all a lover, and I would argue that, as with the figure of Adonis, it is in fact Achilles' premature death and failure to mature and marry that makes him such an erotic figure. Another fragment of Sappho unites the imagery of the lamented warrior and the bridegroom that we have been exploring:

> τίωι σ', ὦ φίλε γάμβρε, κάλως ἐικάσδω;
> ὄρπακι βραδίνωι σε μάλιστ᾽ ἐικάσδω.
>
> (FRAGMENT 115V)

To what, dear bridegroom, can I best compare you?
To a slender shoot, I most liken you.

Here the metaphor of the dead warrior as a plant cut down before reaching maturity is combined with erotic image of the warrior as a bridegroom (and vice versa). Heroes like Iphidamas, Protesilaos, Hektor, and Achilles are all prototypes for the warrior as bridegroom. Sappho then compares the beautiful potential of the young bridegroom to the *anthos* and *hêbê* of a young warrior, an image that as we have seen is full of *pothos* (as befits a wedding song) but also *penthos* (as befits a lament).

A final passage from the *Iliad* suggests once again that the idea of a bridegroom in the prime of youth is potentially and perhaps even inherently a theme of lament. The image of the bridegroom is poignantly conjured when Achilles laments Patroklos in *Iliad* 23. This time, however, Achilles is in the role of a father:

> ὡς δὲ πατὴρ οὗ παιδὸς ὀδύρεται ὀστέα καίων
> νυμφίου, ὅς τε θανὼν δειλοὺς ἀκάχησε τοκῆας,
> ὣς Ἀχιλεὺς ἑτάροιο ὀδύρετο ὀστέα καίων.
>
> (*Iliad* 23.222–24)

73. Himerius *Or.* 1.16.
74. See Nagy 1974, 134–39 and 1999, 28–29.

As when a father mourns while burning the bones of his son
who is a bridegroom, and in death he brings sorrow to his miserable
    parents,
so did Achilles mourn while burning the bones of his comrade.

This simile, because it is applied to Patroklos, should perhaps suggest that
the death of a young bridegroom is the saddest death of all, and such a
death necessarily occurs whenever a warrior is cut down in the prime of
hêbê.

In the preceding argument I have tried to show that the death of heroes in
battle is a focal point of ancient Greek women's song traditions, encompass-
ing both love and loss. These women's traditions about figures like Achilles
and Hektor likewise suffuse the *Iliad* and the *Odyssey,* revealing that such
essential themes as the mortality of the hero and immortality in song have
their origins in the lament poetry of women. These same themes form the
core of the laments of Aeschylus' *Persians.* The Persian dead are lamented as
flowers prematurely cut down and as doomed bridegrooms. Both themes
come together in the word *habros,* merging the semantic and conceptual
realms of death in battle and athletic victory, the everlasting glory of *kleos*
and the luxuriance of lamentation.

Secondarily, however, the word *habros* in the *Persians* evokes *hubris.* When
the Persian queen and elders conjure the ghost of Xerxes' father Darius (the
Persian king who attacked Greece in 490), he informs them that the Persian
disaster is retribution for the *hubris* of Xerxes and his army. This *hubris* is
twofold. It begins when Xerxes dares to bridge the Hellespont, a famous
story that is also narrated in Herodotus:[75]

νῦν κακῶν ἔοικε πηγὴ πᾶσιν ηὑρῆσθαι φίλοις.
παῖς δ᾽ ἐμὸς τάδ᾽ οὐ κατειδὼς ἤνυσεν νέῳ θράσει·
ὅστις Ἑλλήσποντον ἱρὸν δοῦλον ὣς δεσμώμασιν
ἤλπισε σχήσειν ῥέοντα, Βόσπορον ῥόον θεοῦ,
καὶ πόρον μετερρύθμιζε, καὶ πέδαις σφυρηλάτοις
περιβαλὼν πολλὴν κέλευθον ἤνυσεν πολλῷ στρατῷ,
θνητὸς ὢν θεῶν τε πάντων ᾤετ᾽, οὐκ εὐβουλίᾳ,
καὶ Ποσειδῶνος κρατήσειν.

(*Persians* 743–50)

---

75. See Herodotus 7.10–57.

Now it seems that a fountain of evils has been found for all those near
    and dear to me.
My son unknowingly accomplished these things in youthful boldness.
He thought he could hold the flowing sacred Hellespont
with chains as though it were a slave, the Bosporus, the channel of the
    god,
and also he made a new kind of road, and casting fetters fashioned with
    hammers
he built a great path for a great army.
Although he is mortal he thought—and he did not reason well—
that he could overpower all the gods, including Poseidon.

Xerxes thought he could overpower Poseidon and cross the Hellespont to
invade Greece. This is an act of more-than-human boldness and reckless
audacity.

The *hubris* of Xerxes moreover spreads to his army, who, after crossing
the Hellespont, show no restraint in their initial success. They go too far in
victory:

οὗ σφιν κακῶν ὕψιστ᾽ ἐπαμμένει παθεῖν,
ὕβρεως ἄποινα κἀθέων φρονημάτων·
οἳ γῆν μολόντες Ἑλλάδ᾽ οὐ θεῶν βρέτη
ᾐδοῦντο συλᾶν οὐδὲ πιμπράναι νεώς·
βωμοὶ δ᾽ ἄιστοι, δαιμόνων θ᾽ ἱδρύματα
πρόρριζα φύρδην ἐξανέστραπται βάθρων.
τοιγὰρ κακῶς δράσαντες οὐκ ἐλάσσονα
πάσχουσι, τὰ δὲ μέλλουσι, κοὐδέπω κακῶν
κρηνὶς ἀπέσβηκ᾽ ἀλλ᾽ ἔτ᾽ ἐκπιδύεται.

                                              (*Persians* 807–15)

The greatest of evils is in store for them to suffer,
retribution for *hubris* and godless thoughts.
Going to the Greek land they were not ashamed
to despoil wooden images of the gods or burn temples;
altars disappeared, and the buildings of the divinities
were toppled root and branch in utter chaos.
Therefore having committed evil deeds they will suffer
nothing less, and they will continue to suffer, nor is the spring
of evils yet quenched; it still gushes forth.

Here we see the savage side of *hubris,* a *hubris* that likewise characterizes the Persians in Herodotus when they sack the Lydian city of Sardis.[76] As I will argue in future chapters, the plundering of a defeated city is one of the primary contexts in which *hubris* manifests itself.

The botanical aspects of *hubris,* so important to the imagery of *habros* that pervades the play, come to the surface at the climax of Darius' condemnation of Xerxes and the Persian army:

ὕβρις γὰρ ἐξανθοῦσ᾽ ἐκάρπωσεν στάχυν
ἄτης, ὅθεν πάγκλαυτον ἐξαμᾷ θέρος.

(*Persians* 821–22)

For *hubris* blossoms and brings forth as its fruit a crop
of disaster, from which it reaps a harvest of lamentation.[77]

In this way the negative associations of the word *habros* with the aggressive and violent overgrowth conveyed in the word *hubris* are woven into the dominant imagery of the play, with its floral/botanical metaphors for the fallen Persian warriors. The luxuriance of the Persians has a dark side. Under the direction of the impetuous and arrogant Xerxes the *habrosunê* of the Persian people becomes *hubris,* which results in utter disaster being inflicted by the gods.

PRAISE OF THE WAR DEAD
AND THE LAMENTATION OF ELDERS

But while Darius' speech certainly sets up the defeat of the Persians as punishment for a wrongful attack on the part of Xerxes, the Persian war dead, as we have seen, are consistently lamented in terms that humanize and glorify

76. See Nagy 1990a, 267 and Herodotus 1.89.2 (spoken by the Lydian king, Croesus): Πέρσαι φύσιν ἐόντες ὑβρισταὶ ("the Persians [are] by nature men of *hubris*").

77. Cf. Ferrari 2000, 148, comparing these lines to *Agamemnon* 659–60: ὁρῶμεν ἀνθοῦν πέλαγος Αἰγαῖον νεκροῖς / ἀνδρῶν Ἀχαιῶν ναυτικοῖς τ᾽ ἐρειπίοις ("We saw the Aegean sea blossoming with the corpses / Of Achaean men and wreckage of ships" [trans. Ferrari]). Ferrari notes: "The focal image here [in *Persians* 821–22] is established by the word ἐξαμᾷ, referring to mowing or reaping. *Hubris* blossoms into *ate* as stalks of grain flower into ears of corn, but its crop is death. Similarly, in the *Agamemnon* the corpses strewn over the sea are the flowering of *hubris*, producing blooms of *ate*." See also below, where the significance of this parallel between the *atê* of the two armies is discussed further.

the fallen warriors. And while the predominant song medium of the play is the Greek woman's lament, with perhaps special reference to the laments of Greek epic, Mary Ebbott has recently shown that a specifically Athenian kind of praise of war dead is employed as well.

In lines 302–30 the messenger catalogues the Persian dead in a list that is similar to Athenian casualty lists. Ebbott argues that "the framing discourse of tragedy changes the meaning conveyed by the form: instead of a roster designating those celebrated in a special grave, [the list] becomes a disturbing listing of war dead who are not honored and not even buried."[78] The implications of Ebbott's argument for the present discussion are several. The Persians are praised for their deaths in battle in terms that are uniquely Athenian, thereby denying their otherness. Even more significantly, the Athenians are made to think about the fact that the Persians, despite these praises and the laments that glorify them throughout the tragedy, have not been given a hero's burial.

Here we come to the heart of Aeschylus' *Persians*. The play is not a victory song in celebration of the Persian defeat, nor is it a universalization of the experience of defeat, such that the Athenians and Persians are all one in their humanity and mortality. Rather the Athenians are asked to see their enemy with all of its foreignness and otherness, and witness not only the commonalities between them, but also the injustices in which the Athenians themselves have taken part. Tragedy allows the Athenians to reenact and reexperience the events of Salamis from the perspective of the defeated. In this way the *Persians,* the earliest tragedy that has come down to us, perfectly illustrates a principle that operates in many tragedies still to come, in which the plight of the defeated is a central preoccupation.

I have argued throughout this chapter that the *Persians* is remarkable in that it narrates the Battle of Salamis from the perspective of those left behind. From the entrance song of the Persian elders to the final extended antiphonal lament between the chorus and Xerxes, the focus of the play is on the emotions and experiences of the bereaved widows and parents of the deceased warriors. It is not surprising then that the laments of the Persians have a great deal in common with the laments of captive women that I will be examining in future chapters. In this case the Persians were the invading army. Because Persia was the aggressor, the Persian widows are not in the same precarious position as, for example, the Trojan women are. They have not been abandoned to the enemy, they do not face immediate enslavement, and their young sons have not been systematically killed. Nevertheless,

78. Ebbott 2000, 83.

the similarities are many, and suggest once again that the *Persians* is not an exultant play, but one which is keenly attuned to the suffering of the defeated.

What is at first glance surprising about the Persian laments is that they are not sung by the widowed Persian women, as the laments evidently were in Phrynichus' play four years earlier. Instead the Persian elders and Xerxes himself take center stage as the voice of Persia's grief. In this way the Persians might be said to be effeminized by Aeschylus, made to perform actions far more characteristic of Greek women than men. As I have already suggested in my introduction to this chapter, the effeminization of the Persians may be a device whereby Aeschylus casts them as an other. That is, he portrays them as recognizably Persian, by making them recognizably not Greek, and the dichotomy between male and female is an obvious way to achieve this polarization.

But even this hypothesis goes too far in its separation of Greeks and Persians and male and female. Structurally, the *Persians* resembles Aeschylus' *Agamemnon,* in which the chorus of Argive elders express their fears and anxiously await news of the youth who have been in Troy for ten years.[79] We might also compare to the Persian elders the chorus of old men in Euripides' *Herakles,* who likewise anxiously await the return of Herakles at the beginning of the play, and express their fears for Herakles' family in terms that evoke a lament:

> ὦ τέκεα, τέκεα πατρὸς ἀπάτορ',
> ὦ γεραιὲ σύ τε τάλαινα μᾶ-
> τερ, ἃ τὸν Ἀίδα δόμοις
> πόσιν ἀναστενάζεις.
>
> (EURIPIDES, *Herakles* 115–18)

Oh children, children without a father,
Oh poor old man, and you afflicted
mother, you who lament the husband that is
now in Hades' house!

---

79. The similarities between the *Persians* and Aeschylus' *Oresteia* trilogy are many. To cite just two obvious examples, the dream of Atossa and her exchange with the chorus of elders may be compared to Clytemnestra's interaction with the Argive elders in the *Agamemnon,* and Electra's and Orestes' conjuring of their dead father in the *Libation Bearers* is reminiscent of the consultation of the ghost of Darius in the *Persians.* For more parallels of structure and theme, see Ferrari 2000, 143–50 as well as Anderson 1997, 107 and 111.

The plot of Sophocles' *Trachinian Women* has a similar structure, in that it too is dominated by longing for the absent hero.[80] This longing on the part of the elders of the community is yet another means by which the Persian war dead are assimilated to Greek heroes like Herakles, whose sufferings were enacted on the tragic stage and whose untimely deaths were ritually lamented throughout the Greek world.

The vast majority of Aeschylus' play then collapses the barriers between the constructions of male, female, Greek, and non-Greek. Despite elaborate costuming, exotic Persian movements, and foreign-sounding music, the Persians are shown, at least at the moment of death in battle, to be as Greek as any Athenian.

---

80. These plays have affinities with the *nostos* ("homecoming") traditions of epic. For the *Persians* as a homecoming drama see Hall 1996, 18. Ferrari (2000, 144–47) discusses the allusive relationships between the *nostos* themes of the *Persians*, the *Agamemnon*, and the Epic Cycle. See also Anderson 1997, 114–27.

CHAPTER THREE

ATHENIANS AND TROJANS

Before we can examine the laments and plight of the captive Trojan women in Euripides' Trojan War plays in a meaningful way, it is first necessary to establish an understanding of the Athenians' particular relationship with the Trojan War. What associations does the Trojan War as a theme carry with it? How are Trojans and the fall of Troy represented in Athenian literature and art?

As we will see, the Athenians are not categorically a part of the Achaean collective tradition and cannot necessarily be assimilated with the Greeks of the *Iliad*.[1] Athenian participation in the Trojan War has only a tenuous place at best in the Greek tradition, and although there were efforts made to strengthen Athenian ties to this tradition, particularly in Athenian monumental art, in the course of history Athens seems to have maintained a complicated association with its Trojan "past." This complex relationship with the Trojan War myths at various points in Athenian history has important consequences for our interpretation of Archaic and Classical literature and art that treats the fall of Troy—a complexity that has been too easily overlooked in studies that trace the opposition between East and West in Greek thought.

In the *Iliad* that has come down to us, the Athenians are barely mentioned.[2] They do, however, have a place in the Catalogue of Ships, the

1. The papyrus numbers referred to in this chapter are those of Dué, Ebbott, and Yatromanolakis 2001–, with the exception of the unpublished papyri that are included in West's 1998 edition of the *Iliad* and numbered by him. For these unpublished papyri I have used West's numeration, followed by a W.

In the arguments that follow I am indebted throughout to the work of Anderson (1997), Higbie (1997), and Ferrari (2000). On the distinction between Achaeans—the word most commonly used to designate the Greek collective forces at Troy—and Athenians, see Ferrari 2000, 127–28.

2. Athenians or the Athenian hero Menestheus are mentioned in *Iliad* 2.546–56, 558; 4.327–28; 12.331 and 373; 13.195–96 and 689–91; 15.331. Menestheus is also thought to appear in the Hesiodic *Catalogue of Women* (fragment 200.3 W).

definitive roster of record for participants in the Trojan War. The Catalogue
has been shown to reflect, for the most part, the political geography of
Bronze Age Greece.[3] The city of Athens did exist in the Bronze Age; Athens
was inhabited from Neolithic times onward, and in the late Bronze Age a
Mycenaean citadel occupied the Acropolis.[4] There is therefore no reason to
think that a modest Athenian contingent should not have been part of the
epic tradition.

In the catalogue, Athens is a well-built citadel under the aegis of Athena
and the Athenians' native hero Erechtheus. The Athenian contingent of
ships is led by the somewhat obscure hero Menestheus:

οἳ δ' ἄρ' Ἀθήνας εἶχον ἐϋκτίμενον πτολίεθρον
δῆμον Ἐρεχθῆος μεγαλήτορος, ὅν ποτ' Ἀθήνη
θρέψε Διὸς θυγάτηρ, τέκε δὲ ζείδωρος ἄρουρα,
κὰδ δ' ἐν Ἀθήνης εἷσεν ἑῷ ἐν πίονι νηῷ·
ἔνθα δέ μιν ταύροισι καὶ ἀρνειοῖς ἱλάονται
κοῦροι Ἀθηναίων περιτελλομένων ἐνιαυτῶν·
τῶν αὖθ' ἡγεμόνευ' υἱὸς Πετεῶο Μενεσθεύς.
τῷ δ' οὔ πώ τις ὁμοῖος ἐπιχθόνιος γένετ' ἀνὴρ
κοσμῆσαι ἵππους τε καὶ ἀνέρας ἀσπιδιώτας·
Νέστωρ οἶος ἔριζεν· ὃ γὰρ προγενέστερος ἦεν·
τῷ δ' ἅμα πεντήκοντα μέλαιναι νῆες ἕποντο.

Αἴας δ' ἐκ Σαλαμῖνος ἄγεν δυοκαίδεκα νῆας,
στῆσε δ' ἄγων ἵν' Ἀθηναίων ἵσταντο φάλαγγες.

(*Iliad* 2.546–56)

And they that held the well-built citadel of Athens—
the people of great Erechtheus, whom once Athena
the daughter of Zeus raised, and who was born of the life-giving soil
    itself,
and Athena established him at Athens in her own rich sanctuary;
there, with bulls and rams
the Athenian youths worship him as the years circle around—
of these men Menestheus, the son of Peteos, was commander.
There was no man on earth like him
for marshaling chariots and shield-bearing men.
Nestor alone rivaled him, for he was older.
With this man there came fifty black ships.

3. See Allen 1921, Page 1959, and Simpson-Lazenby 1970.
4. For Bronze Age Athens see Iakovidis 1983, 73–90; Hurwit 1999, 67–84.

Here I call attention to Menestheus, who at first glance seems like a strange choice. Why not the Athenians' beloved culture-hero Theseus? Theseus seems to have had no connection whatsoever to the Trojan cycle of myth, and thus his absence might confirm a prevailing view of antiquity that the Athenians are a late addition to the Catalogue.[5] Modern scholars, on the contrary, have thought it more likely that Menestheus is part of a much older tradition than the Theseus myths.[6] The verses of the *Iliad* about Menestheus, canonical as they were, resulted in the incorporation of Menestheus into later Athenian genealogical traditions and myths about the death of Theseus before the Trojan War, which reconciled the Menestheus of the *Iliad* with the central Athenian traditions about Theseus.[7]

It seems that the Athenians, small as their role was in the tradition as a whole, were nevertheless a venerable component of the Achaean forces, and that their hero Menestheus was as integrated into the oral tradition as any of the other minor figures that have been woven into the fabric of the narrative. But despite these claims to participation in the Trojan War, the Athenians were accused in antiquity of forging their place in the *Iliad*. Plutarch records two instances where verses that mention Theseus or the Athenians were said to be inserted by the Athenians themselves or by others.[8] Plutarch's *Life of Solon* records the sixth-century Athenian statesman's attempts to secure control of the island of Salamis for the Athenians, who were struggling over it with the city of Megara. After several years of war the two cities asked the Spartans to arbitrate:

οὐ μὴν ἀλλὰ τῶν Μεγαρέων ἐπιμενόντων πολλὰ κακὰ καὶ δρῶντες ἐν τῷ πολέμῳ καὶ πάσχοντες, ἐποιήσαντο Λακεδαιμονίους διαλλακτὰς καὶ δικαστάς. οἱ μὲν οὖν πολλοὶ τῷ Σόλωνι συναγωνίσασθαι λέγουσι τὴν Ὁμήρου δόξαν· ἐμβαλόντα γὰρ αὐτὸν ἔπος εἰς νεῶν κατάλογον ἐπὶ τῆς δίκης ἀναγνῶναι·

5. Theseus' sons Akamas and Demophon are featured in the *Little Iliad* and the *Sack of Troy*, where they come to Troy in order to rescue Theseus' mother, Aithra, whom the Dioscuri had abducted while rescuing their sister Helen, who had been abducted by Theseus; see Gantz 1993, 298; Anderson 1997, 97–101; and Jenkins 1999. In the Classical period the rescue of Aithra is represented in several works of Athenian art. See further below.

6. See, e.g., Page 1959, 145ff.; Simpson-Lazenby 1970, 56; and Kirk 1985 *ad* 2.552.

7. See Gantz 1993, 298. This is not the place to discuss the history of the transmission of the *Iliad*. It is my view that the process of transmission over generations of composers was generally conservative, with the result that difficult verses were more likely to be reinterpreted over time than discarded, although certainly the system was always to some extent in a state of flux; see Dué 2001. Formulas are slow to enter the overall system of epic diction, and they are likewise slow to drop out of it.

8. See Higbie 1997 for a detailed discussion of these two incidents. On insertion of verses see also Haslam 1997, 83.

Αἴας δ᾽ ἐκ Σαλαμῖνος ἄγεν δυοκαίδεκα νῆας,
στῆσε δ᾽ ἄγων ἵν᾽ Ἀθηναίων ἵσταντο φάλαγγες.

(PLUTARCH, *Solon* 10.1 [*Iliad* 2.557–58])

Notwithstanding all this, when the Megarians persisted in their opposition, and both sides inflicted and suffered many injuries in the war, they made the Lacedaemonians arbitrators and judges of the strife. Accordingly, most say that the reputation of Homer favored the contention of Solon; for he himself inserted a verse into the Catalogue of Ships and read the passage at the trial:

Ajax brought twelve ships from Salamis,
and stationed them where the Athenians placed their phalanxes.

This same story is related by Strabo with additional details, including the verses that the Megarians claimed Solon had replaced.[9] Strabo seems to have had multiple sources for his account; he states in addition that some claim it was the Athenian tyrant Peisistratus who inserted the verse, while others say it was Solon. The belief that an Athenian inserted a verse that he composed himself into the *Iliad* must have had some currency in antiquity. Verse 558 is omitted in several of the ancient papyri and medieval manuscripts, including such important editions as the Hawara papyrus and the tenth-century Venetus A (Marcianus Graecus 454).[10]

A similar allegation of interpolation is made in Plutarch's *Life of Theseus.* Plutarch notes that a verse in *Odyssey* 11 that praises Theseus and Peirithoos was inserted "to please the Athenians."[11] In this case, the claim of insertion seems to have had no effect on the transmission of the verse; it is present in all manuscripts. But other verses in the *Iliad* that mention the Athenians, such as *Iliad* 1.265, had a difficult reception in the textual tradition, with the result that they are omitted in many of the papyri and medieval manu-

---

9. Strabo 9.1.10. See Higbie 1997.

10. *Iliad* 2.558 is omitted in papyrus 2, 38, 104, 866W, and 868W, as well as manuscripts A, F, and Y.

11. *Life of Theseus* 20.2: τοῦτο γὰρ τὸ ἔπος ἐκ τῶν Ἡσιόδου Πεισίστρατον ἐξελεῖν φησιν Ἡρέας ὁ Μεγαρεύς, ὥσπερ αὖ πάλιν ἐμβαλεῖν εἰς τὴν Ὁμήρου νέκυιαν τὸ Θησέα Πειρίθοόν τε θεῶν ἀριδείκετα τέκνα [*Odyssey* 11.631] χαριζόμενον Ἀθηναίοις ("Hêreas the Megarian says that Peisistratus removed this verse from the poetry of Hesiod, just as he inserted into the Nekuia of Homer [*Odyssey* 11.631] the verse: 'Theseus and Peirithoos, distinguished children of the gods'").

scripts.[12] These manuscript omissions suggest that there was a great deal of doubt in antiquity as to whether the Athenians had any role at all in the Achaean expedition against Troy.

The Athenians themselves, however, do not seem to have doubted their place in the epic tradition. Several works of Athenian art emphasized their relationship with the Trojan expedition by highlighting the role of Menestheus or by depicting the rescue of Theseus' mother, Aithra, by Theseus' sons.[13] Three works in particular stand out: a giant bronze representation of the Trojan horse on the Acropolis, the monumental wall painting of the sack of Troy by Polygnotus in the Painted Stoa, and the metopes on the north side of the Parthenon.[14] Each of these works might be said to celebrate the Athenian role in the Trojan War.[15] The colossal bronze statue of the Trojan horse, for example, stood in the sanctuary of Artemis Brauronia on the Acropolis.[16] According to Pausanias (1.23.8), Menestheus, Teucer (the brother of Ajax), and the sons of Theseus (Akamas and Demophon) were depicted looking out from the horse. As several scholars have pointed out, these figures are not the warriors named, for example, in the Odyssean description of the Trojan horse (4.271–89), but the heroes specifically connected to Athens.[17]

12. *Iliad* 1.265 (Θησέα τ᾽ Αἰγεΐδην, ἐπιείκελον ἀθανάτοισιν) is quoted by both Dio and Pausanias, but it is absent from many papyri (56, 122, 278, 377, 529, 531, 761W, 762W, 765W, 766W) and is found in only a minority of medieval manuscripts (O; it is added into the margins of T², H, and V). Modern scholars assume it to be an interpolation of Athenian propaganda (see Kirk 1985 *ad loc.*). West (1998) does not print the verse in the main text of his edition at all, even in brackets.

13. For Akamas, Demophon, and the rescue of Aithra in Greek art see Kron 1981a, 426–27 and 1981b and Anderson 1997, 242–45. For Menestheus, see Simon 1992.

14. Here again I am heavily indebted to the discussion of these works in Ferrari 2000. On the Trojan horse (of which only the statue base survives), see Plutarch 1.23.8 and Hurwit 1999, 198 and fig. 168 on p. 195. On the painting of Polygnotus in the Painted Stoa, see Pausanias 1.15.1–3 and Plutarch, *Life of Cimon* 4.5–6. Polygnotus also painted a larger version of his *Ilioupersis* ("Sack of Troy") in the Cnidian *Lesche* at Delphi, on which see Pausanias 10.25–31, Robert 1893, Kebric 1983, and Stansbury-O'Donnell 1989.

15. This is by far the most common interpretation; see, e.g., Hall 1989, 68–69 and Hurwit 1999, 228–31. Ferrari (2000) has challenged this interpretation. See further below.

16. It was dedicated by a man named Khairedemos around 420 B.C. See note 14 above.

17. The only ancient literary source that includes Menestheus in the story of the Trojan Horse is the fourth-century A.D. poet Quintus of Smyrna (12.305–30). See Higbie 1997, 291 as well as Ferrari 2000, 119. In addition to *Odyssey* 4.271–89 see 8.500–520 and 11.523–32. On the significance of having Teucer and Menestheus depicted together see the discussion above (with reference to Athenian claims to Salamis based on the Catalogue of Ships in the *Iliad*), as well as Higbie 1997, 290–91.

Recent scholars, however, have shown that the representation of the sack of Troy in Athenian art is usually anything but celebratory. Anderson's study of the sack of Troy in Greek poetry and vase painting finds that the destruction of Troy is consistently represented as a sacrilege that rouses the retribution of the gods.[18] Ferrari's analysis of the Parthenon metopes reveals that in the wake of the Persian sack of Athens in 480 the Athenians seem to have identified more with the Trojans than with the Achaeans. The representation of the sack of Troy on the Parthenon as a hubristic and unjustified act in fact resonates with Athenian literature and art in which the fall of Troy is depicted as a great sacrilege on the part of the Achaeans in the context of which many atrocities were committed. The Athenian heroes Menestheus, Akamas, and Demophon are celebrated as the Athenian link to the collective *kleos* of Homeric song. But as Ferrari points out, the point of representing the sack of Troy in fifth-century B.C. Athens was not to praise the Athenians, but to blame the Achaeans.[19]

Depictions of the sack of Troy in Greek literature and art consistently juxtapose in varying combinations the same core set of episodes: the killing of Priam, the king of Troy, by Neoptolemus at the altar of Zeus *Herkeios;* the death of Hektor's infant son Astyanax (at the hands of either Odysseus or Achilles' son Neoptolemus); the rape of Cassandra in the sanctuary of Athena by Ajax, son of Oileus (in the course of which Cassandra is dragged away by force from the cult statue of Athena, which she holds in supplication); the leading away of Polyxena (who will be sacrificed to Achilles); the recovery of Helen; and the departure of Aeneas.[20] The Parthenon is no exception. Although the north metopes are for the most part lost or severely damaged, included on them are likely to have been the leading away of Polyxena, the recovery of Helen, the rescue of Aithra by Akamas and Demophon, and Aeneas' escape with his son Ascanius. Also most likely included were the deaths of Priam and Astyanax and the rape of Cassandra.[21] A scene that seems to be a council of the gods may represent the moment where the gods plot

18. Anderson 1997. The fall of Troy is one of the most popular subjects in Attic vase painting from the mid sixth century B.C. to the mid fifth century B.C., with representations increasing significantly after 490 (the year of the first Persian invasion). See, in addition to Anderson, Schefold and Jung 1989, 283–85 and Ferrari 2000, 120. On the fall of Troy (including the death of Astyanax and the capture of women) as a recognizable theme already in Archaic art, see also Friis Johansen 1967, 26–30 and 35–36 and citations below, note 20.

19. Ferrari 2000, 139.

20. For a survey see Ferrari 2000, 122–24 or Anderson 1997, 192–207. See also Ahlberg-Cornell 1992, 77–85 and Gantz 1993, 646–61.

21. For the contents of the north metopes see Ferrari 2000, 130–32, whose reconstructions I follow here.

destruction for the Achaeans on their journey home, as punishment for the outrages that they have committed.[22]

In interpreting the significance of the sack of Troy on the Parthenon metopes it is important to keep in mind the historical circumstances of the building of this temple. When the Athenians retreated to Salamis in 480, the Persians swept through Attica, took over the Acropolis of Athens, and burned it, destroying its sanctuaries and temples. The monumental building program of the fifth century B.C. was not only a necessary rebuilding, but also the Athenians' testament to their own survival and to the continuity of their city-state in the face of utter devastation—as well as to their ultimate victory over a would-be oppressor. As a memorial of the sacrilege committed by the Persians, the ruins of the burned temples were incorporated into the new building program. The ruins of the old temple of Athena were left in full view and never rebuilt.[23]

These same historical circumstances have led most scholars to interpret the presence of the sack of Troy on the Parthenon as an emblem of victory over the Persians, of West over East.[24] But as Ferrari has argued, such an interpretation requires a radical reinterpretation of the traditional significance of the sack of Troy. Ferrari asks:

> Would a subject that came trailing so heavy a baggage of pejorative connotations be chosen, unless that baggage was crucial to its charge? The thesis of this paper is that the Ilioupersis was deployed on the Parthenon precisely because it was the paradigm of wrongful conquest. The images invited comparison with the Persian invasion of Greece, not, however, in the sense that the Trojans prefigure the Persians. Rather, the recent sack of Athens is seen through the image of the epic sack of Troy.[25]

If Ferrari's interpretation is correct (and I believe that it must be), then the Athenians of the first half of the fifth century B.C. are not to be unequivo-

---

22. Cf. Proclus' summary of the *Sack of Troy:* ἔπειτα ἀποπλέουσιν οἱ Ἕλληνες, καὶ φθορὰν αὐτοῖς ἡ Ἀθηνᾶ κατὰ τὸ πέλαγος μηχανᾶται. ("Then the Achaeans sail off, while Athena plots destruction for them on the seas"). Ferrari (2000, 132) cites as parallels to a council in which the will of Zeus is asserted Euripides' *Trojan Women* 80–81 and Quintus of Smyrna 14.422–72. On Athena's anger, see also chapter 5.

23. See Ferrari 2002a.

24. See note 15 above.

25. Ferrari 2000, 126. She points out (p. 124) that Castriota (1992) questions how the Ilioupersis ("Sack of Troy") representations in postwar Athens can possibly be interpreted as patriotic depictions of victory over the barbarian, but then reaffirms that they must.

cally equated with the Achaeans of Homeric epic. Rather they are a separate entity altogether, more likely to identify with the conquered Trojans than to take pride in the excesses of the victorious Achaeans. Their marginal status in the Iliadic tradition allows Athenian local heroes to maintain a certain distance from the actions of such figures as Odysseus, Ajax (son of Oileus), and Neoptolemus, despite the fact that they are clearly on the Greek side.

I don't mean to suggest, however, that the Athenians' relationship with the Trojan War tradition and the sack of Troy in particular can be so simply explained. As I noted above, the Athenians believed that they had been a part of the collective Greek expedition. At times this was a source of pride for Athens, as the monumental bronze horse dedication on the Acropolis indicates.[26] Moreover, we know of at least one instance in antiquity where the actions of Menestheus at Troy were cited as a parallel for the victory of the Athenians over the Persians. In the fifth century B.C., three herms were set up in the Athenian Agora to commemorate Cimon's victory against the Persian forces at Eion in 475.[27] The inscriptions on the herms compared the valor of the Athenians to that of Menestheus at Troy. The following is one of the three inscriptions, as reported by Aeschines (3.185):

ἔκ ποτε τῆσδε πόληος ἅμ' Ἀτρείδῃσι Μενεσθεὺς
ἡγεῖτο ζάθεον Τρωικὸν ἂμ πεδίον,
ὅν ποθ' Ὅμηρος ἔφη Δαναῶν πύκα χαλκοχιτώνων
κοσμητῆρα μάχης ἔξοχον ἄνδρα μολεῖν.
οὕτως οὐδὲν ἀεικὲς Ἀθηναίοισι καλεῖσθαι
κοσμητὰς πολέμου τ' ἀμφὶ καὶ ἠνορέης.

Once from this city Menestheus together with the sons of Atreus
was the leader to the plain of Troy that is beloved of the gods.
Of this man Homer once said that of all the Danaans with their bronze
　chitons
he excelled in marshaling troops for battle.
Thus it is in no way unseemly for the Athenians to be called
marshals in war and in manhood.[28]

---

26. For a patriotic Athenian interpretation of the Trojan War as a great and collective Greek victory over barbarians, see Isocrates, *Panegyricus* 159. Isocrates seems to me, however, strikingly isolated in his assimilation of the Trojans with barbarians.

27. On the herms of Eion see Connor (forthcoming).

28. For the inscriptions on the three herms see, in addition to Aeschines 3.183–85, Plutarch, *Life of Cimon* 7.4–6.

The herms must have been set up sometime in the mid to late 470s, not long before the production of Aeschylus' *Persians,* and in fact around the time of the production of Phrynichus' *Phoenician Women* in 476, which also dramatized the aftermath of the Battle of Salamis. In the previous chapter I argued that very soon after the Persian invasion the Athenians were able to sympathize in a remarkable way with the sufferings of their defeated enemy through the medium of tragedy. The ability to transcend hostilities and reexperience Salamis from the other side, however, does not mean that the Athenians did not condemn the Persian attack and in particular the destruction of the Acropolis, or that they did not take pride in their own victory.

The Athenians seem to have been all too aware that in the act of sacking a city one is particularly susceptible to committing hubristic outrage.[29] Herodotus, while not an Athenian, marked the Persians as exemplifying *hubris* when they sacked Sardis, the capital city of the Lydians.[30] The Athenians themselves were in a position to act as the Persians did on many occasions in the fifth century B.C. In 475, after besieging and capturing the city of Eion, they sold the entire population into slavery and established a colony there.[31] Eion is the first of many cities to be enslaved by the Athenians in the fifth century, with some victories more brutal than others.[32] Thus the sack of Troy must have resonated with the Athenians on many levels. On the one hand it prefigures the sack of their own city and the desecration of their temples at the hands of a foreign aggressor. On another level, the myth is a warning against the excesses of brutality that often come with victory.

That the depiction of the sack of Troy on the Parthenon is a negative exemplum of a sacrilegious and hubristic assault is, I would argue, supported by Polygnotus' wall paintings of the fall of Troy in the Painted Stoa in Athens and in the Cnidian *Lesche* (meeting hall) in Delphi.[33] Neither painting survives, but they are both described in detail by Pausanias. Like the Parthenon, the paintings' emphasis is on the outrage that pervaded the Trojan assault and its aftermath. I quote here Pausanias' entire description of the Painted Stoa:

αὕτη δὲ ἡ στοὰ πρῶτα μὲν ᾿Αθηναίους ἔχει τεταγμένους ἐν Οἰνόῃ τῆς ᾿Αργεία; ἐναντία Λακεδαιμονίων· γέγραπται δὲ οὐκ ἐς ἀκμὴν ἀγῶνος

29. Cf. Winkler 1985, 37 and Croally 1994, 47.
30. Herodotus 1.89.2. See chapter 2.
31. For sources, see Connor (forthcoming).
32. See further below.
33. On the Painted Stoa see Wycherley 1953 and Meritt 1970. On the Cnidian *Lesche* see Kebric 1983 and Anderson 1997, 247–55.

οὐδὲ τολμημάτων ἐς ἐπίδειξιν τὸ ἔργον ἤδη προῆκον, ἀλλὰ ἀρχομένη τε
ἡ μάχη καὶ ἐς χεῖρας ἔτι συνιόντες. ἐν δὲ τῷ μέσῳ τῶν τοίχων Ἀθηναῖοι
καὶ Θησεὺς Ἀμαζόσι μάχονται. μόναις δὲ ἄρα ταῖς γυναιξὶν οὐκ ἀφήρει
τὰ πταίσματα τὸ ἐς τοὺς κινδύνους ἀφειδές, εἴ γε Θεμισκύρας τε
ἁλούσης ὑπὸ Ἡρακλέους καὶ ὕστερον φθαρείσης σφίσι τῆς στρατιᾶς,
ἣν ἐπ᾽ Ἀθήνας ἔστειλαν, ὅμως ἐς Τροίαν ἦλθον Ἀθηναίοις τε αὐτοῖς
μαχούμεναι καὶ τοῖς πᾶσιν Ἕλλησιν. <u>ἐπὶ δὲ ταῖς Ἀμαζόσιν Ἕλληνές
εἰσιν ᾑρηκότες Ἴλιον καὶ οἱ βασιλεῖς ἠθροισμένοι διὰ τὸ Αἴαντος ἐς
Κασσάνδραν τόλμημα· καὶ αὐτὸν ἡ γραφὴ τὸν Αἴαντα ἔχει καὶ γυναῖκας
τῶν αἰχμαλώτων ἄλλας τε καὶ Κασσάνδραν.</u> τελευταῖον δὲ τῆς γραφῆς
εἰσιν οἱ μαχεσάμενοι Μαραθῶνι· Βοιωτῶν δὲ οἱ Πλάταιαν ἔχοντες καὶ
ὅσον ἦν Ἀττικὸν ἴασιν ἐς χεῖρας τοῖς βαρβάροις. καὶ ταύτῃ μέν ἐστιν ἴσα
⟨τὰ⟩ παρ᾽ ἀμφοτέρων ἐς τὸ ἔργον· τὸ δὲ ἔσω τῆς μάχης φεύγοντές εἰσιν
οἱ βάρβαροι καὶ ἐς τὸ ἕλος ὠθοῦντες ἀλλήλους, ἔσχαται δὲ τῆς γραφῆς
νῆές τε αἱ Φοίνισσαι καὶ τῶν βαρβάρων τοὺς ἐσπίπτοντας ἐς ταύτας
φονεύοντες οἱ Ἕλληνες. ἐνταῦθα καὶ Μαραθὼν γεγραμμένος ἐστὶν
ἥρως, ἀφ᾽ οὗ τὸ πεδίον ὠνόμασται, καὶ Θησεὺς ἀνιόντι ἐκ γῆς εἰκασμένος
Ἀθηνᾶ τε καὶ Ἡρακλῆς· Μαραθωνίοις γάρ, ὡς αὐτοὶ λέγουσιν, Ἡρακλῆς
ἐνομίσθη θεὸς πρώτοις. τῶν μαχομένων δὲ δῆλοι μάλιστά εἰσιν ἐν τῇ
γραφῇ Καλλίμαχός τε, ὅς Ἀθηναίοις πολεμαρχεῖν ᾕρητο, καὶ Μιλτιάδης
τῶν στρατηγούντων, ἥρως τε Ἔχετλος καλούμενος, οὗ καὶ ὕστερον
ποιήσομαι μνήμην.   (PAUSANIAS I.15.1–3)

This portico contains, first, the Athenians arrayed against the Lacedaemonians at Oenoe in the Argive territory. What is depicted is not the
crisis of the battle nor when the action had advanced as far as the display
of deeds of valor, but the beginning of the fight when the combatants
were about to close. On the middle wall are the Athenians and Theseus
fighting with the Amazons. So, it seems, only the women did not lose
through their defeats their reckless courage in the face of danger, if after
Themiscyra was taken by Herakles, and afterward the army that they
dispatched to Athens was destroyed, they nevertheless came to Troy to
fight all the Greeks as well as the Athenians themselves. <u>After the Amazons
come the Greeks when they have taken Troy, and the kings assembled on
account of the outrage committed by Ajax against Cassandra. The painting
includes Ajax himself, other captive women, and Cassandra.</u> At the end of
the painting are those who fought at Marathon; the Boeotians of Plataea
and the Attic contingent are coming to blows with the barbarians. In this
place neither side has the better, but the center of the fighting shows the

barbarians in flight and pushing one another into the marsh, while at the end of the painting are the Phoenician ships, and the Greeks killing the barbarians who are scrambling into them. Here is also a portrait of the hero Marathon, after whom the plain is named, of Theseus represented as coming up from the underworld, of Athena, and of Herakles. The Marathonians, according to their own account, were the first to regard Herakles as a god. Of the fighters the most conspicuous figures in the painting are Callimachus, who had been elected commander-in-chief by the Athenians, Miltiades, one of the generals, and a hero called Echetlus, of whom I shall make mention later.[34]

What I find striking in the description of this painting is its concern for the defeated Trojans, and in particular the captive Trojan women. If it were not for this important detail, it would be natural to interpret the defeat of the Trojans as a victory for the Greeks on par with the victory at Marathon, which was the subject of the adjacent painting.[35] But the paintings are not parallel. We are told that Polygnotus chose to depict not only the plight of the captive women, but the aftereffects of one of the most notorious outrages of the Greeks, the forced removal of Cassandra by Ajax from the sanctuary of Athena. The outrage of the assault, moreover, is exacerbated by the Greeks as a collective when they fail, after deliberating about the matter, to properly punish Ajax. It is the failure to properly condemn Ajax that incites Athena's wrath against the Greeks and leads to their destruction on the voyage home.[36] And it is this moment of deliberation that Polygnotus' painting illustrates.[37]

The Painted Stoa, built in the 460s B.C., was one of the most well known and frequented monuments in Athens, and the paintings inside were revered

34. Translation after Jones and Ormerod (1918), as are all subsequent translations of Pausanias in this chapter.

35. This is how Hall 1989, 68–69 interprets the painting. See also Erskine 2001, 71: "The Trojans of the Painted Stoa are tainted by their context." Erskine likewise interprets the painting of Polygnotus in the Cnidian *Lesche* (discussed below) as anti-Persian in sentiment.

36. This cause of Athena's wrath is suggested by Proclus' summary of the *Sack of Troy* in the Epic Cycle (see note 22 above). See also Euripides, *Trojan Women* 69–73; Anderson 1997, 77–80; and chapter 5 below.

37. It is certainly possible, of course, that Pausanias has not described every aspect of the painting, on which point see further below. It is clear, however, that the sack itself was not represented, but rather the Greeks *after they have taken Troy* (ἠρηκότες ˇΙλιον)—i.e., the tragic aftermath.

in antiquity.[38] Polygnotus is said to have contributed his paintings for free as a gift to the city of Athens.[39] Wycherley has suggested that Polygnotus' work may have even influenced the vase painters, who worked not far from the Stoa. It is important therefore to take this particular version into account when considering the thematic importance of the sack of Troy in Greek poetry and art. Polygnotus' painting of the fall of Troy in the Painted Stoa, moreover, is actually a smaller, excerpted version of the very large Ilioupersis that he painted for the Cnidian *Lesche* at Delphi. This monumental painting, which was accompanied by an equally large painting of Odysseus' journey to the underworld, was likewise famous in antiquity. Although its intended audience was not Athenian, this larger painting by Polygnotus, described in great detail by Pausanias, can shed even further light on the aims and composition of the somewhat more truncated version in the Painted Stoa in Athens.

Pausanias' description of the larger *Ilioupersis* of Polygnotus makes it very clear that the painting's subject is the aftermath of the sack of Troy and the suffering that resulted for the Trojans. The Greeks are sailing away or preparing to depart; Menelaus' ship is putting out to sea. The next scene depicts the first of two groups of captive women:

> Βρισηὶς δὲ ἑστῶσα καὶ Διομήδη τε ὑπὲρ αὐτῆς καὶ Ἴφις πρὸ ἀμφοτέρων ἐοίκασιν ἀνασκοπούμενοι τὸ Ἑλένης εἶδος. κάθηται δὲ αὐτή τε ἡ Ἑλένη καὶ Εὐρυβάτης πλησίον· τὸν δὲ Ὀδυσσέως εἶναι κήρυκα εἰκάζομεν, οὐ μὴν εἶχεν ἤδη γένεια. θεράπαινα δὲ Ἠλέκτρα καὶ Πανθαλίς, ἡ μὲν τῇ Ἑλένῃ παρέστηκεν, ἡ δὲ ὑποδεῖ τὴν δέσποιναν ἡ Ἠλέκτρα· διάφορα δὲ καὶ ταῦτα τὰ ὀνόματα ⟨ἢ⟩ Ὅμηρος ἔθετο ἐν Ἰλιάδι, ἔνθα καὶ Ἑλένην καὶ ἰούσας ὁμοῦ τῇ Ἑλένῃ τὰς δούλας ἐπὶ τὸ τεῖχος πεποίηκεν.
>
> (PAUSANIAS 10.25.4)

Briseis is standing with Diomêdê above her and Iphis in front of both, examining the form of Helen. Helen herself is sitting, and so is Eurybates near her. We inferred that he was the herald of Odysseus, although he had yet no beard. One handmaid, Panthalis, is standing beside Helen; another, Electra, is fastening her mistress' sandals. These names too are different from those given by Homer in the *Iliad,* where he tells of Helen going to the wall with her slave women.

Briseis, Diomede, and Iphis are part of a group of women whom Achilles took captive in his raids in and around the Troad and the neighboring islands

---

38. See Wycherley 1953.
39. Plutarch, *Life of Cimon* 4.

before our *Iliad* begins. These raids were narrated in the *Cypria* and no doubt other epic traditions.⁴⁰ In the painting, these women contemplate Helen, who might be interpreted as the cause of their suffering. Helen herself is now to some extent a captive woman, as are her attendants, and they await their fate at the hands of the victorious Greek soldiers.⁴¹

A second, far larger group of captive women appears later in Pausanias' description. Their sheer number and their position in the description suggest that they were a prominent component of the painting. Here is approximately the first half of Pausanias' description of the captive women:

γυναῖκες δὲ αἱ Τρῳάδες αἰχμαλώτοις τε ἤδη καὶ ὀδυρομέναις ἐοίκασι. γέγραπται μὲν Ἀνδρομάχη, καὶ ὁ παῖς οἱ προσέστηκεν ἑλόμενος τοῦ μαστοῦ — τούτῳ Λέσχεως ῥιφθέντι ἀπὸ τοῦ πύργου συμβῆναι λέγει τὴν τελευτήν· οὐ μὴν ὑπὸ δόγματός γε Ἑλλήνων, ἀλλ' ἰδίᾳ Νεοπτόλεμον αὐτόχειρα ἐθελῆσαι γενέσθαι—, γέγραπται δὲ Μηδεσικάστη, θυγα-τέρων μὲν Πριάμου καὶ αὕτη τῶν νόθων, ἐξῳκίσθαι δὲ ἐς Πήδαιον πόλιν φησὶν αὐτὴν Ὅμηρος Ἰμβρίῳ Μέντορος παιδὶ ἀνδρὶ [ἐς Πήδαιον] συνοικοῦσαν. ἡ μὲν δὴ Ἀνδρομάχη καὶ ἡ Μηδεσικάστη καλύμματά εἰσιν ἐπικείμεναι, Πολυξένη δὲ κατὰ τὰ εἰθισμένα παρθένοις ἀναπέπλεκται τὰς ἐν τῇ κεφαλῇ τρίχας· ἀποθανεῖν δὲ αὐτὴν ἐπὶ τῷ Ἀχιλλέως μνήματι ποιηταί τε ᾄδουσι καὶ γραφὰς ἔν τε Ἀθήναις καὶ Περγάμῳ τῇ ὑπὲρ Καΐκου θεασάμενος οἶδα ἐχούσας ἐς τῆς Πολυξένης τὰ παθήματα.

(PAUSANIAS 10.25.9–11)

The Trojan women are represented as already captives and lamenting. Andromache is in the painting, and nearby stands her boy grasping her breast; this child Lesches says was put to death by being flung from the tower, not that the Greeks had so decreed, but Neoptolemus, of his own accord, wanted to be his killer. In the painting is also Medesikastê, another of Priam's illegitimate daughters, who according to Homer left her home and went to the city of Pedaeum to be the wife of Imbrius, the son of Mentor. Andromache and Medesikastê are wrapped in veils, but the hair of Polyxena is braided after the custom of maidens. Poets sing of her death at the tomb of Achilles, and I have seen with my own eyes paintings both at Athens and at Pergamon on the Caicus depicting the suffering of Polyxena.

40. See Dué 2002, 61–64. In the *Iliad* we are told that Briseis comes from Lyrnessos (2.690, etc.), Diomede from Lesbos (9.664), and Iphis from Skyros (9.667).

41. Cf. the choral odes in Euripides' *Hecuba* (444–83) and *Trojan Women* (177–233), in which the chorus of captive Trojan women contemplate where in Greece they might be taken.

The captive women are painted in such a way that Pausanias can actually *see* them lamenting, and he mentions that Andromache is grasping her breast in a gesture of lamentation. The women are called *aikhmalotidês,* the traditional word for war captives.[42] The fate of Andromache and her son and the sacrifice of Polyxena, two scenes that appear in most representations of the sack of Troy, are emphasized here as specific examples of the suffering of the Trojan women.

Already at this point in the description we can see that Polygnotus has drawn on a storehouse of traditions about the fate of the captive women of Troy for the composition of this painting. Throughout his description of the painting Pausanias uses his knowledge of epic traditions—most often the *Sack of Troy* attributed to Lesches—to interpret what he sees. In the previous passage Pausanias' note about the names of Helen's attendants tells us that the figures were labeled. But it also tells us that Polygnotus' source of inspiration was not necessarily the *Iliad* as it was known to Pausanias and to us, but rather other traditions in which these women played a role. This is only to be expected, given the significant amount of time that elapsed between the creation of Polygnotus' painting and Pausanias' viewing of that painting.[43]

I propose that there were already a variety of traditions about the captive Trojan women current in Polygnotus' day. Pausanias says that he himself had seen a number of paintings that depicted the sacrifice of Polyxena. As we will see in the following chapters, captive women were the protagonists and formed the choruses of many tragedies. Women's love song and lament traditions, with their own particular perspective on the Trojan War myths, may also have been an important source of inspiration for poets and painters in the Archaic and Classical periods. Pausanias is aware of the more canonical epic traditions about Troy, but he does not seem to have access to the other media that may have influenced Polygnotus and other artists of the fifth century B.C.[44]

We have still not come to the end of Pausanias' description of the captive women, however. As the passage continues we catch still further glimpses

42. Sophocles composed a tragedy of that name, which is thought to have centered on Briseis and the other women taken captive by Achilles in the raids. See Blumenthal 1927.

43. On the evolution and multiformity of Greek epic traditions (as well as the relationship between epic and visual narratives) see Dué 2002, 21–36.

44. For more on women's song traditions, see chapter 1. See also Doherty 1996 and Pache 1999, who discuss the women's song traditions that are incorporated into Odysseus' catalogue of heroines in *Odyssey* 11.

of the many traditions about the women of Troy that were current in antiquity:

τῶν δὲ γυναικῶν τῶν μεταξὺ τῆς τε Αἴθρας καὶ Νέστορος, εἰσὶν ἄνωθεν τούτων αἰχμάλωτοι καὶ αὗται Κλυμένη τε καὶ Κρέουσα καὶ Ἀριστομάχη καὶ Ξενοδίκη. Κλυμένην μὲν οὖν Στησίχορος ἐν Ἰλίου πέρσιδι κατηρίθμηκεν ἐν ταῖς αἰχμαλώτοις· ὡσαύτως δὲ καὶ Ἀριστομάχην ἐποίησεν ἐν Νόστοις θυγατέρα μὲν Πριάμου, Κριτολάου δὲ γυναῖκα εἶναι τοῦ Ἱκετάονος· Ξενοδίκης δὲ μνημονεύσαντα οὐκ οἶδα οὔτε ποιητὴν οὔτε ὅσοι λόγων συνθέται. ἐπὶ δὲ τῇ Κρεούσῃ λέγουσιν ὡς ἡ θεῶν μήτηρ καὶ Ἀφροδίτη δουλείας ἀπὸ Ἑλλήνων αὐτὴν ἐρρύσαντο, εἶναι γὰρ δὴ καὶ Αἰνείου τὴν Κρέουσαν γυναῖκα· Λέσχεως δὲ καὶ ἔπη τὰ Κύπρια διδόασιν Εὐρυδίκην γυναῖκα Αἰνείᾳ. γεγραμμέναι δὲ ἐπὶ κλίνης ὑπὲρ ταύτας Δηινόμη τε καὶ Μητιόχη καὶ Πεῖσίς ἐστι καὶ Κλεοδίκη·

(PAUSANIAS 10.26.1–2)

Above the women between Aithra and Nestor are other captive women, Klymenê, Creusa, Aristomakhê, and Xenodikê. Now Stesichorus, in the *Sack of Troy,* includes Klymenê in the number of the captives; and similarly, in the *Homeward Voyages [Nostoi],* he speaks of Aristomakhê as the daughter of Priam and the wife of Kritolaos, son of Hiketaon. But I know of no poet, and of no prose-writer, who makes mention of Xenodikê. About Creusa the story is told that the mother of the gods and Aphrodite rescued her from slavery among the Greeks, as she was, of course, the wife of Aeneas. But Lesches and the *Cypria* make Eurydikê the wife of Aeneas. Beyond these are painted on a couch Deinomê, Metiokhê, Peisis, and Kleodikê.

Each of the women depicted in the painting has a story behind her. Pausanias knows many of the stories, though not all. We can see from a passage like this that there is a vast corpus of narratives about the fall of Troy that is now lost to us, but that must have informed the experience of any spectator of ancient Greek art or tragedy. Just as Pausanias can see and almost hear the laments of the captive women in the painting he describes, so any Athenian of Polygnotus' day would have been able to draw on a vast corpus of women's song traditions and song traditions about women when viewing the Painted Stoa or the metopes of the Parthenon, or hearing the laments of a tragic chorus of captive women.

There are several more aspects of Polygnotus' painting that are relevant to this discussion of Athenian interpretations of the fall of Troy. First, Theseus' son Demophon is represented as contemplating the rescue of his grandmother

Aithra. Pausanias does not mention this episode in his description of the smaller painting in the Painted Stoa in Athens, but it is almost certain to have been painted there too. In the Cnidian *Lesche* at Delphi Demophon and Akamas are also included among the soldiers painted near the head of the Trojan horse. Other parts of the Delphi painting may have been depicted in the Stoa also, since Pausanias' description of the Stoa is far briefer than his description of the Cnidian *Lesche*. For example, Pausanias mentions the deliberation about the rape of Cassandra in his description of the Stoa. For the *Lesche* he also describes Cassandra holding onto the wooden statue of Athena, as well as the various Greek soldiers present, including Ajax, who is giving an oath. It is difficult to say how many of the captive women described in the *Lesche* may have been painted in the Stoa, but Pausanias tells us that there were some in the vicinity of Cassandra, and there may have been more.

Near the end of Pausanias' description of Polygnotus' painting comes a list of corpses. Dead Trojans litter the painting. Priam is among the dead. It is not clear whether Priam is depicted at the altar of Zeus, but this is likely to have been the case, since Pausanias does mention the alternative version in which Neoptolemus drags Priam from the altar and kills him in the doorway. Here again the sheer number of the corpses suggests that the central theme of this painting is the suffering of the Trojans and the utter brutality of the Greeks. The painting is not about the experience of the victors, but that of the losers, whose men are killed and women taken as captives.

I submit that the fuller description of the Cnidian *Lesche* allows us to interpret the painting in the Painted Stoa along similar lines. It is tempting to view the Stoa as a "hall of victory" of sorts, especially in the light of the nearby painting of the Battle of Marathon.[45] But as I have been arguing, for an Athenian audience the sack of Troy had far more complicated meanings than that, as indeed seems to have been the case throughout the Greek world from Archaic times onward.

As we turn back to Greek tragedy in the ensuing chapters, we will see that the concern for the defeated that is evident in Greek monumental art of the fifth century B.C. is likewise an important theme of the tragedies that deal with the Trojan War.[46] In these tragedies the captive women of Troy take

45. The phrase "hall of victory" is Wycherley's (1953, 27).

46. Many tragedies dealing with Trojan War themes were produced in the second half of the fifth century B.C., but curiously, the sack of Troy as a subject of vase painting becomes less and less common. After 420 it nearly ceases to be represented. See Boardman 1989, 229.

center stage, and through the traditional medium of lament they draw the Athenian audience into their suffering. As with the Persians of Aeschylus' drama, the historical circumstances in which these plays were produced must have elicited a complex array of emotions from the Athenian audience. But as the fifth century progressed, the Athenians increasingly became the aggressors in the ongoing hostilities between cities that pervaded the century, with the result that the relationship between history and tragedy is now quite different as we approach the Trojan War tragedies.

The Parthenon was completed in 432, just before the outbreak of the Peloponnesian War. It is a monument that must have evolved in its intentions and significance over the course of Athens' fifth-century building program. Conceived of as a dedication to Athena and a monument to victory over the Persians, it took on further significance as Athens became leader of an empire over the course of the fifth century B.C. The building was famously financed by Athens' imperialist efforts: Athens moved the treasury of what was originally the Delian League, formed to drive the Persians out of Greece, from the sacred and neutral island of Delos to Athens itself. That act is symbolic of the transformation of the Delian League into the Athenian Empire.

Now the Athenians become the sackers of cities and the captors of women and children. In the last three decades of the fifth century B.C. the Athenians systematically subjugated several cities that revolted from their enforced alliance or that refused to join them as allies in the Peloponnesian War that broke out in 431. In 427 the Athenian assembly of citizens voted to kill all the men of Mytilene and enslave all the women and children. Thucydides tells us that the next day, however, the Athenians reconsidered, and instead killed only more than a thousand of the leading conspirators in the revolt.[47] But in 421 the Athenians were not so generous with the people of Scione. There they did kill all the men and enslave the women and children.[48] In 416 they did the same for the city of Melos. But Melos had never been a member of the Delian League or Athenian Empire; they were a colony of Sparta that was attempting to remain neutral. Thucydides' famous Melian dialogue highlights the Athenian atrocity: after a lengthy debate in which the Melians justify their decision to remain neutral, the Athenians besiege the city anyway, and upon taking it, kill the men and enslave the women and children.[49]

This complex dynamic of democracy, empire, civic pride, and wartime suffering is crucial for our understanding of the force of the captive woman's la-

47. Thucydides 3.50.
48. Thucydides 5.32.
49. Thucydides 5.84–116.

ment in late-fifth-century tragedy and the potential multiplicity of responses such laments evoked. The *Hecuba* and the *Andromache* are both thought to have been composed and produced in the mid 420s, several years after the outbreak of the Peloponnesian War.[50] The *Trojan Women* on the other hand was produced in 416, just after the destruction of Melos, and just before the disastrous Sicilian expedition.[51]

How does the representation of the victims of Troy in tragedy resonate with the contemporary events of the Peloponnesian War, in which the Athenians are the destroyers of cities and the enslavers of women? Are the Athenians being asked to confront their Trojan past, this time in the role of the Achaeans, as a mirror image of their current actions? Modern critics have often interpreted the Trojan War plays of Euripides, and particularly the *Trojan Women,* as a protest of the Peloponnesian War on the part of Euripides. Edith Hamilton went so far as to call him "a pacifist in Periclean Athens" and the *Trojan Women* "the greatest piece of anti-war literature there is in the world."[52] While such a reading is obviously far too simplistic, the question remains: Why would it be effective for Euripides to put Trojan captives and their extended laments on the tragic stage several times over the course of the Peloponnesian War? What was the emotional force of these laments and on what level were the Athenians supposed to relate to them, if at all?

Very much connected to these questions is the significance for an Athenian audience of the Trojan nationality and the slave status of the captive women in the tragedies under discussion. What relationship exists between these characters and the Greek concept of the barbarian? Does the slavery that marks the Trojan women after the fall of Troy alienate them from the Athenians and render them morally inferior and unsympathetic? We might expect this to be the case, given the polarized categories of male/female, free man/slave, and Greek/barbarian that have been shown to operate in Greek thought.[53] But in fact the Trojan women defy such binary oppositions and confound expectations.

---

50. It should be noted that the *Andromache* may not have been first produced in Athens, if the scholiast on line 445 who states this can be trusted. It is a complicated question, on which see the recent discussion in Allan 2000, 149–60, with further references there. On the *Andromache*'s relationship to Athens and contemporary events see also below.

51. On the importance of the Peloponnesian War as the cultural context for Euripides' *Trojan Women,* see Croally 1994. For the *Hecuba,* see the edition of Gregory (1999, *passim*).

52. Hamilton 1971, 1. See also Delebecque 1951, 245–62. On the play's relationship to contemporary events see also Westlake 1953; Goossens 1962, 520–34; and Maxwell-Stuart 1973.

53. See the introduction.

Historians of slavery have found that the Trojans of tragedy exemplify a preoccupation on the part of the tragedians with the concept of conventional, as opposed to natural, slavery.[54] As Nancy Rabinowitz in particular has pointed out, the Trojan War plays explore the accident of fate and reversal of fortune by which queens and princesses become servants. She notes: "through highborn Trojan characters, the plays emphasize the possibility that the slave might remain noble in character."[55] Rabinowitz argues that for the Athenian male spectators, the captive Trojan women exemplify a loss of freedom. The fear of slavery on the part of the male audience is to some extent mitigated by the fact that the Trojan captives are female, but their nobility exposes the reality of war, where anyone can be enslaved, regardless of their nature or status.[56] In this way Greeks and Trojans are shown to have a common vulnerability that transcends nationality or natural law.

Questions of natural and conventional slavery in Greek thought are inherently connected with questions of ethnicity, and the portrayal of the Trojan women in tragedy likewise raises many questions about how the Athenians would have perceived their foreignness.[57] Edith Hall, whose work on the concept of the barbarian I have discussed in chapter 2, argues as a central thesis that Greek tragedy marks a radically new portrayal of the Trojans. Whereas in Greek epic there is little distinction made between Greeks and Trojans, tragedy establishes them as *barbarian*—the other and opposite of the ideal Greek.[58] This is achieved by assimilating the Trojans with the Persians of the fifth century B.C. (as the Greeks conceived of them), and by

---

54. See especially Croally (1994, 97–103) and Rabinowitz (1998), who take these terms from Aristotle's discussion of slavery (*Politics* 1252ff.). Aristotle argued that some people were by nature free and others by nature slaves. For Aristotle and other Greek thinkers of the Classical period, women and barbarians belonged to the latter category; for ancient citations, see Croally 1994, 103. As Rabinowitz shows, Aristotle is most interested in the concept of natural slavery, but tragedy is more suited to depicting what happens to individuals when faced with a sudden reversal of fortune. The Trojan women are not by nature slaves, they are made slaves by circumstances beyond their control. For a historical analysis of the practice of enslaving prisoners of war in ancient Greece see Garlan 1987 with references in note 1.

55. Rabinowitz 1998, 59. Rabinowitz' insights into the interplay of class and gender in the Trojan War plays of Euripides are too complex to be done justice here.

56. Rabinowitz 1998, 59. Rabinowitz goes on to argue that the Trojan captives also embody a fear of slave resistance, a fear that is itself mitigated when the Trojan women are shown to identify with their masters across class boundaries and along gender lines.

57. For an excellent discussion, see again Croally 1994, 97–115.

58. Hall 1989, 1. On the Trojans of Greek epic, see Mackie 1996 and Erskine 2001, 51–60. Erskine, however, following Hall (1989), sees a radical shift in the Classical period in the interpretation of the Trojans and the Trojan War. See also the similar line of argument in Harrison 2002, 3–4.

ascribing to them foreign clothing, speech, customs, and behavior.[59] But as several other scholars have forcefully demonstrated, very often the Trojans of tragedy are portrayed as quite Greek. Hall herself is forced to admit that there is a significant subgroup of "noble barbarians" in Greek tragedy who break the pattern that she describes elsewhere in her work.[60] The vast majority of these so-called noble barbarians are in fact Trojan women.[61] Not only are the Trojans and other captives of war presented sympathetically, the Trojan women are often morally superior to the Greeks who have enslaved them.[62]

Because the Trojan War plays of Euripides are the subject of the next chapter, I will adduce just two important passages here that show how completely Greek and Trojan identity can be merged or even reversed in these plays. In the *Trojan Women,* the Greek Helen is vilified by all sides as a treacherous wife, the perfect barbarian, while the Trojan Andromache emerges as the embodiment of Greek wifely virtues. Andromache's description of her marriage to Hektor characterizes her as more Greek than Greek:[63]

> ἃ γὰρ γυναιξὶ σώφρον᾽ ἔσθ᾽ ηὑρημένα,
> ταῦτ᾽ ἐξεμόχθουν Ἕκτορος κατὰ στέγας.
> πρῶτον μέν, ἔνθα (κἂν προσῇ κἂν μὴ προσῇ
> ψόγος γυναιξίν) αὐτὸ τοῦτ᾽ ἐφέλκεται
> κακῶς ἀκούειν, ἥτις οὐκ ἔνδον μένει,
> τούτου παρεῖσα πόθον ἔμιμνον ἐν δόμοις·
> ἔσω τε μελάθρων κομψὰ θηλειῶν ἔπη
> οὐκ εἰσεφρούμην, τὸν δὲ νοῦν διδάσκαλον
> οἴκοθεν ἔχουσα χρηστὸν ἐξήρκουν ἐμοί.
> γλώσσης τε σιγὴν ὄμμα θ᾽ ἥσυχον πόσει
> παρεῖχον· ᾔδη δ᾽ ἁμὲ χρῆν νικᾶν πόσιν,
> κείνῳ τε νίκην ὧν ἐχρῆν παριέναι.

(*Trojan Women* 645–56)

What things have been found to be sensible for women,
at these things I toiled in Hektor's home.

60. Hall 1989, 211–23. Croally (1994, 111–13) gives a detailed critique of Hall's efforts to explain these noble barbarians. See further below.

61. Hall also discusses foreigners who are divinely inspired as an important group of noble barbarians.

62. Segal 1993, 171. See also Aélion 1983; Croally 1994, 103–15; Anderson 1997, 106; Vidal-Naquet 1997, 114; Ferrari 2000, 127–28; and Saïd 2002.

63. See Croally 1994, 90. For Andromache as the paradigm of the lamenting wife and widow in epic, see Segal 1971 and Dué 2002, 67–74.

First of all, if a woman does not stay inside—
whether or not blame has already attached itself to that woman—
this by itself causes people to speak badly of her.
Giving up my longing for this then I stayed in the house.
And I didn't allow entry to the clever words of women,
but having my mind as a sufficient teacher
at home, I contented myself with that.
I kept a silent tongue and a fixed eye for my husband.
And I knew in what things I could be victorious over my husband,
and in what things I had to yield victory to that man.

Andromache goes on to say that her wifely virtue was her ruin—her Greek captors are so captivated by her reputation as a wife that Neoptolemus, the son of her husband's killer, chooses her for himself.

My second example comes from the *Hecuba,* in which, as in the *Trojan Women,* the spectator is presented with a parade of Trojan suffering, voiced in the haunting laments of both the protagonists and the chorus. Such laments evoke the pity of the Greek audience and, by means of this quintessential emotion of tragedy, draw them into the experience of the Trojan women. But in an extraordinary passage, the Trojan women imagine and pity the suffering of the Greek women who have lost their loved ones in war:

πόνοι γὰρ καὶ πόνων
ἀνάγκαι κρείσσονες κυκλοῦνται
κοινὸν δ' ἐξ ἰδίας ἀνοίας
κακὸν τᾷ Σιμουντίδι γᾷ
ὀλέθριον ἔμολε συμφορᾷ τ' ἐπ' ἄλλων.
ἐκρίθη δ' ἔρις, ἃν ἐν Ἰ-
δᾳ κρίνει τρισσὰς μακάρων
παῖδας ἀνὴρ βούτας,

. . .

ἐπὶ δορὶ καὶ φόνῳ καὶ ἐμῶν μελάθρων λώβᾳ·
στένει δὲ καί τις ἀμφὶ τὸν εὔροον Εὐρώταν
Λάκαινα πολυδάκρυτος ἐν δόμοις κόρα,
πολιάν τ' ἐπὶ κρᾶτα μάτηρ
τέκνων θανόντων
τίθεται χέρα δρύπτεται παρειάν,
δίαιμον ὄνυχα τιθεμένα σπαραγμοῖς.

(*Hecuba* 638–56)

Pain and compulsion,
even more powerful than pain, have come full circle;

and from one man's thoughtlessness came a universal
woe to the land of Simois,
destructive disaster resulting in disaster for others.
The strife was decided, the contest which
the shepherd, a man, judged on Ida
between three daughters of the blessed gods,
. . .

resulting in war and bloodshed and the ruin of my halls;
and on the banks of the beautifully flowing Eurotas river,
some Spartan maiden too is full of tears in her home,
and to her grey-haired head a mother
whose sons are slain
raises her hands and she tears her cheeks,
making her nails bloody in the gashes.

Just as tragedy collapses the boundaries between slave and free, so too
the distinction between Greek and foreigner is blurred and even subverted.
It is my contention that whereas Trojans are often characterized as foreign
and sometimes even themselves call attention to the fact that they are "barbarians," the contrast set up between Greek and Trojan often serves only to
highlight the commonality of their suffering.[64] As I will argue in the next
chapter, the laments of the Trojan women are fundamentally Greek in form
and theme, and their very Greekness overrides the otherness of ethnicity and
social status. The effect is not to wholly collapse all distinctions between
Greek and foreigner, male and female, slave and free individual, but to do
so just enough that within the strict confines of the tragic performance these
distinctions can be questioned, explored, and experienced by the audience
of Greek citizens.

We may ask why and how such questioning of the distinctions between
Greek and foreigner came about at the end of the fifth century B.C. It has
been suggested by Hall and others that a radical intellectual movement
circulating in Athens may have promoted a theory about the unity of mankind.[65] In his treatment of the *Trojan Women,* N. T. Croally argues instead

64. Cf. Gregory 1999 on the passage cited above. The commonality between Greek
and Trojan is also articulated by Odysseus elsewhere within the *Hecuba:* εἰσὶν παρ' ἡμῖν
οὐδὲν ἧσσον ἄθλιαι / γραῖαι γυναῖκες ἠδὲ πρεσβῦται σέθεν, / νύμφαι τ' ἀρίστων νυμφίων
τητώμεναι, / ὧν ἥδε κεύθει σώματ' Ἰδαία κόνις ("Among us are grey-haired old women
and aged men no less miserable than you, and brides bereft of excellent bridegrooms,
whose bodies this Trojan dust has covered"; *Hecuba* 322–25).

65. See Baldry 1965; Hall 1989, 215–23; and Croally 1994, 112–13.

for another solution, namely that in the late fifth century the distinction between Greek and barbarian in ordinary life was simply being eroded. He goes on to point out that if it was the Persian Wars that established the opposition of Greek and barbarian in the Greek mind, the Peloponnesian War initiated the disintegration of this concept: "Our questions must be: how will a tragic treatment of the Trojan War, written during the Peloponnesian War, represent these Greeks against the Trojans? In what ways are the Greeks distinguished from the barbarians? And will the Peloponnesian War, rather than the Persian War, prove to be the narrative that informs the play's treatment of the barbarian?"[66]

Hall too argues that the Spartan enemy forces a reinterpretation of the Greek/barbarian dichotomy. In the *Andromache*, Andromache is constantly denigrated as a slave and a barbarian by the Spartan Hermione, who is jealous of her husband's affection for his captive concubine and plots the death of Andromache and her young son. Yet it is clearly Hermione—referred to throughout the play as "the Spartan"—who is the villain of the play, and her actions are universally denounced, while Andromache retains the sympathy of all.[67] Hall argues: "When the Peloponnesian or Theban characters turn into 'enemies,' the logic of the tragic narrative dictates that the barbarians almost imperceptibly turn into 'friends,' and assume the role of surrogate Athenians; *Andromache* and *Troades* fight the Peloponnesian War on a mediated poetic plane."[68]

But is this the whole story? In Hall's reading, the Trojan women are the innocent victims of a Spartan adulteress and a Spartan invasion by Agamemnon and Menelaus, the Spartan aggressors. The Peloponnesian War context causes a radical shift in emotional alliances for the Athenians: the Trojan barbarians are suddenly no longer a demonized other, and the Athenians can now sympathize with them against a common enemy.

This thesis is attractive, but I argue that it requires modification in the light of my preceding arguments. As I have attempted to show in this chapter, the Trojans are portrayed sympathetically in the vast majority of Greek

66. Croally 1994, 104; see also pp. 113–15.

67. As I will show in the next chapter, it is through her laments that Andromache obtains pity and admiration from the Greeks in the play.

68. Hall 1989, 214. Hall does not include the *Hecuba* in this statement, on which see chapter 4. See also Hall 1989, 213: "It is significant that the plays where Greeks are shown in a poor light are always concerned not with Athenians but with their enemies in the Peloponnesian War, especially the family of the Atridae (increasingly associated not with Argos but with Sparta), or Thebans." Erskine 2001 interprets the *Andromache* along similar lines.

poetry and art throughout the fifth century B.C. The sympathetic Trojans of Euripides are not a new phenomenon, but rather represent a continuity of treatment from the earliest Greek epic poetry onward.[69] We need only think once again of Odysseus, who in the tears he sheds upon hearing the tale of the capture of Troy is compared to a lamenting Trojan widow as she is led off into captivity.

It is certainly true that in tragedy, and especially in Sophocles, the Trojans were given foreign attributes and were even assimilated at times to fifth-century B.C. Persians.[70] This characterization, however, does not seem to have alienated them from the Athenian audience emotionally. And as I have argued in chapter 2, the Athenians were capable of sympathizing with even their worst enemy, the Persians, less than a decade after the Battle of Salamis. In that play the Persians are characterized as foreign in every way, except when it comes to their suffering. In their tears and lamentation, they are shown to be incredibly Greek, or perhaps simply all too human. Similarly, the Trojans may be foreign in dress, language, and other customs, but are nevertheless subject to the same laws and consequences of war as the Greeks.

In this chapter I have also tried to suggest that the Athenians cannot be separated from the Trojan expedition so easily. I do not deny that Agamemnon, Menelaus, Hermione, and Orestes are referred to as Spartans and are portrayed particularly negatively in the Trojan War plays of Euripides, especially in the *Andromache*. But Odysseus comes off hardly better,[71] and it is Neoptolemus (with the support of the Athenian heroes Akamas and Demophon) who kills the revered Polyxena in the *Hecuba*. The fact is that Spartans are at the heart of the Trojan War myths, and of course it is the Spartan Helen who is the traditional cause of the entire war.[72]

Nevertheless, visual and literary representations of these myths make it clear that the Greeks *as a collective* are responsible for the atrocities commit-

69. Hall (1989, 213) also suggests continuity of epic traditions as an explanation for why the Trojans are portrayed sympathetically in tragedy—a suggestion that contradicts her arguments elsewhere.

70. For Sophocles' attribution of foreign language and clothing to the Trojans, see Hall 1989, 120–21. For Euripides, see Bacon 1961, 125ff.; Segal 1993, 171 (with note 6); and Saïd 2002.

71. See, e.g., *Iphigeneia at Aulis* 526–27; *Hecuba* 131–33 and 254–57.

72. Sophocles' *Ajax* almost certainly predates the Peloponnesian War, and a major crisis of that play is the attempt by the Spartans Agamemnon and Menelaus to deny the burial of Ajax. This attempt, had it been successful, would have been yet another sacrilege committed in connection with the end of the Trojan War by the Greeks, and it is clearly represented as the wrong course of action in the play.

ted during and after the sack of Troy. And since the Athenians considered themselves to have been a part of that collective, they are necessarily to some extent implicated in the events depicted by Euripides. Therefore I submit that the victims presented on the tragic stage must have struck a special chord with the Athenians, who in the course of the fifth century B.C. became sackers of cities and enslavers of women. The Athenians were not merely being invited to transfer their hatred of the Spartans to the legendary past and a war in which they themselves played no part. They were being forced to confront the actions of the legendary Achaean victors at Troy, and to evaluate the behavior of the Greeks as a collective in victory, in relation to the Athenians' own aggressive wartime policies.

Edith Hall has observed that Troy "functioned as a mythical prism through which the fifth century refracted its own preoccupation with military conflict."[73] If this is true, what did Troy and the sack of Troy signify? In this chapter I have argued that Athenian monumental art of the fifth century condemns the *hubris* of victory displayed by both the Achaeans of Greek epic traditions and the Persians of the recent past. These representations likewise warn the Athenians against going too far in their own victories of the fifth century, and the Athenians are in fact at the height of victory and power as the Parthenon is being built. Greek tragedy—particularly the Trojan War tragedies of Euripides—acutely questions the extent to which the Athenians have heeded their own warning.

The *Hecuba, Trojan Women,* and the *Andromache* have all received a great deal of negative criticism in modern times, even though we know that the *Hecuba* and *Trojan Women* were revered in antiquity, and that all three plays were chosen as school texts. Recent scholars have rehabilitated these plays, particularly the *Trojan Women;* the *Hecuba* and *Andromache* are still considered problematic on many levels.[74] In the past century, the sufferings of the Trojan women have been the key to the plays' performative power. The *Hecuba* and the *Trojan Women* have been produced on numerous occasions in explicit protest of contemporary wars.[75]

But what was it about the Trojan captives that moved the Athenians? If, as I propose, the laments of the Trojan women were a crucial factor in eliciting the pity, fear, and ultimately sorrow of the audience, what can this tell us

73. Hall 2000, ix.

74. For the *Andromache,* see Anderson 1997, 133–55 and Allan 2000; for the *Hecuba* see Kovacs 1987, Mossman 1995, and the edition of Gregory (1999); for the *Trojan Women* see Croally 1994 and the edition of Barlow (1986).

75. See Hall 2000 and Loraux 2002.

about the Athenians' conception of the Trojan War?[76] What relationship, if any, can we find between the experiences of the Trojan women and those of the contemporary Athenians, who were themselves engaged in a protracted war during the years in which these plays were first performed?[77]

In the coming chapter I propose to analyze the laments of the captive Trojan women of Euripides within the context of the tragedies that they occupy. As I analyze each play individually, I will pay particular attention to the effect that the laments have on the other characters (particularly the Greeks) within the play and consider the possible reactions of the audience. As in my discussion of Aeschylus' *Persians* in chapter 2, in which I argued that the traditional features of Greek lament in the songs of the Persians allowed the Athenians to sympathize with their defeated enemy, in the following chapters I will concentrate on the traditional Greek features in the laments of the Trojan women and their emotional effect. Both formal laments as well as passages that employ the language of lament will be analyzed, in order to assess the thematic significance of the captive women of Troy. I will argue again that the "Greekness" of these laments and the continuity of form and meaning inherited from epic portrayals of Trojan suffering invite the audience to transcend the ethnic and political boundaries that divide nations at war. In this way the Athenians can explore their own sorrows by witnessing the suffering of others, including that of their own victims.

76. I have worded this statement carefully, because I am not attempting to suggest that the lamentation of the Trojan women is the only element of these plays that elicits pity. Rhetorical arguments, which were so crucial to the education and life of the Athenian citizen, play an important role in all three plays (a feature that has been criticized in modern assessments). These arguments and such plot elements as the endangerment of children were equally important components of the structure of these plays. On the connection between pity and sorrow, see the conclusion.

77. The *Andromache,* we are told by a scholiast, was not first produced in Athens. Any discussion of the play in its contemporary setting must take this possibility into account, although of course not all scholars accept the statement of the scholiast. See the discussion of Allan (2000, 149–60) and chapter 6.

CHAPTER FOUR

THE CAPTIVE WOMAN'S LAMENT AND HER REVENGE IN EURIPIDES' *Hecuba*

Hecuba, a wretch forlorn and captive, when she saw Polyxena first slaughtered, and her son, her Polydorus, on the wild sea-beach next met the mourning woman's view, then reft of sense did she bark like a dog; such mighty power had grief to wrench her soul.

—DANTE, *Inferno*, CANTO 30.16–21[1]

Woe, woe is me! What words can I utter? What sorrow, what lamentation, the wretchedness of wretched old age, and slavery that I cannot bear or endure! Woe is me! Who will defend me? What family, and what city? Aged Priam is gone; gone are my children. Which way am I to go, this or that? Where can I be safe? Where is any god or power divine to help me?

—EURIPIDES, *Hecuba* 154–65[2]

I would like to begin my discussion of the laments of captive Trojan women in Euripides by examining Euripides' *Hecuba*, which is thought to have been produced first during the mid-420s B.C., at the height of the first phase of the Peloponnesian War.[3] Hecuba was famously all-suffering, and of all the victims at Troy she was portrayed as having lost the most. She was the queen of Troy, and gave birth to many, many children, only to witness

1. Ecuba, trista, misera e cattiva, / poscia che vide Polissena morta, / e del suo Polidoro in su la riva / del mar si fu la dolorosa accorta / forsennata latrò sì come cane: / tanto il dolor le fe' la mente torta (translation after Cary [1914]).

2. οἲ ἐγὼ μελέα, τί ποτ' ἀπύσω; / ποίαν ἀχώ, ποῖον ὀδυρμόν, / δειλαία δειλαίου γήρως, / δουλείας [τᾶς] οὐ τλατᾶς, / [τᾶς] οὐ φερτᾶς; οἴμοι. / τίς ἀμύνει μοι; ποία γέννα, / ποία δὲ πόλις; φροῦδος πρέσβυς, / φροῦδοι παῖδες. / ποίαν ἢ ταύταν ἢ κείναν / στείχω; ποῖ δὴ σωθῶ; ποῦ τις θεῶν / ἢ δαιμόνων ἐπαρωγός; / ὦ κάκ' ἐνεγκοῦσαι, / Τρῳάδες ὦ κάκ' ἐνεγκοῦσαι / πήματ', ἀπωλέσατ' ὠλέσατ'· οὐκέτι μοι βίος / ἀγαστὸς ἐν φάει.

3. On the complicated assemblage of evidence used to date this play, see the excellent summary provided in the edition of Gregory (1999, xii–xv).

the death of her husband and sons. Priam, Hecuba's husband and the king of Troy, died in the sack of Troy, but Hecuba lived on, to experience even more suffering, lose still more children, and become the slave of her family's killers.

In the first half of the *Hecuba,* she loses her virgin daughter Polyxena to the violence of the Greeks. Polyxena is sacrificed as an offering at the tomb of Achilles, who, as a powerful hero after his death, has apparently demanded some kind of prize before the Greeks can leave Troy.[4] In the second half of this play she finds out that her only remaining and youngest son, Polydorus, whom she and Priam had sent away from Troy for his protection, has been killed by Polymestor, king of Thrace, who was supposed to be protecting him. At the end of the play Hecuba watches another daughter, Cassandra, be led off as a concubine, in full knowledge that Cassandra is going to die when she reaches Greece. The play's climax occurs when Hecuba and her fellow captive Trojan women lure Polymestor and his two young sons into the women's tents in the Achaean postwar camp in nearby Thrace.[5] The women blind Polymestor using the pins from their dresses and kill Polymestor's two boys.

The plot of the *Hecuba,* therefore, has two main parts, each taking up half the play, and many questions of interpretation revolve around how the two fit together. Three acts of extraordinary violence form the backbone of this plot: the murder of Polydorus before the play begins, the sacrifice of Polyxena by the Greek soldiers, and the simultaneous blinding of Polymestor and killing of his sons by Hecuba and her fellow captive women. Men's violence against women in war in the first half of the play (in the form of the killing of Polydorus and Polyxena) turns into women's violence against men in the second. Through it all, Hecuba is onstage, the unifying element.[6]

Scholars are divided in their assessments of the character and actions of Hecuba. Closely tied to these questions of interpretation is the transformation that is predicted for Hecuba in the closing lines of the play: Polymestor foretells that Hecuba will be transformed into a "dog with fiery eyes" (*Hecuba* 1265), that is, the landmark known as Cynossema, "the sign/tomb of the

4. It is not clear in the play itself whether Achilles has specified Polyxena as the one to be sacrificed, nor is it absolutely certain that the sacrifice is a prerequisite to the Greeks' leaving Troy. For a survey of the difficulties, see, e.g., Kovacs 1987, 112–14 and Gregory 1999.

5. The play's setting in Thrace is another difficult issue, given that Achilles' tomb should be in Sigeum. See again Kovacs 1987, 112–14.

6. In fact, she leaves stage briefly twice, at 628 and 1022.

dog."[7] Perhaps the most common view of the transformation is that it is emblematic of the degradation caused by war.[8] A few scholars have challenged this interpretation, instead proposing that the significance of the female dog is that it is fiercely maternal.[9] These scholars argue that the play is about Hecuba's strength of character through suffering, and that the symbolism of the dog casts her as an ever-watchful protector of her children. We may compare *Odyssey* 20.14–15, adduced by Justina Gregory: "[Odysseus'] heart barked within him, just as a dog standing over her feeble puppies barks at strangers and is eager to fight."[10] Nicole Loraux argues similarly:

> Hecuba then acts: she performs a woman's *ergon;* and if the Trojan women who kill with pins are "bitches" for Polymestor, it would be a good idea to keep in mind that a female dog is an Erinys only because she is complete motherhood. Later on, moreover, Hecuba will become a bitch on the boat taking her to Greece. The mourning mother has fulfilled her fate.[11]

In order to accept this second, more sympathetic interpretation of Hecuba's character, her actions, and her transformation, we must fully appreciate the lament-filled speeches and songs of the principal characters. Also important for this argument are the choral odes of the play and their concern for the fate of the captive Trojan women. These songs make us sympathetic to the grief of the victims of the war, the innocent women, who even after the war is over continue to be brutalized. They evoke the pity of the Greeks within the play, and this proves to be a decisive element in the plot of Hecuba's revenge. But are the Athenians in the audience to be expected to react as the Greek soldiers do to these laments, or should we expect a response from the external audience that is entirely different from the internal one? The emotional dynamic of the captive woman's lament plays a crucial role in some of the critical interpretive issues of the drama.

7. For more on the term *sêma* ("sign, symbol; tomb"), see discussion below.

8. See, e.g., Kirkwood 1947, Abrahamson 1952, Conacher 1967, Reckford 1985, Nussbaum 1986, Michelini 1987, and Segal 1993.

9. See especially Kovacs 1987, Burnett 1994, Loraux 1998, and Gregory 1999. See also Mossman (1995) and Burnett (1998), who rightly argue that Hecuba's revenge would not have been as problematic for the Athenian audience as it is for modern critics. Burnett 1994 explores the full range of connotations that the dog may convey in ancient sources.

10. Gregory 1999, xxxiv. Translation is Gregory's.

11. Loraux 1998, 50. On Hecuba as an Erinys see also Burnett 1994 and Mossman 1995, 196–97.

Hecuba herself is the embodiment of grief. From her initial sung exchange with the chorus that follows the prologue, Hecuba's voice is one of lament:

οἲ ἐγὼ μελέα, τί ποτ᾽ ἀπύσω; / ποίαν ἀχώ, ποῖον ὀδυρμόν, / δειλαία
δειλαίου γήρως, / δουλείας [τᾶς] οὐ τλατᾶς, / [τᾶς] οὐ φερτᾶς; οἴμοι. /
τίς ἀμύνει μοι; ποία γέννα, / ποία δὲ πόλις; φροῦδος πρέσβυς, / φροῦδοι
παῖδες. / ποίαν ἢ ταύταν ἢ κείναν / στείχω; ποῖ δὴ σωθῶ; ποῦ τις θεῶν / ἢ
δαιμόνων ἐπαρωγός; / ὦ κάκ᾽ ἐνεγκοῦσαι, / Τρωάδες ὦ κάκ᾽ ἐνεγκοῦσαι
/ πήματ᾽, ἀπωλέσατ᾽ ὠλέσατ᾽· οὐκέτι μοι βίος / ἀγαστὸς ἐν φάει.

(*Hecuba* 154–68)

Woe, woe is me! What words can I utter? What sorrow, what lamentation, the wretchedness of wretched old age, and slavery that I cannot bear or endure! Woe is me! Who will defend me? What family, and what city? Aged Priam is gone, gone are my children. Which way am I to go, this or that? Where can I be safe? Where is any god or power divine to help me? Ah, Trojan women! bringers of evil tidings! bringers of evil pain! you have made an end, an utter end of me; life in the light is no longer desirable for me.

I singled this passage out at the very outset of this chapter because Hecuba's words are in fact a perfect example of the captive woman's lament as I have outlined it in the introduction and in chapter 1. Hecuba's song has all the features of what Fowler has called the desperation speech and what I have called the language of lament, the most marked feature being the rhetorical questions that are posed and (either explicitly or implicitly) rejected. In addition to the questions, the essence if not the actual use of the perfect tense is conveyed here by the repetition of the adjective *phroudos* ("gone"). Finally, Hecuba expresses her longing for death as she proclaims that life is no longer desirable for her. As I noted in chapter 1, these same features are typical of women's laments for the dead, to which the desperation speech—perhaps better termed the desperation song—is very likely heavily indebted. But Hecuba's questions here about where she can turn, coupled with the use of *phroudos*, also evoke laments for fallen cities. The desperation speech in the form that Hecuba's takes is particularly appropriate for captive women, who have lost husbands, fathers, and homeland all at once.[12]

Hecuba's song is her reaction to the news delivered by chorus that her daughter Polyxena is going to be sacrificed by the Greeks. Polyxena's death

12. On this particular variation of the desperation speech, see Dué 2000.

is yet one more blow for the grieving Hecuba, who thought she could sink no further in her sorrow. In terms of plot Polyxena's suffering and death in the play are subordinated to their larger purpose, which is to bring Hecuba one step closer to her breaking point of grief. But though subordinated, the character of Polyxena makes an extraordinary impression on those around her, and thus contributes an important dimension to our interpretation of the play as a whole. Because she goes knowingly and in her mind willingly to her death, she has the opportunity to lament her own death and construct her own interpretation of its significance. She chooses death in place of the marriage she can no longer attain, and death instead of slavery.

As I noted in the introduction, in the course of choosing to die Polyxena narrates her life history and the hopes she had for her future in a form that is typical of women's laments:

τί γάρ με δεῖ ζῆν; ᾗ πατὴρ μὲν ἦν ἄναξ / Φρυγῶν ἁπάντων· τοῦτό μοι
πρῶτον βίου· / ἔπειτ' ἐθρέφθην ἐλπίδων καλῶν ὕπο / βασιλεῦσι νύμφη,
ζῆλον οὐ σμικρὸν γάμων / ἔχουσ', ὅτου δῶμ' ἑστίαν τ' ἀφίξομαι· /
δέσποινα δ' ἡ δύστηνος Ἰδαίαισιν ἦ / γυναιξί, παρθένοις τ' ἀπόβλεπτος
μέτα, / ἴση θεοῖσι πλὴν τὸ κατθανεῖν μόνον· / νῦν δ' εἰμὶ δούλη. πρῶτα
μέν με τοὔνομα / θανεῖν ἐρᾶν τίθησιν οὐκ εἰωθὸς ὄν· / ἔπειτ' ἴσως ἂν
δεσποτῶν ὠμῶν φρένας / τύχοιμ' ἄν, ὅστις ἀργύρου μ' ὠνήσεται, / τὴν
Ἕκτορός τε χἀτέρων πολλῶν κάσιν, / προσθεὶς δ' ἀνάγκην σιτοποιὸν
ἐν δόμοις, / σαίρειν τε δῶμα κερκίσιν τ' ἐφεστάναι / λυπρὰν ἄγουσαν
ἡμέραν μ' ἀναγκάσει· / λέχη δὲ τἀμὰ δοῦλος ὠνητός ποθεν / χρανεῖ,
τυράννων πρόσθεν ἠξιωμένα. / οὐ δῆτ'· ἀφίημ' ὀμμάτων ἐλευθέρων /
φέγγος τόδ', Ἅιδη προστιθεῖσ' ἐμὸν δέμας.

(*Hecuba* 349–68)

Why should I go on living? I whose father was lord of all the Phrygians? This was the most important thing in life for me. Then I was nursed on fair hopes to be a bride for kings, the center of fierce jealousy among suitors, to see whose home I would make my own; and over each woman of Ida I was queen, ah me! a maiden marked amid women and girls, equal to the gods, save for death alone. But now I am a slave. That name first makes me long for death, so strange it sounds; and then maybe my lot might give me to some savage master, one that would buy me for money—me, the sister of Hektor and many other princes—who would make me knead his bread within his halls, or sweep his house or set me working at the loom, leading a life of misery; while some slave, bought I know not whence, will defile my bed, once deemed worthy of royalty. No, never!

Here I close my eyes upon the light, free as yet, and I consign my body to
Hades.

Here Polyxena, like the chorus elsewhere in the play, speculates about her
future life, home, and master. Her lament is perfectly constructed so as to
highlight the contrast between past and present and to justify her decision
to die. Whereas in traditional laments for the dead the contrast between
past and present is invoked alongside a longing for death, Polyxena's lament
makes that wish a reality. It is in many ways a speech-act.

This speech-act accomplishes several purposes beyond ensuring Polyxena's
death on her own terms. First, her words win the admiration and pity of
all present. Odysseus himself regrets that the Greeks must kill her (395).
Moreover, the language she uses of herself evokes the heroes of Greek epic
and specifically Achilles—"equal to the gods, save for death alone."[13] Death
gives Polyxena the opportunity to confer herolike status upon herself, while
condemning the Greeks for the life and assault they would have subjected
her to.[14] The messenger Talthybius reports to Hecuba that Polyxena gave
another similar speech just before the Greeks killed her. Again her words
evoke pity and an unwillingness to kill her: Neoptolemus is described as
"both unwilling and willing in his pity for the girl" as he prepares to kill
her (οὐ θέλων τε καὶ θέλων οἴκτῳ κόρης, 566). Talthybius too sheds tears
of pity, both witnessing and relating the events (518–20).

The efficacy of Polyxena's proleptic lament for herself is confirmed by
the reaction that Greeks have to her death. As Talthybius tells it, once her
throat is slit, the Greeks hasten to honor the corpse:

ἐπεὶ δ᾽ ἀφῆκε πνεῦμα θανασίμῳ σφαγῇ, / οὐδεὶς τὸν αὐτὸν εἶχεν Ἀργείων
πόνον· / ἀλλ᾽ οἳ μὲν αὐτῶν τὴν θανοῦσαν ἐκ χερῶν / φύλλοις ἔβαλλον,
οἳ δὲ πληροῦσιν πυρὰν / κορμοὺς φέροντες πευκίνους, ὁ δ᾽ οὐ φέρων
/ πρὸς τοῦ φέροντος τοιάδ᾽ ἤκουεν κακά· / Ἕστηκας, ὦ κάκιστε, τῇ
νεάνιδι / οὐ πέπλον οὐδὲ κόσμον ἐν χεροῖν ἔχων; / οὐκ εἶ τι δώσων τῇ

---

13. Among Achilles' primary traditional epithets in the *Iliad* are *theoeikelos* and *theois
epieikelos,* each meaning "equal to the gods." An even closer parallel is *daimoni îsos,* "equal
to a *daimôn,*" applied to Patroklos as well as other warriors at critical moments as they approach death. So also is *îsos Arêi,* "equal to Ares," applied, e.g., to Patroklos at *Iliad* 11.604,
just as he takes the first steps that set in motion his fatal impersonation of Achilles. On
the application of *theoeikelos* to Hektor and Andromache on their wedding day see Nagy
1974, 134–39 and Dué 2002, 59. Polyxena's description of herself as a bride sought after by
many suitors also of course evokes Helen.

14. On Polyxena's attempt to achieve a warrior's death and its consequent *kleos,* see
Loraux 1987.

περίσσ' εὐκαρδίῳ / ψυχήν τ' ἀρὶστη; τοιάδ' ἀμφὶ σῆς λέγων / παιδὸς
θανούσης, εὐτεκνωτάτην τέ σε / πασῶν γυναικῶν δυστυχεστάτην θ'
ὁρῶ.   (*Hecuba* 571–82)

As soon as she had breathed her last through the fatal gash, each Argive
set his hand to different tasks, some strewing leaves over the dead woman
in handfuls, others bringing pine-logs and heaping up a pyre; and he who
brought nothing would hear from him who did such things as these,
"You stand there, worthless, with no robe or ornament to bring for the
maiden? Are you not going to give anything to her who showed such
peerless bravery and excellence of spirit?" Such is the tale I tell about your
daughter's death, and I look upon you as the most successful all mothers,
yet the most unfortunate of all women.

Although Polyxena's compressed second speech (as it is reported by Talthybius) is less clearly a lament than her speech to Odysseus, the Greeks react
as if they too had heard her previous words. Immediately upon killing her,
they begin to heap up a hero's funeral pyre and bring offerings. The final
description of Polyxena completes the transformation: "peerless in bravery
and the best (*aristê*) in regard to her spirit (*psukhê*)." Hecuba, moreover, is
labeled the most fortunate of mothers for having Polyxena (*euteknôtatên*,
581), even if she is the most unfortunate with respect to all else.

   The reaction of the Greeks gives us an indication of how the audience
might be expected to be affected by Polyxena's words and subsequent death.
Certainly the concept of freedom, *eleutheria*, invoked prominently in both
speeches, might have resonated with an Athenian audience at war. But I
submit that the form as well as the content of Polyxena's words, particularly
in the first speech, arouse the sympathy of those who hear her. Polyxena
performs a traditional Greek lament for her own death. The traditionality
of the lament is by no means undercut by the fact that she is lamenting
herself—this is, as we have seen, a common feature of epic and tragedy.[15]

   In using the language of lament to speak out and construct a legacy
for herself, Polyxena resembles not only a woman like Tecmessa, who in
Sophocles' *Ajax* seeks to legitimate her position in the community through
lament, but also the women of modern Greek traditions, who employ the
public voice allowed them at funerals to manipulate the community of
listeners and protect themselves in a time of uncertainty by inspiring pity.[16]

   15. See the introduction.
   16. For Tecmessa, see the introduction. For modern Greek funerals, I am thinking here
especially of the work of Herzfeld (1993); see also the introduction and chapter 1.

In the end, Polyxena proves to be a consummate lamenter, winning with her song the admiration of all and a hero's burial.

It is appropriate that a tragedy about the Trojan War evoke the heroic quest for glory that constitutes epic poetry. The *Hecuba* does this by assimilating the figures of Polyxena and Achilles, for whom she dies. Just as beautiful, however, is the way that Euripides conjures epic lamentation as well. As Polyxena leaves her mother, she is overcome with tears. She "melts":

> κόμιζ, Ὀδυσσεῦ, μ᾿ ἀμφιθεὶς κάραι πέπλους,
> ὡς πρὶν σφαγῆναί γ᾿ ἐκτέτηκα καρδίαν
> θρήνοισι μητρὸς τήνδε τ᾿ ἐκτήκω γόοις.

> (*Hecuba* 432–34)

Come, Odysseus, veil my head with my garment and take me away;
for now, even before my slaughter, my heart is melted
by my mother's laments, and I in turn melt hers with my own laments.

The metaphor of lamentation as melting derives ultimately from epic and the traditional imagery of Homeric similes. In *Odyssey* 8.522, when Odysseus weeps upon hearing the song of the sack of Troy, the Greek word is τήκετο: he too melts. It is precisely at that moment that Odysseus is compared to a lamenting woman who, after watching her husband die fighting for his city, is being led off into slavery.

The full resonance of the metaphor of melting, however, can be understood only within the context of other epic similes.[17] The more complete image can be found in *Odyssey* 19.204–9, where Penelope's face, upon hearing one of Odysseus' "Cretan lies," is said to melt:

> τῆς δ᾿ ἄρ᾿ ἀκουούσης ῥέε δάκρυα, τήκετο δὲ χρώς·
> ὡς δὲ χιὼν κατατήκετ᾿ ἐν ἀκροπόλοισιν ὄρεσσιν,
> ἥν τ᾿ Εὖρος κατέτηξεν, ἐπὴν Ζέφυρος καταχεύῃ·
> τηκομένης δ᾿ ἄρα τῆς ποταμοὶ πλήθουσι ῥέοντες·
> ὡς τῆς τήκετο καλὰ παρήϊα δάκρυ χεούσης,
> κλαιούσης ἑὸν ἄνδρα παρήμενον.

> (*Odyssey* 19.204–9)

The tears flowed from her as she listened, and her skin melted.
As the snow wastes upon the mountain tops

---

17. On the traditionality of epic similes and the associations that they carry throughout the contexts in which they are employed, see Muellner 1990.

when the East wind has melted it, after the West wind has heaped it up
and the rivers run full with the water from the melted snow,
even so did her beautiful cheeks melt as she shed tears
weeping for the husband who was all the time sitting beside her.

It is clear from the simile that the word "melt" refers to the liquid of tears,
which is compared to the liquid of melted snow. In other words, the tears
are a critical piece of the puzzle. "To melt" does not mean "to be overcome,"
as one translator handles it, but "to produce tears."[18]

In the *Hecuba,* Polyxena and Hecuba each melt in reaction to the laments
of the other. The most common Greek terms for songs of lament, *goos* and
thrênos, are used to describe the kind of speech and song the women employ.[19]
This grief is specifically associated with both the tears of epic and the sorrow
of a captive woman, in what is undoubtedly a traditional image, but which
may also be an allusion to one of the most striking similes ever applied to
Odysseus.

But while I see an attempt on the part of Polyxena to construct a heroic
identity for herself in death, an attempt that is reinforced by the epic and
heroic resonances in her laments, I am very sympathetic to the work of a
number of scholars who argue that Polyxena's quest for *kleos* is undercut
in a variety of ways, particularly in the scene that narrates her death. A
feminist reading of this play would say that Polyxena, as a Trojan captive
woman, dies to liberate herself—that is to save herself from servitude and
sexual degradation. But at the same time, we the audience are compelled to
view the sacrifice through the gaze of the soldiers. Her death is narrated by
Talthybius, so that technically we hear first and then visualize by means of
this soldier's words. And this narration, according to many interpretations,

18. Cf. *Iliad* 16.2–4, in which the tears of Patroklos are compared to a spring trickling
down a rock, and *Andromache* 116 (discussed below). In English the metaphor of melting
is connected with the idea of coldness. We say "the heart is warmed" or "I warmed up to
him." By extension, a hard or inflexible person "melts." The concept of coldness seems to
be there in the Greek as well, but I would argue that the liquid is equally important (cf.
Page 1936 on Andromache's lament, discussed below). Odysseus melts, and in the same
verse "wets the cheeks under his eyelids with tears" (δάκρυ δ' ἔδευεν ὑπὸ βλεφάροισι
παρειάς, 522). Similarly, Penelope "pours down tears." The translation "was overcome" is
that of Samuel Butler.

19. For the terminology of Greek laments see Alexiou 1974, 11–12; Sultan 1993, 93–94;
Derderian 2001, chapter 1; and Tsagalis 2004, chapter 1. *Goos* is usually applied to the laments
of nonprofessional female relatives, while *thrênos* is used of lament "especially composed
and performed at the funeral by nonkinsmen" (Alexiou 1974, 12). In tragedy, however,
there is little distinction between the two terms. For one explanation of the merging of
the terms in tragedy, see Nagy 1994–1995a.

very much eroticizes her death, with the result that to a certain extent Polyxena is degraded anyway by the lustful gaze of the soldiers.[20]

The text of the play itself supports the idea that Polyxena has been sexually violated by the slitting of her throat, an act which is repeatedly referred to as a wedding in death or else as a substitute for a wedding. Hecuba, in asking her fellow captives to lay out the corpse of Polyxena, calls her "my child—a bride but not a bride, a maiden and not a maiden" (νύμφην τ' ἄνυμφον παρθένον τ' ἀπάρθενον, 611–12), suggesting that Polyxena has now become a *gunê,* but in the most twisted of circumstances.[21]

As Charles Segal has pointed out, many modern critics of the *Hecuba* have fallen into "Euripides' trap," appearing to view the sacrifice of Polyxena with the same lustful gaze as the soldiers, and seeming unable to separate the nobility of the victim from the horror of the act.[22] In my analysis I am attempting to walk a fine line: I seek to point out the powerful emotional effect that Polyxena, her lament, and her death have on both the soldiers within the play and the ancient audience, while at the same time placing the sacrifice within the larger context of the representations of the fall of Troy in Greek poetic and artistic traditions. I submit that viewed within that context, Polyxena herself may be pitied but also admired, even while the sacrifice itself is condemned as one of the sacrileges that mark the victory of the Greeks. When we recognize that Polyxena is employing the traditional language of lament to articulate the significance of her own death, we can better understand why the Greeks within and outside of the play react to her death in the way that they do.

I think there is even more to be seen in the gaze of the soldiers, however. In chapter 3, following such scholars as Gloria Ferrari and Michael Anderson, I argued that Greek art of the Archaic and Classical periods almost universally depicts events connected with the fall of Troy as a series of sacrilegious and abominable acts that anger Athena and set in motion the disasters experienced by the Greeks on their return voyages. Moreover, these depictions were on display in many prominent places around Athens, including the Parthenon on the Acropolis and the Painted Stoa in the Agora. Euripides seems all too conscious of the significance of Polyxena's death and Hecuba's suffering in Greek art, and calls our attention to it in two crucial passages. In the first of these two passages, Talthybius relates that just before Neoptolemus kills

20. See especially Rabinowitz 1993, 54–62; Segal 1993, 172; and Steiner 2001, 206. For the eroticization of the sacrifice, see further below.

21. See Loraux 1987, 39 as well as Rabinowitz 1993, 54–56 and Sissa 1990, 99. For death as a wedding, see chapter 1.

22. Segal 1993, 174, with references there.

may well have adorned Athens when the *Agamemnon* was produced, and the sacrifice was certainly represented in vase paintings and other media.[26] But as we saw in the previous chapter, Pausanias says that in paintings depicting the fall of Troy the Trojan captives could be *seen lamenting*. In other words, the paintings could speak.[27]

The similarities between the Polyxena and Iphigeneia passages go even beyond the comparison of these two sacrificial virgins to artwork.[28] Both deaths are portrayed as a substitute for marriage.[29] The thematic and visual connections between the two sacrifices, particularly the evocative description of their robes and the comparison to artwork, set them up as bookends of one another, the two framing sacrileges of the Trojan War. Iphigeneia's

26. Examples include a proto-Attic krater by the Nessos Painter from the early seventh century B.C. (Boston 6.67, but identification is not certain) and a white-ground lekythos by Douris from the fifth century (Palermo NI 1886). See also the Apulian red-figure krater from the fourth century B.C. (London F 159) and London 1206, a sculpted column drum from Ephesus, also from the fourth century B.C. Pliny (*Natural History* 35.73) describes the late-fifth-century B.C. painter Timanthes' famous painting of the sacrifice, in which the grief of each of the figures is portrayed in different, striking ways. For more on the artistic and literary representations of this myth in antiquity see Ahlberg-Cornell 1992, 52–53; Gantz 1993, 582–88; and Woodford 2003, 4–9.

27. Collard (1991 *ad loc.*) suggests that Euripides has been influenced in his depiction of Polyxena by Polygnotus' painting in the Painted Stoa (on which see chapter 3). The idea of women in a painting who can be seen lamenting by the spectator calls to mind a well-known quotation of Simonides in Plutarch's *Moralia* (346): "Simonides called painting silent poetry and poetry painting that speaks." For a full explication of this statement see Ferrari 1997, 1ff. (translation is Ferrari's). Note also *Hecuba* 836–40 (discussed below in note 36), in which Hecuba wishes that Daedalus could place a voice in her arms and hands and hair—in other words that he make her a lamenting statue. For more on Hecuba and figures in tragedy who are likened or liken themselves to statues see Steiner 2001 (on Hecuba, see especially pp. 51–53). On tragedy's engagement of the visual arts see also Zeitlin 1995 and note 33 below. For a recent study of the "poetics of appearance" that unites the imagery of tragedy with Archaic sculpture see Stieber 2004.

28. For further points of comparison, see Rabinowitz 1993, 54.

29. For Iphigeneia as a bride see Seaford 1987, 108–10 and 124–25. On this point I am struck by the fact that Mary Stieber (2004) links the Archaic *korai* on the Acropolis, sometimes termed in accompanying inscriptions and hence in scholarship *agalmata*, with grave memorials for young women who have died just before or in the first years of marriage. Stieber devotes her final chapter to the famous statue Phrasikleia, whose accompanying inscription notes that she will forever have the name *kore* ("maiden") *in place of marriage;* see especially Stieber 2004, 178. Additionally, among those who interpret the Attic *korai* as *agalmata*—that is, as delightful gifts for Athena—Robin Osborne (1994) has associated them with "the world of exchange of precious objects." As Stieber points out, this world of exchange included women. Polyxena, Iphigeneia, and Helen (see below) are all objects of exchange, used, in the words of Osborne of Attic *korai*, "to mark the relationship between men and gods." See Stieber 2004, 21–23 and Osborne 1994, 90–91.

Polyxena, she bared her breasts and begged him to strike her in the che
at the throat (he chooses the latter):

κἀπεὶ τόδ᾽ εἰσήκουσε δεσποτῶν ἔπος,
λαβοῦσα πέπλους ἐξ ἄκρας ἐπωμίδος
ἔρρηξε λαγόνας ἐς μέσας παρ᾽ ὀμφαλόν,
μαστούς τ᾽ ἔδειξε στέρνα θ᾽ ὡς ἀγάλματος
κάλλιστα

(*Hecuba* 557–61)

And she, when she heard her captors' words,
took her robe and from the shoulder
to the waist tore it open,
displaying a breast and bosom as beautiful
as a statue's [*agalma*].

Polyxena is at this moment compared to a statue, an *agalma*. Few com-
mentators have failed to be reminded of Iphigeneia in Aeschylus' *Agamemnon*,
who is compared to a painting when she "pours down towards the ground"
her robes as her sacrificers hold her, gagged, over the altar (*Agamemnon* 239).[23]
Iphigeneia too is an *agalma:* Agamemnon calls her the "*agalma* of the house"
when he agonizes over the decision to kill her (*Agamemnon* 208).

The many similarities in the two situations and in the two passages highlight their differences: whereas Iphigeneia is bound and gagged so that she
cannot resist or pronounce a curse on the house, Polyxena not only goes willingly but voices her sorrow and her reasons for dying.[24] Iphigeneia, because
she can't speak, is compared to figures in a painting that look as if they might
speak (πρέπουσά θ᾽ ὡς ἐν γραφαῖς, προσεννέπειν θέλουσ᾽, *Agamemnon*
242–43). At the same time the phrase "as in paintings" encourages us to step
back and visualize the poetry and its images as a tableau.[25] Such paintings

23. I imagine, following the arguments of Ferrari 1997, that the robes of Iphigeneia are
flowing toward the ground as she is held over the altar, not that she is actually disrobed,
but this interpretation is certainly open to debate. Euripides may well have had in mind
the latter scenario.

24. Similarly, the Iphigeneia of Euripides' *Iphigeneia at Aulis* professes to die willingly
and is allowed to voice her reasons for doing so—reasons that there too gain the admiration of all within the play.

25. On the visual and metaphorical aspects of this passage see especially Ferrari 1997,
as well as Loraux 1987, vii–ix on imagining through words, and Ferrari 2002b, 61–86 on
the relationship between words and image in metaphor.

death too is an abominable act, fundamentally linked to the fall of Troy. In another choral ode of the *Agamemnon,* Helen is, like Iphigeneia, an *agalma* (741), who seemed unthreatening when she first arrived, but who ultimately destroyed Troy (νυμφόκλαυτος Ἐρινύς, 749).[30]

But already in the opening choral song that depicts Iphigeneia's death, the play makes clear how we are to interpret the act, no matter how necessary it was:

ἐπεὶ δ᾽ ἀνάγκας ἔδυ λέπαδνον / φρενὸς πνέων δυσσεβῆ τροπαίαν / ἄναγνον ἀνίερον, τόθεν / τὸ παντότολμον φρονεῖν μετέγνω. / βροτοὺς θρασύνει γὰρ αἰσχρόμητις / τάλαινα παρακοπὰ πρωτοπήμων. ἔτλα δ᾽ οὖν / θυτὴρ γενέσθαι θυγατρός, / γυναικοποίνων πολέμων ἀρωγὰν / καὶ προτέλεια ναῶν.   (*Agamemnon* 218–26)

But when he had put on the yoke of Necessity, with veering of mind, impious, unholy, unsanctified, from then he changed his intention and began to conceive that deed of uttermost audacity. For wretched delusion, counselor of ill, primal source of woe, makes mortals bold. So then he hardened his heart to sacrifice his daughter so that he might further a war waged to avenge a woman, and as an offering for the voyaging of a fleet![31]

Indeed, it is one of the riddles of the play that even before the Greek expedition from Aulis sets out, Artemis has already conceived wrath for the sack of Troy. In the opening ode Troy is represented in an omen as a pregnant hare, devoured by the two eagles, Agamemnon and Menelaus (*Agamemnon* 109–20), and this sign bodes ill: "an abomination to Artemis is the feast of the eagles" (στυγεῖ δὲ δεῖπνον αἰετῶν, 137).[32]

I have dwelled on the sacrifice of Iphigeneia in the *Agamemnon* because it allows us to see the tradition of poetic representation of the events of the Trojan War within which Euripides is working, as well as a specific treatment of the Trojan War myth to which Euripides seems to allude. The many allusions to Iphigeneia invite comparison of Hecuba with Clytemnestra,

---

30. Translation is adapted from that of Smyth (1926).

31. Translation of this passage is adapted from that of Smyth (1926).

32. Here again I adapt the translation of Smyth, which nicely captures the force of στυγεῖ. On the feast of the eagles, see Ferrari 1997, especially pp. 24–28, and discussion below. It would be impossible here to fully explicate the many thematic and metaphorical connections between the sacrifice of Iphigeneia and the sack of Troy in the *Agamemnon.* For a fuller discussion, see especially Ferrari 1997 (with citations there), as well as Zeitlin 1965 and 1966, Lebeck 1971, and Käppel 1998.

who likewise sought justice through murder. But just as important for my discussion is the way that both Aeschylus and Euripides make reference to artistic traditions about the fall of Troy so that the hearer may better visualize the poetry.[33] In the Polyxena passage, the bare-breasted virgin with her robes fallen around her is compared to a statue, although it is not clear to us what the full force of the comparison is. Is Euripides invoking a visual tradition of similar representations in art? Beth Cohen has argued that bare breasts in Classical sculpture are most often the mark of female victims of physical violence (as in depictions of the battle of Lapiths and Centaurs) and I think that this must be part of the answer.[34]

Elsewhere in the play Hecuba too is connected to visual representations:

> ταῦτ᾽ οὖν ἐν αἰσχρῶι θέμενος αἰδέσθητί με, / οἴκτιρον ἡμᾶς, ὡς γραφεύς
> τ᾽ ἀποσταθεὶς / ἰδοῦ με κἀνάθρησον οἷ᾽ ἔχω κακά. / τύραννος ἦ ποτ᾽
> ἀλλὰ νῦν δούλη σέθεν, / εὔπαις ποτ᾽ οὖσα, νῦν δὲ γραῦς ἄπαις θ᾽ ἅμα,
> / ἄπολις ἔρημος ἀθλιωτάτη βροτῶν.   (*Hecuba* 806–11)

Deem this then a disgrace and show respect for me, have pity on me, and, like a painter standing back from his work, look on me and survey my wretched state. I was once queen, but now I am your slave; a happy mother once, but now childless and old alike, without a city, utterly bereft, the most wretched woman living.

I am particularly interested in the way that the viewing of her suffering as though it were a painting or a sculpture is connected to the emotion of pity. It suggests once again that the visual traditions about the fall of Troy were meant to convey the sorrow of the captive Trojans rather than the victory of the Greeks, and to invite the pity of the viewer.[35]

With these same words, which are spoken to Agamemnon, Hecuba seems to reach the lowest point of grief that she can possibly reach. She has just

---

33. Note also *Trojan Women* 686–87, where Hecuba says that she has never embarked on a ship, but she has seen them in paintings (γραφῇ, 687). I am tempted to read this too as reference to visual traditions about the *Nostoi* and paintings such as that in the Cnidian *Lesche*, discussed in chapter 3, where the Greeks are depicted leaving Troy with their captives. See also Anderson 1997, who, following Burnett (1977), compares the structure of the *Trojan Women* to the practices of visual artists. On Euripides' engagement of the visual arts see Zeitlin 1993 and 1995.

34. See Cohen 1997 and the discussion in Gregory 1999 on this passage, with her citations of the various interpretations. See also Collard 1991 *ad loc.* and note 27 above.

35. On the connection between the emotion of pity and the tears of sorrow see the conclusion.

heard the narrative of her daughter Polyxena's sacrificial death. She sends her maid to get some water to wash the corpse of Polyxena, and the maid finds the corpse of her only remaining son, Polydorus. Hecuba's contrast of past and present echoes Polyxena's lament, and likewise has a powerful effect, as do her allusions elsewhere in the speech to the smoking ruins of Troy and the loss of her sons, a combination which, as we have seen, are the traditional elements of the laments of captive women. Agamemnon's pity, achieved here by way of the captive woman's lament, earns Hecuba the leeway she needs to get revenge on her son's killer, Polymestor.[36]

Now that we have examined the place of the laments of Hecuba and Polyxena and their effect within the drama, we can better explore the end of the *Hecuba* (with its violence and subsequent prophecies) and its implications. I have argued that Polyxena becomes heroized almost before our eyes in the course of Talthybius' narrative about her death, and Euripides' Polyxena does indeed conform to a traditional heroization pattern in which 1) a virgin's life is traded for a military victory or the ending of a plague; 2) the victim is willing; and 3) the sacrifice is carried out and the victim receives cult honors as a *sôtêr*.[37]

Hecuba, however, who remains alive for the duration of Euripides' play, does not become a hero in the course of the play itself. Instead, her death and immortalization are foretold. Polymestor, upon losing his sight at the hands of Hecuba and the Trojan women, becomes prophetic:

Ἑκ. οὐ γάρ με χαίρειν χρή σε τιμωρουμένην;
Πο. ἀλλ᾿ οὐ τάχ᾿, ἡνίκ᾿ ἄν σε ποντία νοτὶς —
Ἑκ. μῶν ναυστολήσῃ γῆς ὅρους Ἑλληνίδος;

36. See *Hecuba* 850–51: ἐγώ σε καὶ σὸν παῖδα καὶ τύχας σέθεν, / Ἑκάβη, δι᾿ οἴκτου χεῖρά θ᾿ ἱκεσίαν ἔχω ("Hecuba, I feel pity for you and your child and your misfortune as well as your suppliant gesture"). On this point see also Steiner 2001, 53. Hecuba employs a number of rhetorical strategies in her speech to Agamemnon here, including lament. The most commented upon of these strategies is no doubt the appeal to Agamemnon's desire for Cassandra, which has been read by many scholars as emblematic of Hecuba's degradation of character (for counterarguments, see Mossman 1995, 126–28 and Scodel 1998). The speech moves to its conclusion with a powerful combination of supplication and lamentation: "If only I had a voice in arms, in hands, in hair and feet, either by the skills of Daedalus or one of the gods, so that they might weep all together and take hold of your knees" (εἴ μοι γένοιτο φθόγγος ἐν βραχίοσι / καὶ χερσὶ καὶ κόμαισι καὶ ποδῶν βάσει / ἢ Δαιδάλου τέχναισιν ἢ θεῶν τινος, / ὡς πάνθ᾿ ὁμαρτῇ σῶν ἔχοιντο γουνάτων / κλαίοντ᾿, 836–40). On the connection between lament and revenge, see chapter 1 and chapter 5.

37. See Larson 1995, 16 and 103–6. In this case it is not a military victory that is achieved but rather the propitiation of the hero Achilles, whose potentially destructive anger is thereby avoided.

Πο. κρύψῃ μὲν οὖν πεσοῦσαν ἐκ καρχησίων.
Ἑκ. πρὸς τοῦ βιαίων τυγχάνουσαν ἁλμάτων;
Πο. αὐτὴ πρὸς ἱστὸν ναὸς ἀμβήσῃ ποδί.
Ἑκ. ὑποπτέροις νώτοισιν ἢ ποίῳ τρόπῳ;
Πο. κύων γενήσῃ πύρσ᾽ ἔχουσα δέργματα.
Ἑκ. πῶς δ᾽ οἶσθα μορφῆς τῆς ἐμῆς μετάστασιν;
Πο. ὁ Θρῃξὶ μάντις εἶπε Διόνυσος τάδε.
Ἑκ. σοὶ δ᾽ οὐκ ἔχρησεν οὐδὲν ὧν ἔχεις κακῶν;
Πο. οὐ γάρ ποτ᾽ ἂν σύ μ᾽ εἷλες ὧδε σὺν δόλῳ.
Ἑκ. θανοῦσα δ᾽ ἢ ζῶσ᾽ ἐνθάδ᾽ ἐκπλήσω μόρον;
Πο. θανοῦσα· τύμβῳ δ᾽ ὄνομα σῷ κεκλήσεται—
Ἑκ. μορφῆς ἐπῳδόν, ἢ τί, τῆς ἐμῆς ἐρεῖς;
Πο. κυνὸς ταλαίνης σῆμα, ναυτίλοις τέκμαρ.

(*Hecuba* 1258–73)

HECUBA: I am avenged on you; have I not cause for joy?
POLYMESTOR: The joy will soon cease, in the day when ocean's flood . . .
HECUBA: Shall convey me to the shores of the Greek land?
POLYMESTOR: No, but close over you when you fall from the masthead.
HECUBA: Who will force me to take the leap?
POLYMESTOR: Of your own accord you will climb the ship's mast.
HECUBA: With wings upon my back, or by what means?
POLYMESTOR: You will become a dog with fiery eyes.
HECUBA: How do you know of my transformation?
POLYMESTOR: Dionysus, our Thracian prophet, told me so.
HECUBA: And did he tell you nothing of your present suffering?
POLYMESTOR: No; otherwise you would never have caught me thus by
    guile.
HECUBA: Will I die or live, and so complete my destiny here?
POLYMESTOR: You will die; and to your tomb will be given a name—
HECUBA: Recalling my form, or what will you tell me?
POLYMESTOR: "The suffering hound's grave [*sêma*]," a mark for
    mariners.

Here, as I noted above, we come to perhaps the most difficult point of interpretation in the play. What are we to make of Hecuba's impending transformation into "the *sêma* of the dog," the landmark known as Cynossema?

A *sêma* is a visual sign or symbol. The tomb of a hero is an especially
meaningful symbol, and "tomb" is one of the meanings of the Greek word

sêma.[38] Hecuba's *sêma* will have an important function as well. It will be a navigational sign for sailors—it will guide them to the right course. The navigation of ships is important in many hero cults (most notably, those of Achilles and Odysseus).[39] It sets up a stark contrast to the Greek soldiers, all of whom will be blown off course on their way home as a result of the wrath of Athena, who is helped by Poseidon.[40] Hecuba's *sêma* will also be a visual sign of her *kleos*. The tomb is a visual code that passersby will interpret and speak about, thus leading to the auditory component of the Greek word for glory or fame, *kleos*, "that which is heard."

Polymestor's prophecies therefore have the force of an aetiology. The landmark of Cynossema (i.e., the *sêma* of the dog) is a geographical entity that existed in the contemporary world of the Athenian audience, one that is familiar to those who have sailed in the Aegean sea.[41] But even beyond aetiology, the symbolism of the dog must also have a literary force within the context of the drama. At the beginning of this discussion I cited the work of such scholars as Justina Gregory and Anne Burnett, who argue that the female dog is a "fiercely maternal" figure, and I have tried to show that the emotional dynamics of the play support such an interpretation. Hecuba then becomes, in this reading, not a portrait of degradation and brutality, but the extreme of motherhood, and a symbol for sailors of endurance through suffering.

These sailors would have been, at the time of the composition and production of this play, young Athenian citizens at war. This fact brings me to my final query: where are the Athenians in all of this? I have argued that

38. See Nagy 1987.

39. See Frame 1978 (Odysseus) and Nagy 1979, 338–47 (Achilles) and 1990a, 231–32 (Odysseus). As Nagy argues, Achilles' tomb is conceived of as a navigational sign, with the result that Achilles is a savior of sailors and the hero of the Hellespont.

40. This part of the Troy saga was narrated in the now-lost epic traditions known as the *Sack of Troy* and the *Homeward Voyages* (*Nostoi*): "The Achaeans sail off, while Athena plots destruction for them on the seas" (from Proclus' summary of the *Sack of Troy*). See also *Odyssey* 3.130–35: αὐτὰρ ἐπεὶ Πριάμοιο πόλιν διεπέρσαμεν αἰπήν, / βῆμεν δ' ἐν νήεσσι, θεὸς δ' ἐσκέδασσεν Ἀχαιούς, / καὶ τότε δὴ Ζεὺς λυγρὸν ἐνὶ φρεσὶ μήδετο νόστον / Ἀργείοις, ἐπεὶ οὔ τι νοήμονες οὐδὲ δίκαιοι / πάντες ἔσαν· τῶ σφεων πολέες κακὸν οἶτον ἐπέσπον / μήνιος ἐξ ὀλοῆς γλαυκώπιδος ὀβριμοπάτρης ("When we had sacked the high city of Priam / and were setting sail in our ships, a god scattered the Achaeans, / and at that point Zeus devised grief for the Argives on their homeward voyage [*nostos*]; / for they had not all been either wise or just, / and hence many came to a bad end / through the wrath of the grey-eyed daughter of a mighty father [= Athena]").

41. For more on the landmark see Burnett 1994, 159–60.

the Greeks within the play first pity and then heroize both Polyxena and Hecuba.[42] Are the Athenians to be equated with the Achaeans of the drama, and to experience the same complicated mix of pity and admiration, regret and necessity as is expressed by such figures as Talthybius, Odysseus, and Agamemnon?

In the case of this play it cannot be argued that the Athenians could separate themselves from the actions of the Achaeans.[43] Athens is mentioned prominently in the play and is thereby connected to the heroic world in which the action takes place. As we saw in the introduction, the chorus speculates that they might be taken there, and optimistically supposes that they will weave the *peplos* of Athena for the Panathenaic festival (*Hecuba* 466–74). Moreover, Theseus' sons Akamas and Demophon are explicitly mentioned early in the play as supporters of the sacrifice of Polyxena (*Hecuba* 123–29).[44] I would like to suggest therefore that in viewing the *Hecuba* the Athenians are being asked to include themselves among the host of warriors at Troy, and so to sympathize with the sufferings of their own victims by witnessing them lament their sorrows and even get revenge on the Athenian stage.

But there is a second step that the audience is being asked to take as well, and that is to reflect upon the current wartime situation in the 420s B.C. by experiencing that of the heroic past. Many have noted the contemporary resonance that the speeches in the play contain: Odysseus is a demagogue who courts the mob, Agamemnon is portrayed as a weak-willed politician who only cares about what others think, instead of a king and the leader of the Greek army that he is.[45] In the next chapter I will explore in more detail the effect of such contemporary resonances and their implications for interpretation. I am not suggesting that the force of the *Hecuba* is directed at any particular event, but it does require of its audience the contemplation of the consequences of war, including the one in which the Athenians were currently participating.

Finally, I submit that the suffering being contemplated in the *Hecuba* is that of the Greeks no less than the Trojans, whose laments narrate the sorrows of Greek and Trojan alike. In the last chapter, I adduced the choral ode at *Hecuba* 638–56, in which the chorus of Trojan women sympatheti-cally imagines the sorrow of a Spartan girl and a mother who has lost her

42. I use the term "heroize" specifically in the sense that their narratives mirror the traditional narratives associated with the Greek heroes of myth and cult.

43. See chapter 3.

44. On this point see King 1985 with chapter 5, note 5 below.

45. See, e.g., *Hecuba* 108–40, 254–66, and 309–20.

sons, as an example of the universality of wartime suffering presented in the play. That comparison is doubly remarkable in that it is spoken by Trojans (the historical victims of the Greeks) about Spartans, the current enemy of the Athenians. (And we should not forget that it is Athenian youths who are playing the role of these Trojan captive women contemplating the suffering of the Spartan women.) Like the *Iliad* therefore, the *Hecuba* can explore the agony of war for the Greeks—Athenian and Spartan alike—by means of the sorrow of the Trojan women, as it is expressed in the captive woman's lament.

CHAPTER FIVE

A RIVER SHOUTING WITH TEARS

EURIPIDES' *Trojan Women*

The *Trojan Women*, first produced in 416 B.C., is both the easiest and the most difficult to interpret of the plays under discussion, and indeed it is this deceptive ease that prompted the writing of this book.

The play is an unrelenting portrait of suffering, and has had a great deal of success in modern productions as a play that protests war.[1] Hecuba is onstage lamenting her losses throughout, interrupted by the appearance and forced removal of her daughter Cassandra and her daughter-in-law Andromache. She learns of the sacrifice of Polyxena after the fact, hears of the resolution to kill her grandson Astyanax, and confronts the woman responsible for the war, Helen. In the end, only Hecuba is left to bury the boy Astyanax, during the course of which she performs an exquisite song of ritual lamentation. The *Trojan Women*, it seems, is a straightforward play that exposes the horrors of war by depicting the sufferings of the innocent victims.

But as I noted in chapters 3 and 4, interpretation becomes more complicated when we try to interpret the play within its own historical and political context and with a view to the possible reactions of an ancient audience. It is tempting to read the *Trojan Women* as a play, as with the *Hecuba,* that explicitly protests recent atrocities committed by both Athenians and Spartans in the context of the Peloponnesian War. But N. T. Croally has well argued that there should and must be more to the *Trojan Women* than simple slogans:

> The various attempts to describe what the *Troades* means or teaches all appear rather tame. Of course the play is about "the dreadful effects of war," war, the great tragedy of society; it may even be a condemnation of purposeless and excessive bellicosity; more arguably, it could be interpreted as a drama of "total nihilism," an anti-war, anti-expansionist harangue with Euripides using the voice of Cassandra to preach his message. The

1. See chapter 3 above. For Sartre's stark adaptation of the *Trojan Women*, see Loraux 2002.

willingness of critics to reduce the play to these slogans is evidence of the power of some of its voices. Yet one could and should say more.[2]

Croally sees the function of tragedy as didactic in nature, its purpose to question ideology. Thus, for him, the *Trojan Women* represents "the consequences of war for the structures of thought, the beliefs, values—the ideology—in which Athenians lived, and in which tragedy and its functions were conceived (and challenged)."[3] In other words, the *Trojan Women* is not about a specific event or set of events, but about larger structures.

Because the *Trojan Women* is so full of lamentation, I will discuss only a few of the passages and major themes here, and then go on to consider their implications for Croally's and my own discussion.[4] The passages I have chosen exemplify the form, content, and emotional dynamic of the laments of captive women in Greek tragedy, and contribute to our understanding of both the play as a whole and its relationship to the larger tradition. I would like to begin with the beginning, where a conversation between the gods most connected to Athens, Poseidon and Athena, situates the plot of the drama within the long history of portrayals of the fall of Troy.

POSEIDON AND ATHENA

From the outset, the emphasis of the narrative is on the wrongs the Greeks have committed against the gods in their sack of the city:

> ἣ νῦν καπνοῦται καὶ πρὸς Ἀργείου δορὸς / ὄλωλε πορθηθεῖσ'· (. . .)
> ἔρημα δ' ἄλση καὶ θεῶν ἀνάκτορα / φόνῳ καταρρεῖ· πρὸς δὲ κρηπίδων
> βάθροις / πέπτωκε Πρίαμος Ζηνὸς ἑρκείου θανών.
>
> (*Trojan Women* 8–9, 15–17)

Now Troy is smoldering and destroyed, sacked by the Argive spear . . .
Groves are deserted and the temples of the gods flow with blood. At the base of the altar of Zeus *Herkeios* ["the protector"], Priam has fallen dead.

Poseidon begins his prologue with the effects that the sack of Troy has had on the gods. Poseidon himself together with Apollo built the walls that were breached (4–6). Temples have been defiled, sacred groves deserted, and the

---

2. Croally 1994, 253. For citations of these various positions, see again Croally.
3. Croally 1994, 254.
4. Several passages from this play are discussed elsewhere in the book.

murder of Priam at the altar of Zeus is singled out immediately as an atrocity. When Athena enters, she reveals her own indignation. Though previously their greatest ally, she now wants "to send upon the army of the Achaeans a bitter homecoming voyage" (66, cf. 75) because they have outraged her temples (69), dragged off Cassandra by force (70), let Ajax go unpunished (71), and sacked Troy (72). Thus the *Trojan Women* signals immediately its participation in and continuation of the traditional sack of Troy themes that we have seen time and again in epic, art, and drama: the canonical list of atrocities committed during the sack, the anger of Athena, and her vengeance upon the Greeks on their return voyage.

In his description of the aftermath of the sack, Poseidon eventually moves from the divine to the human consequences, as he observes the women left behind by the slaughter:

πολλοῖς δὲ κωκυτοῖσιν αἰχμαλωτίδων / βοᾷ Σκάμανδρος δεσπότας κληρουμένων. / καὶ τὰς μὲν Ἀρκάς, τὰς δὲ Θεσσαλὸς λεὼς / εἴληχ᾽ Ἀθηναίων τε Θησεῖδαι πρόμοι.   (*Trojan Women* 28–31)

With great wailings of captive women, the Scamander River shouts, as they are allotted to their masters. Some the Arcadian people take, others the Thessalian people, and others are assigned to Theseus' sons, the Athenian champions.

Here not only are the lamentation and suffering of the Trojan women emphasized, but the sons of Theseus are prominently included as agents in the action and recipients of the captives. In this way the Athenian audience becomes immediately connected with the devastation that has occurred and the events that will transpire in the course of the play.[5] Just as in the *Hecuba*, where Theseus' sons are singled out in the beginning of the play as supporters of Polyxena's sacrifice, the Athenians are asked to imagine the wailing of the Trojan women at the same moment that they hear their own local heroes singled out as part of the Greek victory.

The image of the Scamander river overflowing with wailing so that it "shouts" (29) is striking, and like many metaphors for lament that I have discussed thus far, the natural association of tears and rivers and streams resonates with epic reminiscences. This particular passage recalls and vividly

5. An extreme form of this point has been made in connection with the *Hecuba* by King (1985, 63–64, note 35), who sees the *Hecuba* as a condemnation of the barbarity of the Athenians in the first phase of the Peloponnesian War, and the sack of Mytilene in particular. On the role of Akamas and Demophon in the *Hecuba* see also Gregory 1991, 85–86 and Mossman 1995, 41.

transforms the distress of the river in *Iliad* 21, when Achilles fills it with corpses to the point that it can hold no more. This image of intense sorrow, resonating with epic carnage, previews the bulk of the action of the *Trojan Women.*

After the departure of the gods, the play consists with few exceptions of a series of laments by the principle characters and the chorus. Hecuba and the Trojan women seem at least initially to lament purely out of sorrow; unlike the *Hecuba,* there is nothing to be gained by the use of lament in this play other than the pity of the hearers.[6] Hecuba does not have to plead for the right to bury Astyanax, for example—she is simply allowed to do it. The sorrow of the women, moreover, seems even more stark and raw than in the *Hecuba,* perhaps because the setting is Troy itself and the action is situated directly in the aftermath of the sack, whereas the setting of the *Hecuba* is further removed both geographically and chronologically. The *Trojan Women* quite simply abounds in stunning images of suffering, from which there is no alleviation or hope. When the play ends, Hecuba is led off to her new master like all the other women before her, lamenting in antiphonal exchange with her fellow Trojan captives.

The opening dialogue between Poseidon and Athena, however, makes it clear that the events depicted are not over when the play comes to an end. The songs of sorrow that make up the majority of the play are not without import or effect, as I will now go on to show.

MOTHERS IN MOURNING:
HECUBA AND THE TROJAN WOMEN

Upon the departure of the gods, Hecuba performs a monody that recalls her opening lament in the *Hecuba,* with its traditional images of loss and devastation:

αἰαῖ αἰαῖ. / τί γὰρ οὐ πάρα μοι μελέᾳ στενάχειν, / ᾗ πατρὶς ἔρρει καὶ τέκνα καὶ πόσις; / ὦ πολὺς ὄγκος συστελλόμενος / προγόνων, ὡς οὐδὲν ἄρ᾽ ἦσθα. / τί με χρὴ σιγᾶν; τί δὲ μὴ σιγᾶν; / τί δὲ θρηνῆσαι;

(*Trojan Women* 105–11)

Aiai! Aiai! What is there for me that I do not lament with my song, I for whom country, children, and husband are gone? O great dignity of ancestors, cast down now, how you were nothing after all! Why should

6. Cf. Hecuba's words at 473: τοῖς γὰρ κακοῖσι πλείον᾽ οἶκτον ἐμβαλῶ ("I will inspire greater pity for my sufferings").

I be silent? And why not be silent? Why should I perform a lament [*thrênos*]?

Hecuba begins by adducing the central theme of the captive woman's lament, the combined loss all at once of country, children, and husband. She then questions whether she can even bring herself to lament, her questions to some extent echoing the traditional initial question of the "desperation speech" (τί χρὴ δρᾶν;). But she then continues in earnest, narrating the history of her troubles (122–38).

As we have seen, lament gives women the opportunity to speak out about their own lives, and when incorporated into poetry lament often provides a new perspective on the traditional sequencing of events.[7] Hecuba's song is the tale of Troy from the point of view of the woman who experienced it all and suffered most. The solo portion of the lament culminates in a reflection upon her current state:

ὤμοι, θάκους οἵους θάσσω, / σκηναῖς ἐφέδρους ᾿Αγαμεμνονίαις. / δούλα δ᾿ ἄγομαι / γραῦς ἐξ οἴκων πενθήρη / κρᾶτ᾿ ἐκπορθηθεῖσ᾿ οἰκτρῶς. / ἀλλ᾿ ὦ τῶν χαλκεγχέων Τρώων / ἄλοχοι μέλεαι, / καὶ κοῦραι ⟨κοῦραι⟩ δύσνυμφοι, / τύφεται ῎Ιλιον, αἰάζωμεν. / μάτηρ δ᾿ ὡσεί τις πτανοῖς / ὄρνισιν, ὅπως ἐξάρξω ᾿γὼ / κλαγγάν, μολπάν, οὐ τὰν αὐτὰν / οἵαν ποτὲ δὴ / σκήπτρῳ Πριάμου διερειδομένα / ποδὸς ἀρχεχόρου πλαγαῖς Φρυγίους / εὐκόμποις ἐξῆρχον θεούς.

(*Trojan Women* 138–50)

Alas what sort of seat is this that I have taken, I who am seated before the tents of Agamemnon? As a slave I am led away from my home, an old woman, my head shorn piteously in grief. Ah! wretched wives of the bronze-speared Trojans and maidens, unfortunate brides, Ilium is smoldering, let us cry out! Like some mother bird that over her fledglings screams, so I will lead off the shout, the song and dance; not the same as that I once conducted, as I leaned on Priam's scepter and with loud-sounding beats led the dance for the Phrygian gods.

Hecuba laments on behalf of brides who have lost their husbands and calls on them to weep for Troy. She contrasts her own leading off of the dirge with happier times, when once she was a bride and led dance and song in honor of the gods. The chorus of Trojan women at this point commences an antiphonal exchange with Hecuba (153–96) and eventually proceeds to perform its own lament (197–234).

7. On this point, see also the introduction and chapter 1.

The structure, imagery, themes, and language of Hecuba's opening song embody the captive woman's lament as I have discussed it throughout this book, and her subsequent speeches and songs combine a similar cluster of themes. After the departure of Cassandra, Hecuba says she wants to take the opportunity "to sing out" her previous good fortune one last time (472). She recalls her royal marriage and her preeminent children. But her speech typically switches modes almost instantly in order to contrast the happy past with the miserable present, in which her children have been killed, bridegrooms have been selected in vain, she has witnessed the slaughter of Priam, and she is now a slave (474–97).[8]

But as I argued in my discussion of the *Hecuba,* I see in Hecuba's use of the mother bird metaphor an engagement on the part of Euripides with the lament tradition even beyond the *Agamemnon* of Aeschylus, whose dark, often sinister metaphors and allusions to the events of the Trojan War and its aftermath seem to have had a profound impact on subsequent portrayals.[9] In a passage of the *Agamemnon,* Agamemnon and Menelaus are compared at the outset of the expedition to vultures that fly through the sky, shrieking in lamentation (γόον, 57) because they have lost their young.[10] Now it is Hecuba who shrieks (*Trojan Women* 146–47).

The comparison of Hecuba to a mother bird is taken up by the chorus later in the play:

ἠιόνες δ᾽ ἅλιαι / ἴαχχον οἰωνὸς οἷ-/ον τεκέων ὕπερ βοᾷ, / ᾷ μὲν εὐνάς, ᾷ δὲ παῖδας, / ᾷ δὲ ματέρας γεραιάς.   (*Trojan Women* 826–32)

The shores of the sea cry out like a mother bird shouting for her young, now for husbands, now for children, now for aged mothers.

Here the laments of the Trojan women fill not just a river but an ocean. Their lamentation is compared both metaphorically to the roar of the ocean and by means of a simile to the shriek of a bird. The ocean carries connotations of liquid and hence tears as well as sound, while the bird, in addition to sound, conveys the attachment and intimacy of the mother-child bond. Indeed, the simile of the mother bird is very likely a traditional one in Greek women's

8. Anderson (1997, 158) argues that this speech is an adaptation and hence fulfillment of Priam's vision of the sack of Troy in *Iliad* 22.59–76 (for a discussion of this passage, see Anderson 1997, 28–36).

9. Euripides' *Iphigeneia at Aulis* and *Iphigeneia among the Taurians* (neither of which are discussed extensively in this book) have a similar allusive relationship with both the *Agamemnon* of Aeschylus and the Trojan myth cycle as a whole.

10. See *Agamemnon* 49ff. and further discussion below.

laments for the loss of children.[11] In the *Hecuba,* Polyxena compares herself
to a frightened bird when Hecuba first calls her out onto the stage in order
to tell her of her fate (ὥστ᾽ ὄρνιν θάμβει / τῷδ᾽ ἐξέπταξας, *Hecuba* 178–79).
In the *Trojan Women,* Andromache compares Astyanax to a young bird trying
to hide under her wings when Talthybius comes to announce the decision to
kill him (τί μου δέδραξαι χερσὶ κἀντέχῃ πέπλων, / νεοσσὸς ὡσεὶ πτέρυγας
ἐσπίτνων ἐμάς;, *Trojan Women* 750–51). The metaphor of the mother bird
is only partially relevant here, however, because the shores are crying out
for more than children. Husbands—or, more literally, sexual/marital unions
(εὐνάς)—and mothers are also included in this complex song, because the
captive women of Troy have many things to lament all at once.

Aeschylus' simile of the vultures may itself allude ultimately to *Odyssey*
16.213–19, in which Odysseus and Telemakhos are at long last reunited and
compared in their weeping to "eagles or vultures" that have been robbed of
their young.[12] But later in the *Odyssey,* the simile and the reunification of
father and son take on a new meaning. In *Odyssey* 22.302–6, Odysseus is
compared in his vengeance on the suitors to vultures that swoop down and
kill smaller birds who cannot escape.[13] In *Iliad* 9.323–27, Achilles strikingly
compares his own situation to that of a mother bird who has lost the toil of
raising her young, and the implication there too, I would argue, is that he
is out for revenge.[14]

The traditional resonance of the metaphor of the vultures is therefore
complex and indeed foreboding, and Aeschylus exploits this ambiguity. In
the *Agamemnon* ode, Agamemnon and Menelaus are first vultures who have

11. Cf., e.g., *Herakles* 1039–41, in which Herakles' father, Amphitryon, is compared in
his grief to a mother bird lamenting her young after Herakles has killed his grandsons,
Herakles' own children. Earlier in the play, Megara, fearing for her life and that of her
children, says that she protects her sons "beneath [her] wings, like a bird that puts her
young under her" (*Herakles* 71–72). On the figure of Procne and the mourning song of
the nightingale see Loraux 1998, 55–65.

12. Note, however, that the bird I have translated as "eagles" here is φῆναι, not
αἰετός.

13. See also the final lines of the *Odyssey,* in which Odysseus prepares to swoop down
upon the relatives of the suitors in battle like an eagle (*Odyssey* 24.537–38), on which image see Moulton 1977, 135–39. On the traditional themes, narratives, and connotations
associated with and evoked by particular animal metaphors in Homeric epic see especially
Muellner 1990.

14. Scott (1974, 78) also suggests there may be a link between the Achilles simile and
the *Odyssey* similes in the theme of revenge. Moulton (1977, 101–4) has noted that the
relationship between Achilles and Patroklos is several times described by similes that involve
the parent/children motif, and Achilles is usually cast in the role of the protector. This pattern makes it all the more significant that Achilles here draws on the imagery of women's
laments for children to describe himself, given the central importance of Patroklos' death
(and Achilles' avenging of that death) in the *Iliad.*

lost their young and lament, but just a few lines later in that same passage, they are compared by way of an omen to eagles who devour a pregnant hare (109–20); this omen predicts Troy's destruction. This far more sinister aspect of the simile appears in Euripides' *Andromache*. In yet another transformation of the simile, Menelaus and now his daughter Hermione are the two vultures, who will kill the child of Andromache by Neoptolemus: κτενοῦσί σε δισσοὶ λαβόντες γῦπες ("Two vultures will snatch you up and kill you," *Andromache* 74–75).

But as Gloria Ferrari has demonstrated, the sinister nature of Aeschylus' simile begins not with the eagles that devour the hare, but with the vultures, who sing a *goos* for their lost young. Lament has the power to initiate a cycle of vendetta, and the vultures in their lament are crying out for vengeance.[15] That vengeance is going to come in the form of Clytemnestra—the mother of Iphigeneia—who is herself an incarnation of an Erinys sent from Troy. Whereas initially Aeschylus' lost fledglings symbolize Helen and her theft by Paris, the referent soon changes, and the lost young become Iphigeneia. Her death creates an Erinys that avenges both her death and the sack of Troy at the same time.[16]

When we understand the lament of the vultures to be a call for vengeance, the songs of the Trojan women take on a new dimension. Suddenly they are not the stark, purposeless depictions of sorrow that they seem at first glance. The Trojan women have much to lament, and much to avenge. They have lost not just children, but husbands and city as well. But their vengeance will not come from a human agent, or even a human incarnation of an Erinys, as in the *Agamemnon*. The Greeks kill the last hope of Troy, Astyanax, precisely so that he will not grow up to avenge the Trojans (*Trojan Women* 723). Vengeance comes instead from the gods themselves, Poseidon and Athena, whose wrath and indignation frame the play.

THE BRIDE'S SONG: CASSANDRA

The figure of Cassandra in the *Trojan Women* is very interesting for this discussion precisely because she insists that she does not lament. In her maddened state she reproaches her mother for lamenting when she herself is singing a wedding song (*Trojan Women* 308–22). In this way Euripides has adapted still another form of women's song to the medium of tragedy

---

15. See chapter 1.

16. I have reduced here to a mere outline the subtle and in-depth arguments of Ferrari 1997, 24–35. On the theme of a mother's vengeance see also Slatkin 1991; Rabinowitz 1993, 103–24; Loraux 1998; and Foley 2001, 272–99.

and used it to explore the fate of the captive Trojan women. But of course Cassandra's words are full of references to marriage, and the theme of marriages gone wrong, beginning with Helen's, is one of the major themes of the laments of the play.

Cassandra is not to be simply a "slave to the bride of the Spartan [= Clytemnestra]" but neither is she to be a proper bride herself. Rather, Agamemnon has chosen her for the purpose of "shadowy nuptials in the marriage bed."[17] Moreover, like Polyxena and Iphigeneia, Cassandra is destined to find a wedding in death: "Let me marry my bridegroom in Hades."[18] Cassandra's entrance song, for the audience who knows of her impending doom, is a horrible conflation of a wedding hymn and a funeral dirge.[19] Cassandra, like her mother before her, makes a connection between the song and dance she now performs and the dancing of happier days, providing a meaningful and traditional contrast between past and present: "Raise your foot on high, lead on the dance—Euan, Euoi!—as in the happiest times when my father was alive" (*Trojan Women* 325–28).[20] Hecuba exclaims: "Hephaistos, you bear the torch at the weddings of mortals, but this flame you stir up is full of grief and far outside of my hopes."[21]

Cassandra herself is not deluded either about what her "marriage" means; she proceeds to foretell the murders that await them upon arrival in Argos. Cassandra takes comfort in the knowledge that she will not be unavenged: "For if there is a Loxias, in me the renowned lord of the Achaeans, Agamemnon, will find a more disastrous marriage than Helen's" (εἰ γὰρ ἔστι Λοξίας, / Ἑλένης γαμεῖ με δυσχερέστερον γάμον / ὁ τῶν Ἀχαιῶν κλεινὸς Ἀγαμέμνων ἄναξ, 356–58). Her death is the Trojans' victory: "I will come bearing victory to the dead after destroying the house of Atreus, by whom we have been cut

---

17. See *Trojan Women* 249–53: Τα. ἐξαίρετόν νιν ἔλαβεν Ἀγαμέμνων ἄναξ. / Ἑκ. ἦ τᾷ Λακεδαιμονίᾳ νύμφᾳ / δούλαν; ἰώ μοί μοι. / Τα. οὔκ, ἀλλὰ λέκτρων σκότια νυμφευτήρια ("Talthybius: Lord Agamemnon has chosen her. Hecuba: To be a slave for his Spartan bride? Oh, alas! Talthybius: No, for shadowy nuptials in the marriage bed"). Mary Ebbott (2003) has analyzed the poetic resonance of the word *skotios* ("shadowy") as a metaphor for illegitimacy.

18. ἐς Ἅιδου νυμφίῳ γημώμεθα (*Trojan Women* 445).

19. On the conflation of wedding songs and laments for the dead in the Greek tradition, see chapter 1.

20. πάλλε πόδα / αἰθέριον ἄναγε χορόν· εὐάν, εὐοῖ / ὡς ἐπὶ πατρὸς ἐμοῦ / μακαριωτάταις τύχαις.

21. *Trojan Women* 343–45: Ἥφαιστε, δᾳδουχεῖς μὲν ἐν γάμοις βροτῶν, / ἀτὰρ λυγράν γε τήνδ' ἀναιθύσσεις φλόγα / ἔξω τε μεγάλων ἐλπίδων. Ferrari 1997 demonstrates the close iconographic association between torches and the Erinyes, a connection that is no doubt significant here.

down" (ἥξω δ' ἐς νεκροὺς νικηφόρος / καὶ δόμους πέρσασ' Ἀτρειδῶν, ὧν ἀπωλόμεσθ' ὕπο, 460–61). Her predictions are not confined to the fate of Agamemnon; she also prophesies the wanderings of Odysseus (431–43). In this way Cassandra, like Athena and Poseidon, looks beyond the confines of the play to the disasters that await the Greeks upon their departure from Troy.

Cassandra, too, is therefore the quintessential captive woman, and in her bridal song many important themes come together. Like Polyxena in the *Hecuba*, she stands for the young Trojan women who will never have marriages, but will instead become captive concubines and slaves. She is also set up as the counterpart of Helen. Her "marriage" to Agamemnon will bring death and destruction from Troy to Argos, just as Helen and Paris brought destruction from Greece to Troy. Cassandra perhaps does not lament, but she does get her revenge.

A LAMENT FOR THE DEAD

Perhaps the most moving laments of the play are those for Astyanax, performed first by Andromache when his death is decreed, and second by Hecuba. Here again Euripides draws on epic suffering, particularly in Andromache's lament at lines 740–79. Upon learning of Hektor's death in *Iliad* 22, Andromache predicted that her son would be hurled from the walls of Troy by one of Hektor's enemies; here her predictions come true.[22] Andromache speculates about the life he should have had as the ruler of Asia, envisions his painful death, touches and embraces him for the last time, and then angrily curses both Helen and her captors. It is Hecuba, however, who is responsible for burying him, dressed in his wedding clothes and covered by the shield of his father, Hektor (1218–20).

Hecuba's speech in anticipation of the burial of Astyanax is a lament for the dead, not a captive woman's lament, and as such it exhibits much of the form and content of Greek funeral laments as they have been studied by Alexiou and others. The speech itself, unlike other laments performed by Hecuba, is not sung, but it is immediately followed by an antiphonal exchange with the chorus that continues until the end of the play.[23] This

22. For Andromache's lament in *Iliad* 22, see chapter 1. The death of Astyanax was also related in the *Sack of Troy* in the Epic Cycle.

23. On the metrical sequence of these concluding passages and the emotional dynamic they convey, see Barlow 1986 *ad loc.*

exchange, with its interruptions of syntax, spontaneous interjections, and exclamations of grief, exemplifies the interaction between the mourner and surrounding women documented in studies of modern Greek funerals.[24] In the following brief excerpt I have underlined some examples of this kind of interaction:

Χο. ἒ ἔ, φρενῶν
  ἔθιγες ἔθιγες· ὦ μέγας ἐμοί ποτ᾽ ὢν
  ἀνάκτωρ πόλεως.
Εκ. ἃ δ᾽ ἐν γάμοισι χρῆν σε προσθέσθαι χροῒ
  Ἀσιατίδων γήμαντα τὴν ὑπερτάτην,
  Φρύγια πέπλων ἀγάλματ᾽ ἐξάπτω χροός. . . .
Χο. αἰαῖ αἰαῖ·
πικρὸν ὄδυρμα γαῖά σ᾽, ὦ
  τέκνον, δέξεται.
  στέναζε, μᾶτερ Εκ. αἰαῖ.
Χο. νεκρῶν ἴακχον. Εκ. οἴμοι.
Χο. οἴμοι δῆτα σῶν ἀλάστων κακῶν.

(*Trojan Women* 1216–31)

CHORUS: Ah, ah, you have touched,
you have touched my mind; Oh you who were once for me a great
lord of the city.
HECUBA: The robes that you should have put around your skin
on the day of your marriage to the most outstanding of the women of
    Asia,
these Phrygian adornments I fasten around your skin . . .
CHORUS: Aiai aiai!
The earth will receive you, child,
Bitter source of grief.
Cry out, mother HECUBA: Aiai!
CHORUS: a song for the dead. HECUBA: Alas!
CHORUS: Alas indeed for your unforgettable sorrows.

As we will see in chapter 6, it is in exchanges like these that we find perhaps the closest connections between the stylized language of tragedy and the conventions of actual funerals.

24. On the traditional and formulaic aspects of this kind of response see especially Caraveli-Chavez 1978. On this phenomenon and Caraveli-Chavez' work, see also further discussion in chapter 6.

Hecuba's preceding speech likewise has important connections to Greek funerary laments. It conforms to the traditional structure of both ancient and modern laments for the dead, as outlined by Alexiou, consisting of a direct address, a narrative of the past or future, and then a renewed address accompanied by reproach and lamentation.[25] Hecuba begins with a series of angry rhetorical questions (again, typical of laments for the dead) addressed to the Greeks (1156–66). She then addresses Astyanax directly. She mourns individual body parts,[26] and speculates on the happiness he might have had (1179). When she recalls his mouth, she remembers the past and words that he once spoke, as he promised that he would be the one to bury her with all care (1180–86). She highlights the abnormality of the old woman burying her grandchild, thereby contrasting not only the present and the past (when the normal cycle of birth and death could be taken for granted), but also their respective youth and old age. Taking the place of his mother, Andromache, Hecuba laments the care that was lavished on him in vain, and as she continues to address him, she weaves into her grief images of her own son Hektor, Astyanax's father (1187–99).

THE ANGER OF ANDROMACHE

The fact that Hecuba is a captive Trojan woman and the very Greekness of her speech of lament raise questions similar to those we already have been considering. What is the emotional force of this speech and the antiphonal exchange that brings the play to an end? How might the members of the audience have responded to these evocations of their own funeral rituals? Before I turn to such questions, I would first like to consider the figure of Andromache.

As forceful as the lament of Hecuba must have been for a Greek audience, it is Andromache who delivers some of the most provocative lines of the play—some of which are later echoed in Hecuba's speech: "Greeks who have discovered barbarian evils, why do you kill this child who is in no way to blame?" (ὦ βάρβαρ' ἐξευρόντες Ἕλληνες κακά, / τί τόνδε παῖδα κτείνετ' οὐδὲν αἴτιον;, 764–65). Do Andromache's accusations contain the theme around which Euripides has constructed this drama? Have Greeks and barbarians exchanged places, such that the Trojans are noble and innocent

---

25. Alexiou 1974, 133 and Dué 2002, 67.

26. Compare Agave's lament at Euripides, *Bacchae* 1300ff. Unfortunately there is a lacuna at this point in the received text, but reconstruction of the missing passage from several sources suggests that Pentheus' body parts were lamented in a similar way.

victims of war, and the Greeks savage barbarians without restraint or rever-
ence for the gods?

The *Trojan Women* has certainly been read this way many times, and with
good reason.[27] As I noted in previous chapters, in the same year that the play
was produced, the Athenians killed all the men and enslaved the women and
children of the neutral population of Melos, simply for choosing to remain
neutral. Again in the same year the decision was made to launch the infamous
and disastrous Sicilian expedition, a massive invasion of an island that had
done little or nothing to provoke such an assault. Melos was not an isolated
event, as we have seen, but one component in an imperialist reign of terror
on the part of the Athenians over the course of the fifth century B.C., and the
Spartans were guilty of similar crimes. It would be hard to deny that there
is a relationship, however complex, between the *Trojan Women* and these
contemporary wartime atrocities. N. T. Croally has argued that the *Trojan
Women* challenges the reigning ideology in Athens that would allow these
events to occur. I think this thesis is supported by the early and prominent
reference to the Athenians early in the play as participants in the sack of Troy,
by the framing outrage expressed by Athens' two patron deities, Athena and
Poseidon, and by the Greeks' impending doom at the play's end.

In a recent study of Euripides' so-called political plays (namely, the
Children of Herakles and the *Suppliant Women,* both produced in the 420s),
Daniel Mendelsohn has explored the intersection of the feminine and the
political in the plays. In arguing that these two plays have been unappreci-
ated by critics because they have been misunderstood, Mendelsohn writes:

> In this narrow reading of the political, the emotional, feminine incur-
> sions that we find in the *Children of Herakles* and the *Suppliant Women*
> (Alkmene's rage, Evadne's despair), and that are so typical of Euripidean
> dramaturgy, are bound to appear intrusive and out of place. But careful
> re-evaluation of what is known about these plays indicates that the inclu-
> sion of ostensibly incongruous feminine passions in them was in fact a
> special Euripidean innovation—a self-conscious addition of the feminine
> to mythic narratives that, until Euripides' treatment of them here, had
> indeed focused on the masculine, martial, and "political."[28]

In Mendelsohn's reading, Euripides has used the feminine to problematize
and challenge state ideology: "girls and women are often the representatives
of a disturbing and potentially disruptive otherness within the carefully

27. See, e.g., the edition of Barlow (1986) and the references assembled in Croally 1994,
253.

28. Mendelsohn 2002, 12–13.

constructed world of the drama."[29] Much of Mendelsohn's work, therefore, intersects with that of Croally, and is potentially useful when considering the role of gender in the *Trojan Women*. If we assume that the *Trojan Women* is a play about imperialism (or, more generally, war), and specifically about Athenian imperialism within the context of the Peloponnesian War, we might argue that Euripides has dramatized the effects of war on women in order to challenge the ideology of imperialism.

Continuing this line of argument for a moment, I am now ready to accept that the Athenian audience is indeed being asked in this play to confront on some level recent political decisions by witnessing once again the fall of Troy and the suffering of the Trojan women. Whereas in chapter 2 we saw that shortly after the Persian Wars Athens could identify with Troy as the city wrongfully sacked, the Athenians can now, after more than fifty years of empire, be equated with the Achaeans who did the sacking. But if this is the case, how could they interpret this recent history without adding to it the moral color that the sack of Troy brings with it throughout the history of Greek artistic and poetic traditions? I think it is possible to acknowledge that such coloring is intentional and necessary without insisting that Euripides intended the *Trojan Women* to be a protest of war, or of specific policies or decisions. I am much more inclined, with Croally, to read the *Trojan Women* as a challenge rather than a protest, as a questioning of imperialist ideology rather than a pacifist's prayer for peace.[30] The power of the play lies in its exposition of a universal truth, not in its ties to a specific event.[31]

The *Trojan Women*, like the *Hecuba*, is steeped in the epic and artistic traditions about the Trojan War that condemn the actions of the Greeks and highlight the suffering of the Trojan widows. But rather than separate the Athenians from this tradition, Euripides explicitly involves them in it, thereby challenging the audience to confront the sorrow that their own actions have brought about and to think about how a justified victory can go horribly wrong if the victors are not kept in check.

But the play does more than that, because the laments and language and imagery of the play are traditional and Greek, and thus blur the distinction between Greek and Trojan, winner and loser. As in Aeschylus' *Persians*, the Trojans are labeled (occasionally) "barbarian" and (often) "Phrygian" or

29. Mendelsohn 2002, 20–21.

30. I would interpret the comedies of Aristophanes in a similar way. For similar trends in the interpretation of Herodotus, see chapter 2, note 4.

31. In her book *The Mourning Voice* (2002), Nicole Loraux notes that Sartre's staging of the *Trojan Women*, produced in explicit protest of the Vietnam War, failed to capture much of the emotional intensity of the play precisely because it was too closely tied to a particular political event.

"Asian" only to at the same time universalize their grief.[32] And so a crucial component of the emotional dynamic in this play must be, in addition to pity, fear. I say this not because of Aristotle's famous formulation about the emotions of tragedy, but because the Athenians were on the verge of launching a massive expedition, and were weakened by the plague and protracted hostilities of the past two decades. If the Sicilian expedition failed (as it ultimately did), the smoldering Troy of Euripides' play could be not Mytilene or Scione or Melos, but Athens. This is a reality that Athens had experienced, back in 480. The *Trojan Women* reminds its audience that it could happen again. Cassandra's words in particular are full of dire foreboding when read in the light of contemporary events: the Trojans died gloriously fighting for their country (τὸ κάλλιστον κλέος, 386); they were buried in their native land and lamented by their wives. But as for the Greeks, they lie dead, unburied, uncared for, and unlamented in a foreign land (376–86).[33]

But just as we cannot reduce the complexity of the *Trojan Women* to a simple antiwar slogan, neither can we reduce the emotional dynamic of this tragedy (or any tragedy) to politics and ideology. The women of Troy engage the emotions of their audiences both within and beyond the plays in which they are featured, and they do this by means of their own particular mode of speech and song, the captive woman's lament. Tragedies like the *Hecuba* and the *Trojan Women* were successful and affective at least in part because they allowed their audiences to transcend time and space and weep for the suffering they were witnessing on a universal level.

The Athenians are implicated in the events of the *Trojan Women*, but they are not outright condemned. In fact the chorus hopes that of all the places in Greece, they will be taken to Athens, "the famous and blessed land of Theseus."[34] As far as we know Athens was at war with someone for most of its history up to 416. It is unrealistic and anachronistic to think of Euripides as a pacifist. But the *Trojan Women* is a testament to this poet's capacity to comprehend and make comprehensible to others the true cost of war, however necessary and awful it may be.

---

32. For the Trojans as "barbarians," see, e.g., *Trojan Women* 1021.

33. On the horror connected with the idea of soldiers left unburied in the Greek tradition see Ebbott 2000.

34. τὰν κλεινὰν εἴθ' ἔλθοιμεν / Θησέως εὐδαίμονα χώραν (*Trojan Women* 208–9). Cf. 218–19: τάδε δεύτερά μοι μετὰ τὰν ἱερὰν / Θησέως ζαθέαν ἐλθεῖν χώραν ("These places are second to me after the sacred, holy land of Theseus").

CHAPTER SIX

THE CAPTIVE WOMAN IN THE HOUSE

EURIPIDES' *Andromache*

Euripides' *Andromache* may not have been originally produced in Athens, if we may trust the comment of a scholiast at line 445 of the play, nor can we be certain of the date of its production, which is generally assumed to be the mid 420s.[1] It is, moreover, a complicated drama that has not always been admired, though several recent studies have gone a long way toward better explicating its themes and structure.[2]

I have nevertheless thought it useful to include it in my discussion, because the play contains several components that shed light on the captive woman's lament. First, in Andromache we witness another important dimension of the captive woman's role in Greek tragedy, that of the captive war prize whose introduction into the home initiates death and destruction. As a captive woman, Andromache's safety continues to be in jeopardy even after she is well established in Greece as the sexual slave of Neoptolemus, and she therefore resorts to lament at several points in the play. The play's supposed anti-Spartan sentiment, discussed briefly in chapter 3, also raises new questions about the role of the captive Trojan women in fifth-century tragedy.

I would like to begin this chapter with a brief mention of Cassandra in Aeschylus' *Agamemnon,* which is the earliest extant play to feature prominently the speech and songs of a captive woman. In that play Cassandra, like Andromache, is brought to the home of her Greek captor, but unlike Andromache, she has no one to save her from the murderous designs of her captor's wife. Cassandra's presence onstage in that play is marked by her exceptional lyrics, which she sings in exchange with the spoken words of the

---

1. εἰλικρινῶς δὲ τοὺς τοῦ δράματος χρόνους οὐκ ἔστι λαβεῖν. οὐ δεδίδακται γὰρ Ἀθήνησιν. For the date as well as arguments for and against production outside of Athens see Allan 2000, 149–60.

2. See especially Anderson 1997 and Allan 2000.

chorus. Most of her song consists of prophetic visions of the murder taking place within the house, but there are occasional moments when Cassandra reflects upon her own situation, particularly in the following two passages:

ἰὼ γάμοι, γάμοι Πάριδος, / ὀλέθριοι φίλων. / ἰὼ Σκαμάνδρου πάτριον ποτόν. / τότε μὲν ἀμφὶ σὰς ἀιόνας τάλαιν᾽ / ἠνυτόμαν τροφαῖς· / νῦν δ᾽ ἀμφὶ Κωκυτόν τε κἀχερουσίους / ὄχθους ἔοικα θεσπιῳδήσειν τάχα.

(Agamemnon 1156–61)

Oh marriages, marriages of Paris, so destructive to those near and dear! Oh native river, Scamander! Once upon a time around your banks I, the wretch, grew up. But now by Kokytos and the banks of Acheron, it seems, I will soon sing my prophecies.

ἰὼ πόνοι πόνοι πόλεος / ὀλομένας τὸ πᾶν. / ἰὼ πρόπυργοι θυσίαι πατρὸς / πολυκανεῖς βοτῶν ποιονόμων· ἄκος δ᾽ / οὐδὲν ἐπήρκεσαν / τὸ μὴ πόλιν μὲν ὥσπερ οὖν ἐχρῆν παθεῖν.

(Agamemnon 1167–71)

Oh pains, pains of the city, destructive to all! Oh sacrifices performed by my father before the city sacrifices, full of the slaughter of beasts that feed on grass! But the cure was not strong enough to protect the city so that it did not have to suffer.

In the first passage, Cassandra contrasts her imminent death and existence along the rivers of the underworld with her childhood in Troy along the banks of the Scamander—a river that, as we have seen, carries with it associations with both slaughter and lamentation. This contrast between life and death is a basic theme of traditional laments for the dead, and Cassandra, having foreseen her death, is now lamenting herself. Cassandra blames the marriage of Paris and Helen for her misfortunes, as will all of the Trojan women in their laments in all subsequent tragedies. The multiple marriages of Helen (perhaps emphasized here by the plural γάμοι in 1156) are set up as the destroyer of all Trojan husbands (such as Hektor and Priam), and the cause of the perverted "weddings" of Polyxena and Cassandra, who should have married royalty, as well as that of Andromache, who becomes "the bride of her husband's killers."[3] In the second passage Cassandra remembers the many

---

3. *Andromache* 403. See, e.g., *Hecuba* 265–66, 629–56, 942–51; *Trojan Women* 131–37, 498–99, 766–73, 780–81, 890–1059; *Andromache* 103–16, 602–13. On the perverted marriages of the Trojan captives see Seaford 1987.

sacrifices that were not in the end sufficient to save Troy from destruction. And so, in the midst of her prophetic visions we find in the *Agamemnon* our first glimpse of the captive woman's lament as it will develop in Greek tragedy: a combination of lament for the dead, lament for a fallen city, and lament for present misery, contrasted with previous good fortune.

As I have noted elsewhere, captive women were also featured in the plays of Sophocles, and Tecmessa in the *Ajax* is in many ways the archetypal lamenting captive woman of Greek tragedy.[4] Likewise the plot of Sophocles' *Trachinian Women* resembles that of the *Agamemnon* and the *Andromache* in several respects.[5] The hero, Herakles, is away from home and long awaited by his wife, Deianeira. A group of captive women from a town that Herakles has recently sacked is sent to the home in advance of Herakles' arrival. One of them, Iolê, is immediately recognized by Deianeira as a princess and a rival. From there the plots of the three plays diverge considerably, but as in the *Agamemnon,* death and the destruction of the marriage are the result of the captive woman's arrival in the home.[6]

A choral ode of Euripides likewise highlights the themes we have been tracing:

τὰν μὲν Οἰχαλίᾳ / πῶλον ἄζυγα λέκτρων, ἄναν-/δρον τὸ πρὶν καὶ ἄνυμφον, οἴ-/κων ζεύξασ᾿ ἀπ᾿ Εὐρυτίων / δρομάδα ναΐδ᾿ ὅπως τε βάκ-/χαν
σὺν αἵματι, σὺν καπνῷ, / φονίοισι νυμφείοις / Ἀλκμήνας τόκῳ Κύπρις
ἐξέδωκεν· / ὦ τλάμων ὑμεναίων.

(EURIPIDES, *Hippolytus* 545–54)

There was that maiden in Oikhalia, a filly unyoked and unmarried, husbandless and not yet a bride, whom, unyoking her from Eurytos' house like some running Naiad or Bacchant, amidst blood and smoke and murderous marital vows, Kypris gave as bride to the son of Alkmênê. What a wretched wedding hymn!

As in the case of the captive women of Troy, the "marriage" of Iolê not only brings destruction on the house of her "husband," but is also predicated on

4. See chapter 1.

5. The date of the *Trachinian Women* is unknown, but it is thought to be among the earliest of Sophocles' plays, and was almost certainly produced well after the *Agamemnon* and well before the *Andromache*.

6. See Segal 1995, 69–94. For an illuminating discussion of the relationship of the concubine to the *oikos* in Classical Athens, see Ferrari 2002b, 192–200.

the destruction of her own family and town. Sophocles does not give Iolê a speaking role; if he had, her words no doubt would have had much in common with those of Tecmessa and the Trojan women of Euripides.

That Sophocles has *not* allowed Iolê to lament, then, is perhaps of real significance. This is a question explored recently by Victoria Wohl, who—in contrast to many recent readings—sees Iolê's silence as a form of resistance in the pattern of exchange between men that Wohl traces throughout her book. If Wohl is right, then Sophocles has constructed a role for the captive woman very different from but no less powerful than that of Euripides. In Wohl's reading, Iolê employs a strategy opposite to that of the Trojan women of tragedy, who, through the words of their laments, are allowed to protest their suffering and their role as prizes of war and objects of exchange between warriors.[7]

Whereas in the *Agamemnon* Cassandra laments only sparingly and in the *Trachinian Women* Iolê remains silent throughout, in the *Andromache* lament plays a crucial role. It is the means by which Andromache gains the sympathy of the local women and other characters, her sole defense in a land of strangers against a hostile and indeed murderous mistress. The play begins with a prologue spoken by Andromache in which she narrates her Trojan past, her present life in Phthia as sex slave of Neoptolemus, and the impending danger. Jealous of the fact that Andromache has had a son by her husband, Neoptolemus, the still-childless Hermione threatens to kill both Andromache and her child with the help of her father, Menelaus. The contents of this speech, as we will see, are reshaped in the form of laments at key moments elsewhere in the play.

Immediately following the prologue is a brief conversation with a fellow Trojan captive, after which Andromache introduces an extraordinary lament:

χώρει νυν· ἡμεῖς δ᾽, οἷσπερ ἐγκείμεσθ᾽ ἀεὶ / θρήνοισι καὶ γόοισι καὶ δακρύμασι, / πρὸς αἰθέρ᾽ ἐκτενοῦμεν . . . πάρεστι δ᾽ οὐχ ἓν ἀλλὰ πολλά

---

7. See Wohl 1998, 3–56. See also Wohl's discussion of Cassandra in the *Agamemnon,* whose lack of resistance (despite her speaking role) she contrasts with Iolê (Wohl 1998, 116): "[R]ather than lamenting the sufferings of Iphigeneia, Cassandra merely replicates them in her own person; rather than exposing the logic of fetishism, Cassandra denies and, with her death, reproduces it."

The lack of resistance that Wohl perceives complements my own observation that in the *Agamemnon* Cassandra does not lament, but as we have seen there are a few places in which Cassandra does employ the language of lament to articulate and perhaps protest her own sorrow. On Cassandra's resistance or lack thereof see also Rabinowitz 2000.

μοι στένειν, / πόλιν πατρῷαν τὸν θανόντα θ᾽ Ἕκτορα / στερρόν τε τὸν
ἐμὸν δαίμον᾽ ᾧ συνεζύγην / δούλειον ἦμαρ εἰσπεσοῦσ᾽ ἀναξίως.

(Andromache 91–93, 96–99)

Go now; but I, the things in which I always wrap myself, *thrênoi* and
gooi and tears, I will draw out, lifting them up toward the heavens . . .
For I have not one but many things to lament, my native city and my
dead husband Hektor and the hard *daimôn* to which I am yoked, since I
undeservedly met the day of slavery.

Andromache makes clear that what she is about to sing is a lament; in the
same verse we find not only the two primary terms for laments, *goos* and
thrênos, but also tears (δακρύμασι, 92). The themes of her lament are laid out
clearly as well. Unlike a traditional lament for the dead, which, though often
wide-ranging, is primarily concerned with one source of grief, Andromache has many causes of sorrow. She laments the loss of city, husband, and
freedom, which are as we have seen the defining sorrows of captive women.
In the song that follows, Andromache narrates her own particular past, but
also the pasts of all the Trojan women.

Andromache employs here a striking metaphor: she says that she continu-
ally "wraps herself up in" laments. This metaphor refers not simply to the
frequency of her laments but also to her purpose in lamenting. As Gloria
Ferrari has shown, metaphors of covering or wrapping (as in clothing or cloth)
refer to the concept *aidôs*. *Aidôs,* as Ferrari demonstrates, both constrains
and protects those who are incapable of exercising agency, such as women,
children, and slaves: "the cover of cloth and downcast gaze raise a shield
that in lawful society protects from arbitrary violence persons deprived of
agency."[8] Andromache, both a woman and a slave, employs lament in much
the same way that one uses *aidôs*. By using the publicly sanctioned language
of lament, Andromache earns sympathy and ultimately her safety. As I
noted already in chapter 1, the Greek women of Phthia respond positively
and protectively to the laments of Andromache (ᾤκτιρ᾽ ἀκούσασ᾽, "Upon
hearing [her words], I pity her," 421), but disapprove of her more reasoned
arguments (364).

I turn now to Andromache's elegiac lament, which I give here in full:

Ἰλίῳ αἰπεινᾷ Πάρις οὐ γάμον ἀλλά τιν᾽ ἄταν
    ἀγάγετ᾽ εὐναίαν εἰς θαλάμους Ἑλέναν.

8. Ferrari 1997, 8; see also Ferrari 1990 and 2002b, 54–56 and 73–81. On the concept
of *aidôs* see, in addition to Ferrari, Cairns 1993.

ᾶς ἕνεχ᾽, ὦ Τροία, δορὶ καὶ πυρὶ δηιάλωτον
    εἷλέ σ᾽ ὁ χιλιόναυς Ἑλλάδος ὀξὺς Ἄρης
καὶ τὸν ἐμὸν μελέας πόσιν Ἕκτορα, τὸν περὶ τείχη
    εἷλκυσε διφρεύων παῖς ἁλίας Θέτιδος·
αὐτὰ δ᾽ ἐκ θαλάμων ἀγόμαν ἐπὶ θῖνα θαλάσσας,
    δουλοσύναν στυγερὰν ἀμφιβαλοῦσα κάρᾳ.
πολλὰ δὲ δάκρυά μοι κατέβα χροός, ἁνίκ᾽ ἔλειπον
    ἄστυ τε καὶ θαλάμους καὶ πόσιν ἐν κονίαις.
ὤμοι ἐγὼ μελέα, τί μ᾽ ἐχρῆν ἔτι φέγγος ὁρᾶσθαι
    Ἑρμιόνας δούλαν; ἇς ὕπο τειρομένα
πρὸς τόδ᾽ ἄγαλμα θεᾶς ἱκέτις περὶ χεῖρε βαλοῦσα
    τάκομαι ὡς πετρίνα πιδακόεσσα λιβάς.

                    (EURIPIDES, *Andromache* 103–16)

To lofty Ilium Paris did not conduct a wedding but a curse,
    when he brought Helen into his bridal chamber as a wife.
For her sake, Troy, with spear and fire
    a thousand Greek ships and a swift Ares took you captive
together with my husband Hektor—wretched me—whom around the
        walls
    the son of the sea goddess Thetis dragged, driving his chariot.
But I myself was led away from my bridal chamber to the shore of the
        sea,
    encircling my head with abominable slavery.
My skin poured down many tears, when I left behind
    my city and my bridal chamber and my husband in the dust.
Alas, wretched me! Why was it necessary for me to survive to look
        upon the light
    as Hermione's slave? Worn down by her,
as a suppliant of the goddess I throw my arms around this statue,
    melting like a spring that gushes forth from the rocks.

In this one lament, most if not all of the themes and imagery discussed in this book come together. This accumulation alone suggests that the song is in form and content highly traditional, yet it is in one significant way unique: it is the only lament in the elegiac meter in Greek tragedy. In Greek tragedy elegy and lament are frequently equated, but other than this one no Archaic or Classical elegiac lament survives.[9] It has been argued by Denys Page that a Doric tradition of elegiac lament, of which no text survives, existed in Argos and elsewhere, though many scholars have rejected this theory. Others sug-

9. See Page 1936, 206–10.

gest that Euripides is responsible for the innovation, and that he made the connection between lamentation and elegy. It is not my intention to solve the problem, but rather to point out the highly traditional themes and form of this extraordinary lament. I believe that the arguments that follow could be used to support Page's contention that the elegiac lament is an ancient and well-developed art form, but unfortunately the evidence simply does not allow us to say one way or the other.[10]

The lament begins with the theme of the wedding of Paris and Helen as a curse or plague. This theme pervades the lamentation of the Trojan women in Greek tragedy, and is a more specific form of the general theme of marriage, which plays such an important role in Greek women's laments. In laments for the dead the marriage that is mourned is usually that of the lamenting woman herself, or else if the dead person is of premarital age, the mourner speculates about the marriage the dead person should have had.[11] As I mentioned previously, in both ancient and modern practice young people who die before marriage are buried in wedding clothes. In the laments of the captive women of Troy, by contrast, Helen's marriage is blamed as the destroyer of the marriages that have already taken place, the thwarter of marriages to come, and the cause of all the corrupted wedding rituals surrounding the sexual enslavement of women by the Greek soldiers. Andromache's enslavement in particular becomes a reversal of her own wedding to Hektor, as well as that of Helen's to Paris. Whereas Helen was brought across the Aegean from Greece and conducted in her wedding procession to her bridal chamber in Troy, Andromache was conducted out of her bridal chamber in Troy to the Greek ships and brought across the Aegean to Greece.[12]

In the next couplet Andromache moves from Helen to the city of Troy, which Helen destroyed. The destruction of Troy is as we have seen a crucial component in the laments of the Trojan captive women, even when, as here and in the *Hecuba,* the ruins are not physically present on the scene. Helen and Troy's destruction are inseparably linked in the construction of the lament, as are linked in the next couplet the fall of Troy and the death of Hektor. This chain of causality is traditional and is assumed throughout the *Iliad.* In the fourth couplet the death of Hektor leads inevitably to the enslavement of Andromache, again a traditional theme from the standpoint of the *Iliad.*[13] The contrast between her past status as bride and current slavery is emphasized here again: Andromache, led from her bridal chamber to the

10. See the arguments of Page in Page 1936. For a summary of the counterarguments, see the commentary of Lloyd (1994 *ad loc.*).

11. See, e.g., Euripides, *Herakles* 456–91, where Megara laments her sons in anticipation of their death at the hands of Lykos.

12. Cf. *Andromache* 401–3, as well as *Trojan Women* 569–71. See Seaford 1987, 123–30.

13. See, e.g., *Iliad* 6.447–65 and 24.725–34.

shore of the sea, does not put a veil or any other kind of wedding headpiece around her head, but rather the abominable yoke of slavery (δουλοσύναν στυγερὰν ἀμφιβαλοῦσα κάρᾳ, 110).[14]

The fifth couplet (111–12) is extraordinary for its highly compressed and yet deeply resonant expression of the essence of the captive woman's lament:

πολλὰ δὲ δάκρυά μοι κατέβα χροός, ἁνίκ' ἔλειπον
    ἄστυ τε καὶ θαλάμους καὶ πόσιν ἐν κονίαις.

My skin poured down many tears, while I was leaving behind
    my city and my bridal chamber and my husband in the dust.

The image of the skin pouring tears is evocative of epic lament traditions, as we have seen, and especially of Penelope, who in her role as the faithful wife reunited with her husband is a particularly poignant counterpart here.[15] Later in the ode the epic image is filled out even further, when Andromache says that she "melts," like a rocky spring (τάκομαι ὡς πετρίνα πιδακόεσσα λιβάς, 116).

Verse 111 conjures the heroic suffering of a lamenting wife, while verse 112 captures many of the themes most frequently combined in the laments of captive women, the simultaneous loss of city, home/marriage, and husband. This fifth couplet is highly traditional and almost paradigmatic, in that Andromache's words could be spoken by any of the Trojan women.[16] I note especially the phrase *en koniais* ("in the dust"). In the *Iliad,* the dust is where heroes fall in battle,[17] and when a city is sacked or an army is decisively defeated, a large part of the horror is that the losers are left unburied. Hektor, however, was spectacularly buried; his funeral concludes the *Iliad.* Andromache's lament therefore is not restricted to her own particular story. It becomes a generic lament on behalf of all the women of Troy.

The sixth couplet in Andromache's lament begins with the exclamation ὤμοι ἐγὼ μελέα, which I have crudely translated here and elsewhere as "Alas, wretched me." The phrase echoes verse 107 just a few lines earlier (καὶ τὸν ἐμὸν μελέας πόσιν). Such exclamations have only been touched on in my discussion so far (see especially chapter 5), but I would like to point them out briefly here, because they are probably the phrases that are most closely related to the laments of actual women outside of tragedy and epic.

---

14. Cf. *Iliad* 22.468–72, where Andromache, upon learning of the death of Hektor, tears from her head the veil that Aphrodite gave her on her wedding day.

15. See discussion above in chapter 4.

16. On paradigmatic versus syntagmatic lament narratives see Dué 2002, 5–16.

17. See *LSJ*[9], s.v. κονία.

Because no laments from antiquity survive beyond the stylized examples preserved in literature, it is impossible to conjecture the extent to which the laments of literature and the laments of actual women are related. Nevertheless in chapter 1, I surveyed some modern traditions, including that of modern Greece, that suggest ways in which women's songs may be incorporated into men's traditions. Here, too, the continuities observable in the lament traditions of rural modern Greece may provide some insight. Anna Caraveli-Chavez, building on the work of Margaret Alexiou, has studied the dynamics of interjections and emotional exclamations in modern Greek laments, and argues that they create a parenthetical voice within the primary narrative:

> Ultimately, refrains—even if they consist of only a single syllable—serve as a parallel creation to the main thrust of the song. By breaking a word or line in ways unorthodox to everyday conversational patterns, they provide space for a parenthetical voice to exist which distances the listener from the fixed meaning of words and phrases. Whether the denotative value of words is suspended in this way, or a different aspect of an image or feeling is captured indirectly, or a certain emotion reaches a crescendo through repetition and invocation, two forces are at work here: The force of the main text which moves forward . . . and the complementary force of the refrains which, like a magic chorus, tends to interrupt the linear flow of actions and ideas. Thus directly or indirectly, the *tsakismata* act as a commentary from a different perspective on the main poem.[18]

Caraveli-Chavez goes on to point out that the interchange of two voices—"the dominant and the parenthetical, the solo and the choral"—has its roots in the antiphonal structure of ancient laments, a structure that is present in the laments of the *Iliad,* as we have seen.[19] The laments of tragedy likewise frequently manifest this antiphonal structure, particularly in conjunction with the chorus. And while the emotional interjections of tragedy, such as

---

18. Caraveli-Chavez 1978, 27.

19. On the antiphonal structure of Greek laments, see also Alexiou 1974, 131–60. Caraveli-Chavez's arguments complement very nicely the hypothesis of Page (1936, 219–20)—not likely to have been known to Caraveli-Chavez: "Most important and illuminating is the repetition of ὤμοι ἐγὼ μελέα from καὶ τὸν ἐμὸν μελέας. It seems to me likely that this repetition faintly recalls an ancient elegiac refrain. In the *Iliad* . . . a cry is raised by a chorus of bystanders at the end of a Lament. Now it would be a short step from this to insert such cries at the end of successive stages within a Lament . . . Zacher thinks the word ἔλεγος itself is derived from the word ἔλεγε, a cry of lamentation, repeated as a refrain at regular intervals throughout an 'elegiac' poem."

Andromache's here, are far more stylized than those of modern Greek laments, we can perhaps find in them emotional cues for the audience, for whom such interjections are meaningful and vital, cues that offer a glimpse of the living tradition of lamentation.

I return now to the final couplets of Andromache's elegiac lament. She bewails the fact that she is still alive, living only to serve as the slave of Hermione. This sentiment likely had parallels in contemporary laments as well, since the contrast between the living mourner and the dead is a central theme of the Greek lament tradition.[20] Here the mourner is not only alive and miserable, but she has become a slave. We can see that this traditional contrast is particularly acute when it is employed by captive women, because it is also a contrast between danger and safety, servility and nobility, slavery and freedom.

And finally, as I noted above, Andromache's lament comes to its conclusion in the seventh couplet with a comparison of Andromache to a rocky spring. In her tears she melts:

τάκομαι ὡς πετρίνα πιδακόεσσα λιβάς.

I melt like a spring that gushes forth from the rocks.

This simile is remarkable in that it is likely to have evoked for its ancient audience several archetypal scenes of lamentation in Greek epic and tragedy at the same time. First there is the verb τάκομαι ("I melt"), whose epic contexts I have already discussed in connection with the *Hecuba*. The spring gushing forth from the rock likewise has epic resonance: Patroklos is compared to just such a spring when he laments the suffering of the Greeks in *Iliad* 16.

But the quintessential context for the mourner as a rocky spring is probably the myth of Niobe, who is adduced within the lament-filled final book of the *Iliad* as the ultimate mourner:

νῦν δέ που ἐν πέτρησιν ἐν οὔρεσιν οἰοπόλοισιν
ἐν Σιπύλῳ, ὅθι φασὶ θεάων ἔμμεναι εὐνὰς
νυμφάων, αἵ τ' ἀμφ' Ἀχελώϊον ἐρρώσαντο,
ἔνθα λίθος περ ἐοῦσα θεῶν ἐκ κήδεα πέσσει.

(*Iliad* 24.614–17)

And now somewhere among the rocks in the lonely mountains
in Sipylos, where they say are the haunts of goddesses,

20. See Alexiou 1974, 171–77.

the nymphs who dance around the Acheloos River,
there as a stone she weighs her cares from the gods.

Although it is not specified in the *Iliad* passage that there is a spring of
water trickling down from this rock, it has been assumed since Eustathius
that this was the case.[21] Likewise Sophocles' Antigone compares herself to
Niobe, who, melting away (ταχομέναν, 828), "wets the ridges under her
eyebrows with every sort of weeping" (τέγγει δ᾽ ὑπ᾽ ὀφρύσι παγκλαύτοις
δειράδας, 831–32).[22] Andromache's lament, like the Antigone passage, combines the metaphor of melting with the rocky spring in a way that manages
to suggest Penelope, Patroklos, Niobe, and Antigone all at once. It is difficult to say whether all of these connections could have been readily made
by all members of the ancient audience, but the effect is at the very least to
place Andromache's suffering within the heroic realm, and to maximize the
magnitude of her sorrow.

On this note Andromache's elegiac lament comes to a close. The chorus
of women of Phthia then enters, and reiterates many of the themes of Andromache's lament:

γνῶθι δ᾽ οὖσ᾽ ἐπὶ ξένας
δμωὶς ἐπ᾽ ἀλλοτρίας
πόλεος, ἔνθ᾽ οὐ φίλων τιν᾽ εἰσορᾷς
σῶν, ὦ δυστυχεστάτα,
⟨ὦ⟩ παντάλαινα νύμφα.

(EURIPIDES, *Andromache* 136–40)

Realize that you are
a servant in a foreign city
where there are none of those near and dear to you to turn to,
O most unfortunate of women,
O all-suffering bride.

The chorus understands well Andromache's plight, and having heard her
lament they now pity her, though they are powerless to help. Twice in the

21. See the commentary of Richardson (1993 *ad loc.*). For more on the geographical
landmark and ancient references to it, see the commentary of Jebb (1891 *ad Antigone*
831).

22. See also *Andromache* 532–34, where the image of the spring trickling down from a
rock is used a second time, when in an antiphonal choral ode Andromache and her son
beseech Menelaus to spare them. For Andromache's lament before Menelaus at 383–420
as an attempt to save the life of herself and her son, see chapter 1.

next five lines they express their pity, calling Andromache "most pitiable" (οἰκτροτάτα, 141; see also 144). As in the *Hecuba* it seems that the Greeks within the play (in this case the chorus) point to the expected emotional reaction of the audience. Indeed, Andromache retains the sympathy of all throughout, with the obvious exceptions of the Spartan Hermione and her father, Menelaus.

In contrast to Andromache, Hermione and Menelaus are vilified in the play, and, much as in the *Trojan Women,* there is a stated role reversal between Greek (in this case, Spartan) and barbarian. Hermione repeatedly refers to Andromache as a barbarian and a slave, but then later admits she was wrong, and claims that she was misled by other women.[23] Because Hermione is an admittedly sex-crazed murderess,[24] her denigration of Andromache is severely undercut, thereby blurring once again the distinctions between Greek and Trojan in the Trojan War plays of Euripides.

If we try to place this blurring of Greek and Trojan in its larger context, however, we face some inevitable interpretive difficulties due to our ignorance of the play's intended first performance. Certainly the play was produced during the Peloponnesian War, and as I noted in chapter 3, many have read the vilification of Hermione as anti-Spartan sentiment within this context. Because Hermione and Menelaus are acting on their own and independently of the collective Greek expedition to Troy, I admit here with reservations that it is possible that the *Andromache* would have been appreciated as an anti-Spartan play. There is a danger in taking this hypothesis too far, however, because as in the case of the *Persians,* I do not believe we should reduce the complex drama that is the *Andromache* (or any tragedy) to patriotic propaganda. But if the *Andromache* is an anti-Spartan play, this is possible only because the events that transpire are clearly separated from the Trojan War itself, and because the Trojans were never fully enfolded in the Greek concept of the barbarian. The Athenians (or whatever population was the original intended audience) are not being asked here to examine their own actions against those of the Greeks in a paradigmatic war, but rather to sympathize in a new context with a figure who has always been sympathetic, Andromache, the archetypal lamenting widow and future captive woman we see in the *Iliad.*

---

23. *Andromache* 930–35. For Andromache as a barbarian and slave, see especially 147–80, 243, and 261.

24. *Andromache* 161, 241–42, 245.

CONCLUSION

THE TEARS OF PITY

λόγος δυνάστης μέγας ἐστίν, ὃς σμικροτάτωι σώματι καὶ
ἀφανεστάτωι θειότατα ἔργα ἀποτελεῖ· δύναται γὰρ καὶ φόβον
παῦσαι καὶ λύπην ἀφελεῖν καὶ χαρὰν ἐνεργάσασθαι καὶ ἔλεον
ἐπαυξῆσαι . . . τὴν ποίησιν ἅπασαν καὶ νομίζω καὶ ὀνομάζω
λόγον ἔχοντα μέτρον· ἧς τοὺς ἀκούοντας εἰσῆλθε καὶ φρίκη
περίφοβος καὶ ἔλεος πολύδακρυς καὶ πόθος φιλοπενθής, ἐπ᾽
ἀλλοτρίων τε πραγμάτων καὶ σωμάτων εὐτυχίαις καὶ δυσ-
πραγίαις ἴδιόν τι πάθημα διὰ τῶν λόγων ἔπαθεν ἡ ψυχή.
—GORGIAS, *Encomium of Helen* 8–9

*Speech is a great power, which by means of the smallest and most
invisible form effects the most divine works: it has the power to
stop fear and take away grief and create joy and increase pity . . .
I both consider and define all poetry as speech with meter. Fearful
shuddering and tearful pity and longing that delights in mourning
come upon its hearers, and at the actions and physical sufferings of
others in good fortunes and in evil fortunes the soul experiences a
suffering, through words, of its own.*

Tragedy often forced Athens to confront itself. Athenian tragedy examines
the policies, actions, belief structures, and values of its citizens. It does so,
however, only for the duration of the performance. In the end, for all that
examination and after all the suffering, these same policies, actions, belief
structures, and values are often only reaffirmed for the spectators. In this way
only then might Euripides be called a "pacifist," in that he challenged the
Athenians to witness and consider the suffering that they were not only in
the process of inflicting on others but also might one day experience themselves. Ultimately, though, no tragedy could have affected the course of the
Peloponnesian War, and no tragedy did. Edith Hamilton found Euripides to

be a visionary precisely because no one took the message that she assumed Euripides was trying to send: "In that faraway age a man saw with perfect clarity what war was, and wrote what he saw in a play of surpassing power, and then—nothing happened."[1]

We might make a similar observation about the practice of enslaving captives of war. Joseph Vogt observes of slaves in Euripidean tragedy: "Real slaves, even if they are noble according to their possibilities, never reach the full stature of individuals; nobles on the other hand retain their freedom in captivity, for they are incapable of lowering themselves. Both sides often speak about the fate of slavery, but no one suggests that slavery ought not exist."[2] Tragedy questions and confronts the fundamental institutions of humankind, but it is not designed to preach or dictate policy.[3]

In this book I have argued that the captive woman's lament, particularly as it is employed in the Trojan War plays of Euripides, was a particularly effective vehicle with which to explore and even challenge wartime ideologies. I submit that the lament in tragedy is effective for such an examination because, as Nicole Loraux has emphasized most recently, it is so affective on both a personal and collective level.[4] Though it is often infused with contemporary rhetoric, tragedy is not a political debate in the assembly; it is an emotional experience undergone in common by the citizens of Athens within the city's religious space.[5] The act of viewing tragedy as a notional totality of the citizen body is a necessarily civic event, but I agree with Loraux that there is a deeply emotional dimension as well that has been underemphasized in recent years in favor of the intellectual and the political.[6]

The essential emotions of tragedy, according to Aristotle, are pity and fear, the rousing of which produces a kind of purification (*katharsis*),[7] and

1. Hamilton 1971, 1.

2. Vogt 1975, 21.

3. In saying this I do not mean to deny the profound educational and civic importance that tragedy was accorded by the Athenians themselves, on which see, e.g., Dué 2003 with further bibliography and ancient testimony there.

4. In Plato's *Republic* Socrates argues that tragedy and comedy cannot be admitted into the ideal state because in the context of the theater people allow themselves to react emotionally (either with grief or laughter) to things to which in their individual daily lives they ordinarily would not allow themselves to react. The theater encourages the abandonment of self-restraint, and the spectator is too easily overwhelmed by the collective emotions produced by the shared experience of viewing; see Plato, *Republic* 605c6–606d.

5. Loraux 2002.

6. An important exception to this trend is Segal 1993; see also Stanford 1983.

7. On *katharsis*, see chapter 2, note 8.

at various points in this book I have suggested links between the captive woman's lament and both of these emotions. Gorgias too, a closer witness to the fifth century than Aristotle, noted the powerful emotional effects that speech can have on its hearers. In the extract I quote above, when Gorgias speaks about poetry, he singles out three emotions that I would argue are central to tragic rhetoric (in both its spoken and sung forms): "fearful shuddering and tearful pity and longing (*pothos*) that delights in mourning." As I bring my study to a conclusion, I propose to explore these three emotions and their relationship to the captive woman's lament in Greek tragedy.

Gorgias' comment is perhaps our earliest indication outside of the dramas themselves that for the Athenians the emotion of pity is fundamentally linked to tears (*poludakrus*).[8] Pity is the emotion that makes one cry.[9] Pity, however, can be felt only for people and events that are a few steps removed from the spectator. Aristotle explains that pity may be felt for the misfortunes of an acquaintance, but if the events are too closely connected to the individual, that person experiences fear.[10] The essential difference is that the misfortunes of an acquaintance are merely a *representation* of one's own potential suffering and so elicit pity, whereas one's own suffering brings about the fear that makes one shudder.

And so, following Aristotle's lead, we might say that the otherness of the Trojan women is part of what enables them to elicit tears of pity from a Greek audience.[11] Like other heroes of the tragic stage, they are removed physically, geographically, and chronologically from their Athenian audience. They are also captive slaves and foreign women, and perhaps this increased distance likewise serves an emotional purpose in the complex system of

8. See also Segal 1993, 26. Segal argues that lamentation within tragedy is an emotional cue for the audience.

9. Cf. the anecdote in Plutarch's *Life of Pelopidas* 29 about Alexander, the famously cruel tyrant of Pherae, who abruptly left a performance of the *Trojan Women* because "he was ashamed to be seen by the citizens weeping for sufferings of Hecuba and Andromache, when he had never pitied any of the people that he had killed" (αἰσχυνόμενος τοὺς πολίτας, εἰ μηδένα πώποτε τῶν ὑπ' αὐτοῦ φονευομένων ἠλεηκώς, ἐπὶ τοῖς Ἑκάβης καὶ Ἀνδρομάχης κακοῖς ὀφθήσεται δακρύων). The anecdote again shows the connection between pity and tears. See also Flashar 1956.

10. See Aristotle, *Rhetoric* 1382b26–1383a12, 1385b11–1386b7; Janko 1987 *ad Poetics* 1453a4; and Konstan 2001, 49–74.

11. As Aristotle makes clear in the *Rhetoric,* however, pity can be felt only for misfortune that could happen to oneself or a loved one and seems near (see citations in note 10 above). On the distinction between "one's own" (*oikeia*) and "someone else's" (*allotria*) in Plato's analysis of the emotions of tragedy see also the discussion of Rosenbloom (1995, 101–4).

tragic meaning. The distance inherent in any Trojan War drama seems to have contributed to this dynamic of pity and tears.[12]

But the distance between the world of heroes in the there and then and the world of the audience in the here and now was bridged by the tragic chorus, who maintained a physical connection to the audience (via their location in the orchestra) and mediated between the two worlds.[13] And this chorus could consist of captive women, who, like the tragic protagonists, sang laments, and unlike the protagonists, were nonprofessional Athenian youths. This crucial element, taken together with the contemporary resonance of many tragedies, but especially the Trojan War tragedies, leads me to suggest that the captive woman's lament was also an effective tool for eliciting fear.[14] The fate of the Trojans could be the Athenians', and that same fate certainly was inflicted by the Athenians on others. The plight of the captive woman was very near the Athenians indeed in the latter portion of the fifth century B.C.

I have also argued that Gorgias' third emotion, *pothos philopenthês*, longing that delights in mourning, is an essential feature of tragedy, and perhaps even, *pace* Aristotle, the defining emotion of the Trojan War tragedies.[15] The *pothos* that the captive woman's lament inspires is a complex one. The captive woman longs for her husband, sons, father, city, and freedom. The women around her likewise lament those entities. The Athenian audience, on the other hand, longs for the dead heroes of the remote past who died before Troy, or perhaps for the dead youth who have died in battle far more recently, or perhaps simply for the release through tears that the theater provides—or perhaps all at the same time. The *pothos* of tragedy can be erotic, spiritual, or patriotic, but above all it is full of grief.

And it is this emotion of tearful longing that universalizes the experiences of Greeks, Trojans, Athenians, and barbarians in connection with war. I have argued that the institution of tragedy provided a space for the Athenians in which barriers between Greek and barbarian, male and female, and citizen and slave could be tested and temporarily blurred. In this same space the sufferings of their own enemies and defeated victims could be explored, a

---

12. On the significance of the distance (geographical, chronological, and emotional) built in to the plots of Athenian dramas, a distance seemingly required for the exploration of critical civic issues, see Zeitlin 1990.

13. See chapter 5.

14. See chapter 4.

15. See especially chapters 1 and 2.

possibility that I have found to be extraordinary and that points to an appreciation of shared humanity.[16]

When we consider as a point of comparison the representation in the media of the recent (2003) and ongoing conflict in Iraq, the difference is striking. Americans now have access to news at all times of the day and night on television and on the World Wide Web, with the result that we are bombarded with images of war. The human dimension is central to this media coverage, but it is almost invariably the American (or European) human interest that is the focus. Every American soldier who is taken prisoner, killed, or even wounded is extensively profiled, their picture displayed reverently and their family interviewed. Rarely does the face of an Iraqi soldier or bereaved loved one make it to the television screen.

If we turn back to the ancient world, we find that this appreciation on the part of the fifth-century Athenians may not be so extraordinary after all. On a pithos from the island of Mykonos dated to around 675 B.C., one of the very earliest surviving representations of the fall of Troy in art, a series of panels shows the Trojan women taken captive and their children slain before their eyes.[17] The creator of that pithos, like Euripides, knew what war was, and depicted it with perfect clarity. As is in keeping with the dynamics of myth and an oral tradition that far predates the Athenian institution of tragedy, already in 675 the experiences of the Trojan women were iconic and emblematic of wartime suffering.

Concern for the victims of war, as exemplified by the Trojan women, is one of the many continuities that unite the epic and the tragic poetic traditions. The significance of the Trojan War and the lessons taught by it changed with each new era of history, and yet the emotional dynamic, as evoked by the captive woman's lament, remained remarkably constant.

---

16. Cf. Segal 1993, 26–27: "Such emotional participation enlarges our sympathies and so our humanity. Aristotle's closest approximation to 'humanity' in this sense is his term *to philanthrôpon,* and he associates it with pity and fear in one passage (1452b38) and with the tragic in general in another (1456a21). This expansion of our sensibilities in compassion for others is also part of the tragic catharsis. We can be moved to such compassion because we accept fears as our own and acknowledge that the pity and grief for the tragic protagonist's suffering imply pity and grief for the suffering of all men and women and do, in fact, constitute a concern to 'all the citizens' and 'all' the spectators."

17. This pithos is more famous for the depiction on its neck of the wooden horse. On the Mykonos pithos see Ervin 1963; Caskey (= Ervin) 1976; Hurwit 1985, 173–76; and Anderson 1997, 182–91.

BIBLIOGRAPHY

ABBREVIATIONS

AJA   *American Journal of Archaeology*
AJP   *American Journal of Philology*
BICS   *Bulletin of the Institute of Classical Studies of the University of London*
BMCR   *Bryn Mawr Classical Review*
CA   *Classical Antiquity*
CJ   *Classical Journal*
CP   *Classical Philology*
CQ   *Classical Quarterly*
HSCP   *Harvard Studies in Classical Philology*
JHS   *Journal of Hellenic Studies*
LIMC   H. C. Ackermann and J.-R. Gisler, eds. *Lexicon Iconographicum Mythologiae Classicae*. Zurich: Artemis Verlag, 1981–1997.
QUCC   *Quaderni Urbinati di Cultura Classica*
RE   A. Pauly, G. Wissowa, and W. Kroll, eds. *Realenzyklopädie der klassischen Altertumswissenschaft*. Stuttgart, 1893–.
TAPA   *Transactions and Proceedings of the American Philological Association*

Abrahamson, E. L. 1952. "Euripides' Tragedy of Hecuba." *TAPA* 83: 120–29.

Abu-Lughod, L. 1999. *Veiled Sentiments: Honor and Poetry in a Bedouin Society*. 2d ed. Berkeley: University of California Press.

Adams, S. 1952. "Salamis Symphony: The *Persae* of Aeschylus." In White 1952: 46–54.

Aélion, R. 1983. *Euripide, héritier d'Eschyle*. Paris: Belles Lettres.

Ahlberg-Cornell, G. 1992. *Myth and Epos in Early Greek Art: Representation and Interpretation*. Jonsered, Sweden: Paul Åströms Förlag.

Aitken, E., and J. Maclean, eds. 2001. *Philostratus: Heroikos*. Atlanta, Ga.: Society of Biblical Literature.

———. 2003. *Philostratus: On Heroes*. Atlanta, Ga.: Society of Biblical Literature.

Alden, M. 2000. *Homer beside Himself: Para-Narratives in the Iliad*. Oxford: Oxford University Press.

Alexiou, M. 1974. *The Ritual Lament in Greek Tradition*. Cambridge: Cambridge University Press. 2d ed., ed. P. Roilos and D. Yatromanolakis. Lanham, Md.: Rowman and Littlefield, 2002.

———. 2001. *After Antiquity: Greek Language, Myth, and Metaphor.* Ithaca, N.Y.: Cornell University Press.

Alexiou, M., and P. Dronke. 1971. "The Lament of Jephta's Daughter: Themes, Traditions, Originality." *Studi Medievali,* 3d series, vol. 12: 819–63.

Allan, W. 2000. *The* Andromache *and Euripidean Tragedy.* Oxford: Oxford University Press.

Allen, T. W., ed. 1921. *The Homeric Catalogue of Ships.* Oxford: Clarendon Press.

Anderson, M. J. 1997. *The Fall of Troy in Early Greek Poetry and Art.* Oxford: Clarendon Press.

Anderson, M. J., ed. 1965. *Classical Drama and Its Influence: Essays Presented to H. D. F. Kitto.* London: Methuen.

Arnould, D. 1990. *Le rire et les larmes dans la littérature grecque d'Homère à Platon.* Paris: Belles Lettres.

Atallah, W. 1966. *Adonis dans la littérature et l'art grecs.* Paris: C. Klincksieck.

Bacon, H. 1961. *Barbarians in Greek Tragedy.* New Haven: Yale University Press.

Bailey, C., ed. 1936. *Greek Poetry and Life: Essays Presented to Gilbert Murray on His Seventieth Birthday.* Oxford: Clarendon Press.

Baldry, H. C. 1961. "The Idea of the Unity of Mankind." In Reverdin 1961: 167–95.

Barlow, S., ed. 1986. *Euripides* Trojan Women. Warminster, England: Aris and Phillips.

Bartók, B., and A. B. Lord. 1951. *Serbo-Croatian Folk Songs: Texts and Translations of Seventy-Five Folk Songs from the Milman Parry Collection and a Morphology of Serbo-Croatian Melodies.* New York: Columbia University Press.

Bassi, K. 1998. *Acting Like Men: Gender, Drama, and Nostalgia in Ancient Greece.* Ann Arbor: University of Michigan Press.

Beissinger, M., J. Tylus, and S. Wofford, eds. 1999. *Epic Traditions in the Contemporary World: The Poetics of Community.* Berkeley: University of California Press.

Blok, J. 2001. "Virtual Voices: Toward a Choreography of Women's Speech in Classical Athens." In Lardinois and McClure 2001: 95–116.

Blumenthal, A. von. 1927. "Sophokles." *RE* 3 A 1052.

Boardman, J. 1989. *Athenian Red Figure Vases of the Classical Period.* New York: Thames and Hudson.

Boedeker, D. 1998. "Presenting the Past in Fifth-Century Athens." In Boedeker and Raaflaub 1998: 185–202.

Boedeker, D., and K. Raaflaub, eds. 1998. *Democracy, Empire, and the Arts in Fifth-Century Athens.* Cambridge, Mass.: Harvard University Press.

Borthwick, E. 1976. " 'Flower of the Argives' and a Neglected Meaning of *Anthos.*" *JHS* 96: 1–7.

Bouvrie, S. des. 1990. *Women in Greek Tragedy: An Anthropological Approach.* Oxford: Oxford University Press.

Bowers, J. 1993. "Women's Music and the Life Cycle." *International League of Women Composers Journal* (October): 14–20.

Bremmer, J. 1999. "Transvestite Dionysus." In Padilla 1999: 183–200.

Brown, W. E. 1965–1966. "Sophocles' Ajax and Homer's Hector." *CJ* 65: 118–21.

Burgess, J. S. 2001. *The Tradition of the Trojan War in Homer and the Epic Cycle.* Baltimore: Johns Hopkins University Press.

Burian, P. 1985. *Directions in Euripidean Criticism.* Durham, N.C.: Duke University Press.

Burnett, A. P. 1977. "*Trojan Women* and the Ganymede Ode." *Yale Classical Studies* 25: 291–316.

———. 1994. "Hekabe the Dog." *Arethusa* 27: 151–64.

————. 1998. *Revenge in Attic and Later Tragedy*. Berkeley: University of California Press.

Cairns, D. 1993. *Aidos: The Psychology and Ethics of Honour and Shame in Ancient Greek Literature*. Oxford: Clarendon Press.

Calame, C. 1977. *Les choeurs de jeunes filles en Grèce archaïque*. Rome: Edizioni dell'Ateneo e Bizzarri.

————. 1994–1995. "From Choral Poetry to Tragic Stasimon: The Enactment of Women's Song." *Arion* 3: 136–54.

————. 1999a. *Choruses of Young Women in Ancient Greece: Their Morphology, Religious Role, and Social Function*, trans. D. Collins and J. Orion. Lanham, Md.: Rowman and Littlefield.

————. 1999b. *The Poetics of Eros in Ancient Greece*, trans. J. Lloyd. Princeton: Princeton University Press.

————. 1999c. "Performative Aspects of the Choral Voice in Greek Tragedy: Civic Identity in Performance." In Goldhill and Osborne 1999: 125–53.

Caraveli, A. 1986. "The Bitter Wounding: Lament as a Social Protest in Rural Greece." In Dubisch 1986: 169–94.

Caraveli-Chavez, A. 1978. *Love and Lamentation in Greek Oral Poetry*. Ph.D. dissertation, State University of New York.

————. 1980. "Bridge between Two Worlds: The Women's Ritual Lament as Communicative Event." *Journal of American Folklore* 93: 129–57.

Carlisle, M., and O. Levaniouk, eds. 1999. *Nine Essays on Homer*. Lanham, Md.: Rowman and Littlefield.

Carpenter, T. H. 1991. *Art and Myth in Ancient Greece: A Handbook*. London: Thames and Hudson.

Carson, A. 1986. *Eros the Bittersweet*. Princeton: Princeton University Press.

Cartledge, P. 1993. *The Greeks: A Portrait of Self and Other*. Oxford: Oxford University Press.

————. 1997. " 'Deep Plays': Theatre as Process in Greek Civic Life." In Easterling 1997: 3–35.

————. 1998. "The *Machismo* of the Athenian Empire—or the Reign of the *Phaulus?*" In Foxhall and Salmon 1998b: 54–67.

Cartledge, P., P. Millet, and S. Todd, eds. 1990. *Nomos: Essays in Athenian Law, Politics, and Society*. Cambridge: Cambridge University Press.

Cary, H. F., trans. 1914. *Dante's* Inferno. New York: P. F. Collier.

Caskey, M. E. 1976. "Notes on Relief Pithoi of the Tenian-Boiotian Group." *AJA* 80: 19–41.

Castriota, D. 1992. *Myth, Ethos, and Actuality: Official Art in Fifth-Century B.C. Athens*. Madison: University of Wisconsin Press.

Clerke, A. M. 1892. *Familiar Studies In Homer*. London: Longmans, Green.

Clifford, J. 1986. "Introduction: Partial Truths." In Clifford and Marcus 1986: 1–26.

Clifford, J., and G. Marcus, eds. 1986. *Writing Culture*. Berkeley: University of California Press.

Cohen, B. 1997. "Divesting the Female Breast of Clothes in Classical Sculpture." In Koloski-Ostrow and Lyons 1997: 66–92.

————, ed. 2000. *Not the Classical Ideal: Athens and the Construction of the Other in Greek Art*. Leiden: Brill.

Cohen, D. 1995. *Law, Violence, and Community in Classical Athens*. Cambridge: Cambridge University Press.

Coleridge, E. P., trans. 1891. *The Plays of Euripides*. London: George Bell.

Collard, C. 1991. *Euripides:* Hecuba. Warminster, England: Aris and Phillips.

Conacher, D. J. 1967. *Euripidean Drama: Myth, Theme, and Structure.* Toronto: University of Toronto Press.

———. 1974. "Aeschylus' *Persae*: A Literary Commentary." In Heller 1974: 141–68.

Connor, W. R. Forthcoming. "The Herms of Eion." Center for Hellenic Studies.

Coote, M. 1977. "Women's Songs in Serbo-Croatian." *Journal of American Folklore* 90: 331–38.

———. 1992. "On the Composition of Women's Songs." *Oral Tradition* 7: 332–48.

Corcella, A. 1984. *Erodoteo e l'analogia.* Palermo: Sellerio.

Croally, N. T. 1994. *Euripidean Polemic: The* Trojan Women *and the Function of Tragedy.* Cambridge: Cambridge University Press.

Cropp, M., K. Lee, and D. Sansone, eds. 1999–2000. *Euripides and Tragic Theatre in the Late Fifth Century* (*Illinois Classical Studies* 24–25).

Csapo, E., and W. Slater, eds. 1994. *The Context of Ancient Drama.* Ann Arbor: University of Michigan Press.

Daitz, S. 1971. "Concepts of Freedom and Slavery in Euripides' *Hecuba.*" *Hermes* 99: 217–26.

Danforth, L. 1982. *The Death Rituals of Rural Greece.* Princeton: Princeton University Press.

Davidson, O. M. 2000. *Comparative Literature and Classical Persian Poetics.* Costa Mesa, Calif.: Mazda.

Davies, M., ed. 1988. *Epicorum Graecorum Fragmenta.* Göttingen: Vandenhoek and Ruprecht.

———. 1989. *The Epic Cycle.* Bristol: Bristol Classical Press.

Delebecque, E. 1951. *Euripide et la guerre du Péloponnèse.* Paris: C. Klincksieck.

Derderian, K. 2001. *Leaving Words to Remember: Greek Mourning and the Advent of Literacy* (*Mnemosyne* Suppl. 209). Leiden: Brill.

Detienne, M. 1994. *The Gardens of Adonis: Spices in Greek Mythology,* trans. J. Lloyd. Princeton: Princeton University Press.

Doherty, L. 1996. *Siren Songs: Gender, Audiences, and Narrators in the* Odyssey. Ann Arbor: University of Michigan Press.

Dougherty, C. 1993. *The Poetics of Colonization: From City to Text in Archaic Greece.* New York: Oxford University Press.

Dubisch, J., ed. 1986. *Gender and Power in Rural Greece.* Princeton: Princeton University Press.

Dubois, P. 1984. *Centaurs and Amazons.* Ann Arbor: University of Michigan Press.

Dué, C. 2000. "Tragic History and Barbarian Speech in Sallust's *Jugurtha.*" *HSCP* 100: 311–25.

———. 2001. "Achilles' Golden Amphora in Aeschines' *Against Timarchus* and the Afterlife of Oral Tradition." *CP* 96: 33–47.

———. 2002. *Homeric Variations on a Lament by Briseis.* Lanham, Md.: Rowman and Littlefield.

———. 2003. "Poetry and the Dêmos: State Regulation of a Civic Possession." In C. W. Blackwell, ed., *Dêmos: Classical Athenian Democracy* (A. Mahoney and R. Scaife, eds., *The Stoa: A Consortium for Electronic Publication in the Humanities*) (edition of January 31, 2003). http://www.stoa.org/projects/demos/article_poetry_and_demos?page=1.

Dué, C., M. Ebbott, and D. Yatromanolakis, eds. 2001–. *Homer and the Papyri.* Center for Hellenic Studies. http://chs.harvard.edu/homer_papyri.

Dué, C., and G. Nagy. 2003. "Preliminaries to the *On Heroes* of Philostratus." In Aitken and Maclean 2003: xvii–xliii.

Dunn, F. 1996. *Tragedy's End: Closure and Innovation in Euripidean Drama*. New York: Oxford University Press.

Easterling, P. E. 1984. "The Tragic Homer." *BICS* 31: 1–8.

———. 1987. "Women in Tragic Space." *BICS* 34: 15–26.

———. 1996. "Weeping, Witnessing, and the Tragic Audience: Response to Segal." In Silk 1996: 173–81.

———, ed. 1997. *The Cambridge Companion to Greek Tragedy*. Cambridge: Cambridge University Press.

Ebbott, M. 1999. "The Wrath of Helen: Self-Blame and Nemesis in the *Iliad*." In Carlisle and Levaniouk 1999: 3–20.

———. 2000. "The List of the War Dead in Aeschylus' *Persians*." *HSCP* 100: 83–96.

———. 2003. *Imagining Illegitimacy in Classical Greek Literature*. Lanham, Md.: Lexington Books.

———. 2005. "Marginal Characters in Greek Tragedy." In Gregory 2005.

Erskine, A. 2001. *Troy between Greece and Rome: Local Tradition and Imperial Power*. Oxford: Oxford University Press.

Ervin, M. 1963. "A Relief Pithos from Mykonos." *Archaiologikon Deltion* 18: 37–75.

Ferrari, G. 1990. "Figures of Speech: The Picture of *Aidos*." *Mêtis* V: 185–200.

———. 1997. "Figures in the Text: Metaphors and Riddles in the *Agamemnon*." *CP* 92: 1–45.

———. 2000. "The Ilioupersis in Athens." *HSCP* 100: 119–50.

———. 2002a. "The Ancient Temple on the Acropolis at Athens." *AJA* 106: 11–36.

———. 2002b. *Figures of Speech: Men and Maidens in Ancient Greece*. Chicago: University of Chicago Press.

Figueira, T., and G. Nagy, eds. 1985. *Theognis of Megara: Poetry and the Polis*. Baltimore: Johns Hopkins University Press.

Finkelberg, M. 1988. "Ajax' Entry in the Hesiodic Catalogue of Women." *CQ* 38: 31–41.

Finley, M., ed. 1960. *Slavery in Classical Antiquity: Views and Controversies*. Cambridge: W. Heffer.

———. 1980. *Ancient Slavery and Modern Ideology*. London: Chatto and Windus.

———. 1981. *Economy and Society in Ancient Greece*. Ed. B. Shaw and R. Saller. London: Chatto and Windus.

———, ed. 1987. *Classical Slavery*. London: Frank Cass.

Fisher, N. 1990. "The Law of Hubris in Athens." In Cartledge, Millett, and Todd 1990: 147–65.

———. 1992. *Hybris: A Study in the Values of Honour and Shame in Ancient Greece*. Warminster, England: Aris and Phillips.

———. 1993. *Slavery in Classical Greece*. London: Bristol Classical Press.

Flashar, H. 1956. "Die medizinischen Grundlagen der Lehre von der Wirkung der Dichtung in der griechischen Poetik." *Hermes* 84: 12–48.

Flueckiger, J. 1996. *Gender and Genre in the Folklore of Middle India*. Ithaca, N.Y.: Cornell University Press.

Foley, H. 1978. "Reverse Similes and Sex Roles in the *Odyssey*." *Arethusa* 11: 14–21.

———. 2001. *Female Acts in Greek Tragedy*. Princeton: Princeton University Press.

———. 2003. "Choral Identity in Greek Tragedy." *CP* 98: 1–30.

Foley, J. M., ed. 1990. *Oral Formulaic Theory: A Folklore Casebook*. New York: Garland.

———. 1999. *Homer's Traditional Art*. University Park: Pennsylvania State University Press.

———. 2002. *How to Read an Oral Poem*. Urbana: University of Illinois Press.

Fornara, C. W. 1971a. *Herodotus: An Interpretive Essay*. Oxford: Oxford University Press.

———. 1971b. "Evidence for the Date of Herodotus' Publication." *JHS* 91: 25–34.

Fowler, R. L. 1987. "The Rhetoric of Desperation." *HSCP* 91: 5–38.

Foxhall, L., and J. Salmon, eds. 1998a. *Thinking Men: Masculinity and Its Self-Representation in the Classical Tradition*. New York: Routledge.

———, eds. 1998b. *When Men Were Men: Masculinity, Power, and Identity in Classical Antiquity*. New York: Routledge.

Frame, D. 1978. *The Myth of the Return in Early Greek Epic*. New Haven: Yale University Press.

Friis Johansen, K. 1967. *The* Iliad *in Early Greek Art*. Copenhagen: Munksgaard.

Frisone, F. 2000. *Leggi e regolamenti funerari nel mondo Greco I: Le fonti epigraphiche*. Lecce: Università di Lecce, Scoula di Specializzazione in Archeologia Classica e Medioevale.

Gagarin, M. 1976. *Aeschylean Drama*. Berkeley: University of California Press.

Gamel, M.-K. 1999. "Staging Ancient Drama: The Difference Women Make," in Porter, Csapo, Marshall, and Ketterer 1999: 22–42.

Gantz, T. 1993. *Early Greek Myth*. Baltimore: Johns Hopkins University Press.

Garlan, Y. 1987. "War, Piracy, and Slavery in the Greek World." In Finley 1987: 9–27.

———. 1988. *Slavery in Ancient Greece,* trans. J. Lloyd. Ithaca, N.Y.: Cornell University Press.

Garland, R. 1985. *The Greek Way of Death*. Ithaca, N.Y.: Cornell University Press.

Gellrich, M. 1995. "Interpreting Greek Tragedy: History, Theory, and the New Philology." In Goff 1995: 38–58.

Gennep, A. van. 1960. *The Rites of Passage,* trans. M. Vizedom and G. Caffe. Chicago: University of Chicago Press.

Goetsch, S., and P. Toohey, eds. 1995. *How Is It Played? Genre, Performance, and Meaning* (*Didaskalia* Suppl. 1). http://didaskalia.open.ac.uk/issues/supplement1/index.html.

Goff, B., ed. 1995. *History, Tragedy, Theory: Dialogues on Athenian Drama*. Austin: University of Texas Press.

Goldhill, S. *Reading Greek Tragedy*. 1986. Cambridge: Cambridge University Press.

———. 1988. "Battle Narratives and Politics in Aeschylus' *Persae*." *JHS* 108: 189–93.

———. 1996. "Collectivity and Otherness—The Authority of the Tragic Chorus." In Silk 1996: 244–56.

———. 1997. "The Audience of Athenian Tragedy." In Easterling 1997: 54–68.

Goldhill, S., and R. Osborne, eds. 1993. *Art and Text*. Cambridge: Cambridge University Press.

Goossens, R. 1962. *Euripede et Athènes*. Brussels: Palais des Académies.

Gould, J. 1996. "Tragedy and Collective Experience." In Silk 1996: 217–43.

Graver, M. 1995. "Dog-Helen and Homeric Insult." *CA* 14: 41–61.

Greene, T. M. 1999. "The Natural Tears of Epic." In Beissinger, Tylus, and Wofford 1999: 189–202.

Gregory, J. 1991. *Euripides and the Instruction of the Athenians*. Ann Arbor: University of Michigan Press.

———, ed. 1999. *Euripides:* Hecuba. Atlanta, Ga.: Scholars Press.

———, ed. 2005. *The Blackwell Companion to Greek Tragedy*. Oxford: Blackwell.

Griffin, J. 1977. "The Epic Cycle and the Uniqueness of Homer." *JHS* 97: 39–53.

Griffith, M. 2001. "Antigone and Her Sister(s): Embodying Women in Greek Tragedy." In Lardinois and McClure 2001: 117–36.

Hagedorn, S. 2004. *Abandoned Women: Rewriting the Classics in Dante, Boccaccio, and Chaucer.* Ann Arbor: University of Michigan Press.

Hall, E. 1989. *Inventing the Barbarian: Greek Self-Definition through Tragedy.* Oxford.

———, ed. 1996. *Aeschylus' Persians.* Warminster, England: Aris and Phillips.

———. 2000. "Introduction." In Morwood 2000: ix–xlii.

Hamilton, E. 1971. "A Pacifist in Periclean Athens." In Euripides, *Trojan Women,* trans. E. Hamilton. New York: Bantam.

Harrison, T. 2000. *The Emptiness of Asia: Aeschylus' "Persians" and the History of the Fifth Century.* London: Duckworth.

———, ed. 2002. *Greeks and Barbarians.* New York: Routledge.

Hartog, F. 1988. *The Mirror of Herodotus: The Representation of the Other in the Writing of History,* trans. J. Lloyd. Berkeley: University of California Press.

Haslam, M. 1997. "Homeric Papyri and Transmission of the Text." In Powell and Morris 1997: 55–100.

Hawke, J. 2004. "Review: Flavia Frisone, *Leggi e regolamenti funerari nel mondo Greco I: Le fonti epigraphiche.*" *BMCR* 2004.02.10. http://ccat.sas.upenn.edu/bmcr/2004/2004–02–10.html.

Heath, M. 1987a. *The Poetics of Greek Tragedy.* Stanford: Stanford University Press.

———. 1987b. *"Iure principem locum tenet:* Euripides' *Hecuba."* *BICS* 34: 40–68.

———. 2004. *Aristotle* Poetics: *A Bibliography.* University of Leeds, School of Classics (edition of June 21, 2004). http://www.leeds.ac.uk/classics/resources/poetics/poetbib.htm.

Hedreen, G. 1991. "The Cult of Achilles in the Euxine." *Hesperia* 60: 313–30.

Heller, J., ed. 1974. *Serta Turyniana: Studies in Greek Literature and Palaeography in Honor of Alexander Turyn.* Urbana: University of Illinois Press.

Henderson, J. 1991. "Women and the Athenian Dramatic Festivals." *TAPA* 121: 133–48.

Henrichs, A. 1994–1995. "Why Should I Dance? Choral Self-Referentiality in Greek Tragedy." *Arion* 3: 56–111.

———. 1996. "Dancing in Athens, Dancing on Delos: Some Patterns of Choral Projection in Euripides." *Philologus* 140: 48–62.

Herington, J. 1985. *Poetry into Drama: Early Tragedy and the Greek Poetic Tradition.* Berkeley: University of California Press.

Herzfeld, M. 1993. "In Defiance of Destiny: The Management of Time and Gender at a Cretan Funeral." *American Ethnologist* 20.2: 241–55.

Higbie, C. 1997. "The Bones of a Hero, the Ashes of a Politician: Athens, Salamis, and the Usable Past." *CA* 16: 279–308.

Holst-Warhaft, G. 1992. *Dangerous Voices: Women's Laments and Greek Literature.* New York: Routledge.

Householder, F., and G. Nagy. 1972. *Greek: A Survey of Recent Work (Current Trends in Linguistics* 9). The Hague: Mouton.

Hurwit, J. 1985. *The Art and Culture of Early Greece, 1100–480 B.C.* Ithaca, N.Y.: Cornell University Press.

———. 1999. *The Athenian Acropolis: History, Mythology, and Archaeology from the Neolithic Era to the Present.* Cambridge: Cambridge University Press.

Iakovidis, S. 1983. *Late Helladic Citadels on Mainland Greece.* Leiden: Brill.

Isaac, B. 2004. *The Invention of Racism in Classical Antiquity.* Princeton: Princeton University Press.

Janko, R., ed. 1987. *Aristotle,* Poetics I *with the* Tractatus Coislinianus, *A Hypothetical Reconstruction of* Poetics II, *and the Fragments of the* On Poets. Indianapolis: Hackett.

Jebb, R. C., ed. 1891. *The* Antigone *of Sophocles.* Cambridge: Cambridge University Press.

———, ed. 1893. *The* Ajax *of Sophocles.* Cambridge: Cambridge University Press.

Jenkins, T. 1999. "*Homêros ekainopoiêse:* Theseus, Aithra, and Variation in Homeric Myth-Making." In Carlisle and Levaniouk 1999: 207–26.

Jones, J. 1962. *On Aristotle and Greek Tragedy.* New York: Oxford University Press.

Jones, W. H. S., and H. A. Ormerod, trans. 1918. *Pausanias: Description of Greece.* Cambridge, Mass.: Harvard University Press.

Joshel, S., and S. Murnaghan, eds. 1998. *Women and Slaves in Greco-Roman Culture: Differential Equations.* New York: Routledge.

Jouan, F. 1966. *Euripide et les légendes des "chants cypriens," des origines de la guerre de Troie à l'"Iliade."* Paris: Belles Lettres.

Jowett, B., trans. 1895. *The Dialogues of Plato.* New York: Charles Scribner's Sons.

Judet de la Combe, P. 1995. "Sur la reprise d'Homère par Eschyle." *Lexis* 13: 129–44.

Käppel, L. 1998. *Die Konstruktion der Handlung in der* Orestie *des Aischylos: Die Makrostruktur des "Plot" als Sinnträger in der Darstellung des Geshlechterfluchs* (*Zetemata* 99). Munich: Beck.

Katz, M. A. 1998. "Did the Women of Ancient Athens Attend the Theater in the Eighteenth Century?" *CP* 93: 105–24.

Kebric, R. 1983. *The Paintings in the Cnidian Lesche at Delphi and Their Historical Context.* Leiden: Brill.

Kerewsky-Halpern, B. 1981. "Text and Context in Serbian Ritual Lament." *Canadian-American Slavic Studies* 15: 52–60.

Keuls, E. 1993. *The Reign of the Phallus: Sexual Politics in Ancient Athens.* 2d ed. Berkeley: University of California Press.

King, K. C. 1985. "The Politics of Imitation: Euripides' *Hekabe* and the Homeric Achilles." *Arethusa* 18: 47–66.

Kirk, G. S., ed. 1985. *The* Iliad: *A Commentary* I (Books 1–4). Cambridge: Cambridge University Press.

Kirkwood, G. M. 1947. "Hecuba and Nomos." *TAPA* 78: 61–68.

———. 1965. "Homer and Sophocles' *Ajax.*" In Anderson 1965: 51–70.

Kitto, H. 1961. *Greek Tragedy.* 3d ed. London: Methuen.

Knox, B. M. W. 1961. "The *Ajax* of Sophocles." *HSCP* 65: 1–37.

Koloski-Ostrow, A., and C. Lyons, eds. 1997. *Naked Truths: Women, Sexuality, and Gender in Classical Art and Archaeology.* New York: Routledge.

Konstan, D. 2001a. *Pity Transformed.* London: Duckworth.

———. 2001b. "*To Hellenikon Ethnos*: Ethnicity and the Construction of Ancient Greek Identity." In Malkin 2001: 29–50.

Koskoff, E., ed. 1987. *Women and Music in Cross-Cultural Perspective.* New York: Greenwood Press.

Kovacs, D. 1987. *The Heroic Muse: Studies in the* Hippolytus *and* Hecuba *of Euripides.* Baltimore, Md.: Johns Hopkins University Press.

Kron, U. 1981a. "Aithra I." *LIMC* I.1: 420–37.

———. 1981b. "Akamas and Demophon." *LIMC* I.1: 435–46.

Kurke, L. 1992. "The Politics of Ἀβροσύνη in Archaic Greece." *CA* 11: 90–121.

Lanza, D. 1988. "Les temps de l'émotion tragique: Malaise et soulagement." *Mêtis* III: 15–39.

Lardas, K. 1992. *Mourning Songs of Greek Women.* New York: Garland.

Lardinois, A., and L. McClure, eds. 2001. *Making Silence Speak: Women's Voices in Greek Literature and Society.* Princeton: Princeton University Press.

Larson, J. 1995. *Greek Heroine Cults.* Madison: University of Wisconsin Press.

Lebeck, A. 1971. *The* Oresteia: *A Study in Language and Structure.* Cambridge, Mass.: Harvard University Press.

Lee, K., ed. 1976. *Euripides'* Troades. New York: St. Martin's.

Lipking, L. 1988. *Abandoned Women and Poetic Tradition.* Chicago: University of Chicago Press.

Lloyd, M., ed. 1994. *Euripides'* Andromache. Warminster, England: Aris and Phillips.

Lohmann, D. 1970. *Die Komposition der Reden in der Ilias.* Berlin: de Gruyter.

Longo, O. 1990. "The Theater of the *Polis.*" In Winkler and Zeitlin 1990: 12–19.

Loraux, N. 1975. "HBH et ANΔPEIA: Deux versions de la mort du combattant athénien." *Ancient Society* 6: 1–31.

———. 1986. *The Invention of Athens: The Funeral Oration in the Classical City,* trans. A. Sheridan. Cambridge, Mass.: Harvard University Press.

———. 1987. *Tragic Ways of Killing a Woman,* trans. A. Forster. Cambridge, Mass.: Harvard University Press.

———. 1995. *The Experiences of Teiresias: The Feminine and the Greek Man,* trans. P. Wissing. Princeton: Princeton University Press.

———. 1998. *Mothers in Mourning,* trans. C. Pache. Ithaca, N.Y.: Cornell University Press.

———. 2000. *Born of the Earth: Myth and Politics in Athens,* trans. S. Stewart. Ithaca, N.Y.: Cornell University Press.

———. 2002. *The Mourning Voice: An Essay on Greek Tragedy,* trans. E. Rawlinson. Ithaca, N.Y.: Cornell University Press.

Lord, A. B. 1960. *The Singer of Tales.* Cambridge, Mass.: Harvard University Press, 1960. 2d rev. edition, ed. S. Mitchell and G. Nagy, 2000.

———. 1991. *Epic Singers and Oral Tradition.* Ithaca, N.Y.: Cornell University Press.

———. 1995. *The Singer Resumes the Tale.* Ithaca, N.Y.: Cornell University Press.

Mackie, H. 1996. *Talking Trojan: Speech and Community in the* Iliad. Lanham, Md.: Rowman and Littlefield.

Malkin, I., ed. 2001. *Ancient Perceptions of Greek Ethnicity.* Cambridge, Mass.: Harvard University Press.

Marshall, K., ed. 1993. *Rediscovering the Muses: Women's Musical Traditions.* Boston: Northeastern University Press.

Martin, R. P. 1989. *The Language of Heroes: Speech and Performance in the* Iliad. Ithaca, N.Y.: Cornell University Press.

Martino, E. de. 1958. *Morte e pianto rituale nel mondo antico.* Turin: Einaudi.

Mastronarde, D. 1998. "Il coro euripideo." *QUCC* 60: 55–80.

———. 1999. "Knowledge and Authority in the Choral Voice of Euripidean Tragedy." *Syllecta Classica* 10: 87–104.

————. 1999–2000. "Euripidean Tragedy and Genre: The Terminology and Its Problems." In Cropp, Lee, and Sansone 1999–2000: 23–40.

Maxwell-Stuart, P. 1973. "The Dramatic Poets and the Expedition to Sicily." *Historia* 22: 397–404.

McClure, L. 1999. *Spoken Like a Woman: Speech and Gender in Athenian Drama*. Princeton: Princeton University Press.

Meier, C. 1993. *The Political Art of Greek Tragedy*, trans. A. Webber. Baltimore: Johns Hopkins University Press.

Mendelsohn, D. 2002. *Gender and the City in Euripides' Political Plays*. Oxford: Oxford University Press.

Meritt, L. S. 1970. "The Stoa Poikile." *Hesperia* 39: 233–64.

Michelini, A. 1978. "HUBRIS and Plants." *HSCP* 82: 35–44.

————. 1982. *Tradition and Dramatic Form in the* Persians *of Aeschylus*. Leiden: Brill.

————. 1987. *Euripides and the Tragic Tradition*. Madison: University of Wisconsin Press.

Miles, S., ed. 1986. *Simone Weil: An Anthology*. New York: Wiedenfeld and Nicolson.

Miller, M. 1997. *Athens and Persia in the Fifth Century B.C.: A Study in Cultural Receptivity*. Cambridge: Cambridge University Press.

Mitchell, S., and G. Nagy. 2000. "Introduction to the Second Edition." In Lord 1960 (2000): vii–xxx.

Moles, J. 1996. "Herodotus Warns the Athenians." *Papers of the Leeds International Latin Seminar* 9: 259–84.

Monsacré, H. 1984. *Les larmes d'Achille: Le héros, la femme et la souffrance dans la poésie d'Homère*. Paris: A. Michel.

Morwood, J., ed. 2000. *Euripides'* Hecuba, The Trojan Women, Andromache. Oxford: Oxford University Press.

Mossman, J. 1995. *Wild Justice: A Study of Euripides'* Hecuba. Oxford: Clarendon Press.

Moulton, C. 1977. *Similes in the Homeric Poems*. Göttingen: Vandenhoeck and Ruprecht.

Muellner, L. 1990. "The Simile of the Cranes and Pygmies: A Study of Homeric Metaphor." *HSCP* 93: 59–101.

Munson, R. 2001. *Telling Wonders: Ethnographic and Political Discourse in the Work of Herodotus*. Ann Arbor: University of Michigan Press.

Murko, M. 1990. "The Singers and Their Epic Songs." *Oral Tradition* 5: 107–30.

Murnaghan, S. 1999. "The Poetics of Loss in Greek Epic." In Beissinger, Tylus, and Wofford 1999: 203–20.

Murry, G. 1940. *Aeschylus: The Creator of Tragedy*. Oxford: Oxford University Press.

Nagler, M. 1974. *Spontaneity and Tradition: A Study in the Oral Art of Homer*. Berkeley: University of California Press.

Nagy, G. 1974. *Comparative Studies in Greek and Indic Meter*. Cambridge, Mass.: Harvard University Press.

————. 1979. *Best of the Achaeans: Concepts of the Hero in Archaic Greek Poetry*. Baltimore: Johns Hopkins University Press. 2d ed., 1999.

————. 1985. "Theognis and Megara: A Poet's Vision of His City." In Figueira and Nagy 1985: 22–81.

————. 1987. "The Sign of Protesilaos," *Mêtis* II: 207–13.

————. 1990a. *Pindar's Homer: The Lyric Possession of an Epic Past*. Baltimore: Johns Hopkins University Press.

————. 1990b. *Greek Mythology and Poetics*. Ithaca, N.Y.: Cornell University Press.

————. 1993. "Alcaeus in Sacred Space." In Pretagostini 1993: 221–25.

————. 1994–1995a. "Genre and Occasion." *Mêtis* IX–X: 11–25.

————. 1994–1995b. "Transformations of Choral Lyric Traditions in the Context of Athenian State Theater." *Arion* 3: 41–55.

————. 1996a. *Poetry as Performance*. Cambridge: Cambridge University Press.

————. 1996b. *Homeric Questions*. Austin: University of Texas Press.

————. 1998. "Foreword." In Loraux 1998: ix–xii.

————. 1999. "Epic as Genre." In Beissinger, Tylus, and Wofford 1999: 21–32.

Nenola-Kallio, A. 1982. "Studies in Ingrian Lament." *FF Communications*. Helsinki: Academia Scientiarum Finnica.

Neuberger-Donath, R. 1996. "Τέρεν δάκρυον: θαλερὸν δάκρυον: Über den Unterschied der Characterisierung von Mann und Frau bei Homer." In *Classical Studies in Honor of David Sohlberg*, ed. R. Katzoff, V. Petroff, and D. Schaps, 57–60. Ramat Gan: Bar-Ilan University Press.

Nilsson, M. 1906. *Griechische Feste*. Leipzig: B. G. Teubner.

Nussbaum, M. 1986. *The Fragility of Goodness: Luck and Ethics in Greek Tragedy and Philosophy*. Cambridge: Cambridge University Press.

Ormand, K. 1999. *Exchange and the Maiden*. Austin: University of Texas Press.

Osborne, R. 1994. "Looking On, Greek Style: Does the Sculpted Girl Speak to Women Too?" In *Classical Greece: Ancient Histories and Modern Archaeologies*, ed. I. Morris, 81–96. Cambridge: Cambridge University Press.

Pache, C. 1999. "Odysseus and the Phaeacians." In Carlisle and Levaniouk 1999: 21–33.

Padilla, M. W., ed. 1999. *Rites of Passage in Ancient Greece*. Lewisburg: Bucknell University Press.

Page, D. L. 1936. "The Elegiacs in Euripides' *Andromache*." In Bailey 1936: 206–30.

————. 1959. *History and the Homeric Iliad*. Berkeley: University of California Press.

Parry, A., ed. 1971. *The Making of Homeric Verse: The Collected Papers of Milman Parry*. Oxford: Clarendon Press.

Parry, M. 1932. "Studies in the Epic Technique of Oral Versemaking, II: The Homeric Language as the Language of Oral Poetry." *HSCP* 43: 1–50 [repr. in A. Parry 1971: 325–64].

Patterson, O. 1991. *Freedom*, volume I: *Freedom in the Making of Western Culture*. New York: Basic Books.

Pelling, C., ed. 1997a. *Greek Tragedy and the Historian*. Oxford: Clarendon Press.

————. 1997b. "Aeschylus' *Persae* and History." In Pelling 1997a: 1–20.

————. 1997c. "East Is East and West Is West—Or Are They? National Stereotypes in Herodotus." *Histos* 1. http://www.dur.ac.uk/Classics/histos/1997/pelling.html.

Pickard-Cambridge, A. 1968. *The Dramatic Festivals of Athens*. 2d ed. Oxford: Clarendon Press.

Podlecki, A. J. 1990. "Could Women Attend the Theater in Ancient Athens? A Collection of Testimonia." *Ancient World* 21: 27–43.

Porter, J. R., E. Csapo, C. W. Marshall, and R. C. Ketterer, eds. 1999. *Crossing the Stages: The Production, Performance, and Reception of Ancient Theater* (*Syllecta Classica* 10).

Powell, B., and I. Morris, eds. 1997. *A New Companion to Homer*. Leiden: Brill.

Pozzi, D. 1991. "The Polis in Crisis." In Pozzi and Wickersham 1991: 126–63.

Pozzi, D., and J. Wickersham, eds. 1991. *Myth and the Polis*. Ithaca, N.Y.: Cornell University Press.

Pretagostini, R., ed. 1993. *Tradizione e innovazione nella cultura greca da Omero all'età ellenistica: Scritti in onore di Bruno Gentili.* Rome: Gruppo editoriale internazionale.

Raaflaub, K. 1987. "Herodotus, Political Thought, and the Meaning of History." *Arethusa* 20: 221–48.

Rabinowitz, N. 1993. *Anxiety Veiled: Euripides and the Traffic in Women.* Ithaca, N.Y.: Cornell University Press.

———. 1995. "The Male Actor of Greek Tragedy: Evidence of Misogyny or Gender-Bending?" In Goetsch and Toohey 1995. http://didaskalia.open.ac.uk/issues/supplementɪ/Rabinowitz.html.

———. 1998. "Slaves with Slaves: Women and Class in Euripidean Tragedy." In Joshel and Murnaghan 1998: 56–68.

———. 2000. "Review: Victoria Wohl, *The Intimate Commerce: Exchange, Gender, and Subjectivity in Greek Tragedy.*" *BMCR* 2000.08.28. http://ccat.sas.upenn.edu/bmcr/2000/2000-08-28.html.

Raheja, G., and A. Gold. 1994. *Listen to the Heron's Words: Reimagining Gender and Kinship in North India.* Berkeley: University of California Press.

Reckford, K. 1985. "Concepts of Demoralization in the *Hecuba.*" In Burian 1985: 112–28.

Reed, J. D. 1995. "The Sexuality of Adonis." *CA* 14: 317–47.

———, ed. 1997. *Bion of Smyrna: The Fragments and the Adonis.* Cambridge: Cambridge University Press.

Rehm, R. 1994. *Marriage to Death: The Conflation of Wedding and Funeral Rituals in Greek Tragedy.* Princeton: Princeton University Press.

———. 2002. *The Play of Space: Spatial Transformation in Greek Tragedy.* Princeton: Princeton University Press.

Reverdin, M. 1961. *Grecs et barbares* (Entretiens sur L'Antiquité Classique 8). Geneva: Fondation Hardt.

Reynolds, D. F. 1995. *Heroic Poets, Poetic Heroes: The Ethnography of Performance in an Arabic Oral Epic Tradition.* Ithaca, N.Y.: Cornell University Press.

Richardson, N., ed. 1993. *The* Iliad*: A Commentary.* Vol. VI. Cambridge: Cambridge University Press.

Ridgeway, W. 1910. *The Origin of Tragedy.* Cambridge: Cambridge University Press.

Ridgway, B. 1981. *Fifth Century Styles in Greek Sculpture.* Princeton: Princeton University Press.

———. 1991. *Prayers in Stone: Greek Architectural Sculpture.* Berkeley: University of California Press.

Riemer, P., and B. Zimmerman, eds. 1998. *Der Chor im antiken und modernen Drama.* Stuttgart: J. B. Metzler.

Robert, C. 1893. *Die Iliupersis des Polygnot* (Hallisches Winckelmannsprogram 17). Halle: M. Niemeyer.

Roilos, P., and D. Yatromanolakis, eds. 2002. 2d ed. of M. Alexiou, *The Ritual Lament in Greek Tradition.* Lanham, Md.: Rowman and Littlefield, 2002.

Rose, P. 1995. "Historicizing Sophocles' *Ajax.*" In Goff 1995: 59–90.

Rosen, R., and I. Sluiter, eds. 2003. *Andreia: Studies in Manliness and Courage in Classical Antiquity* (*Mnemosyne* Suppl. 238). Leiden: Brill.

Rosenblatt, P. C., R. Walsh, and A. Jackson, eds. 1976. *Grief and Mourning in Cross-Cultural Perspective.* New Haven: Human Relations Area Files Press.

Rosenbloom, D. 1995. "Myth, History, and Hegemony in Aeschylus." In Goff 1995: 91–130.

Saïd, S. 2002. "Greeks and Barbarians in Euripides' Tragedies: The End of Differences?" In Harrison 2002: 62–100.

Sainte Croix, G. E. M. de. 1981. *The Class Struggle in the Ancient Greek World: From the Archaic Age to the Arab Conquests.* Ithaca, N.Y.: Cornell University Press.

Saxonhouse, A. 1992. *Fear of Diversity: The Birth of Political Science in Ancient Greek Thought.* Chicago: University of Chicago Press.

Scaife, R. "The *Kypria* and Its Early Reception." *CA* 14: 164–92.

Schefold, K., and F. Jung. 1989. *Die Sagen von den Argonauten, von Theben und Troia in der klassischen und hellenistischen Kunst.* Munich: Hirmer.

Schein, S. 1984. *The Mortal Hero: An Introduction to Homer's Iliad.* Berkeley: University of California Press.

Schrier, O. 1998. *The* Poetics *of Aristotle and the* Tractatus Coislinianus: *A Bibliography from about 900 till 1996.* Leiden: Brill.

Scodel, R. 1980. *The Trojan Trilogy of Euripides* (*Hypomnemata* 60). Göttingen: Vandenhoeck and Ruprecht.

———. 1998. "The Captive's Dilemma: Sexual Acquiescence in Euripides' *Hecuba* and *Troades.*" *HSCP* 98: 137–54.

Scott, W. 1974. *The Oral Nature of the Homeric Simile.* Leiden: Brill.

Seaford, R. 1981. "Dionysiac Drama and the Dionysiac Mysteries." *CQ* 31: 252–75.

———. 1987. "The Tragic Wedding." *JHS* 107: 106–30.

———. 1994. *Reciprocity and Ritual: Homer and Tragedy in the Developing City-State.* Oxford: Clarendon Press.

———. 2003. "Aeschylus and the Unity of Opposites." *JHS* 123: 141–63.

Segal, C. 1971. "Andromache's Anagnorisis: Formulaic Artistry in *Iliad* 22.437–76." *HSCP* 75: 33–57.

———. 1990. "Violence and the Other: Greek, Female, and Barbarian in Euripides' *Hecuba.*" *TAPA* 120: 109–31 [reprinted in Segal 1993].

———. 1993. *Euripides and the Poetics of Sorrow.* Durham, N.C.: Duke University Press.

———. 1995. *Sophocles' Tragic World: Divinity, Nature, Society.* Cambridge, Mass.: Harvard University Press.

———. 1996. "Catharsis, Audience, and Closure in Greek Tragedy." In Silk 1996: 149–72.

Seidensticker, B. 1995. "Women on the Tragic Stage." In Goff 1995: 151–73.

Seremetakis, C. N. 1990. "The Ethics of Antiphony: The Social Construction of Pain, Gender, and Power in the Southern Peloponnese." *Ethos* 18: 481–511.

———. 1991. *The Last Word: Women, Death, and Divination in Inner Mani.* Chicago: University of Chicago Press.

Sideras, A. 1971. *Aeschylus Homericus: Untersuchungen zu den Homerismen der aischyleischen Sprache* (*Hypomnemata* 31). Göttingen: Vandenhoeck and Ruprecht.

Silk, M., ed. 1996. *Tragedy and the Tragic: Greek Theatre and Beyond.* Oxford: Clarendon Press.

———. 1998. "Style, Voice, and Authority in the Choruses of Greek Drama." In Riemer and Zimmerman 1998: 1–26.

Simon, E. 1992. "Menestheus." *LIMC* VI.1: 472–75.

Simpson, R. Hope, and J. Lazenby. 1970. *The Catalogue of the Ships in Homer's* Iliad. Oxford: Clarendon Press.

Sissa, G. 1990. *Greek Virginity,* trans. A. Goldhammer. Cambridge, Mass.: Harvard University Press.

Slatkin, L. 1991. *The Power of Thetis: Allusion and Interpretation in the* Iliad. Berkeley: University of California Press.

Smyth, H. W., trans. *Aeschylus.* Cambridge, Mass.: Harvard University Press, 1926.

Sommerstein, A., S. Halliwell, J. Henderson, and B. Zimmerman, eds. 1993. *Tragedy, Comedy, and the Polis.* Bari: Levante editori.

Sourvinou-Inwood, C. 1995. *"Reading" Greek Death: To the End of the Classical Period.* Oxford: Clarendon Press.

Stanford, W. B. 1983. *Greek Tragedy and the Emotions: An Introductory Study.* London: Routledge and Kegan Paul.

Stansbury-O'Donnell, M. 1989. "Polynotos's *Iliupersis*: A New Reconstruction." *AJA* 93: 203–15.

Steiner, D. 2001. *Images in Mind: Statues in Archaic and Classical Greek Literature and Thought.* Princeton: Princeton University Press.

Stieber, M. C. 2004. *The Poetics of Appearance in the Attic Korai.* Austin: University of Texas Press.

Sultan, N. 1993. "Private Speech, Public Pain: The Power of Women's Laments in Ancient Greek Poetry and Tragedy." In Marshall 1993: 92–110.

———. 1999. *Exile and the Poetics of Loss in Greek Tradition.* Lanham, Md.: Rowman and Littlefield.

Taplin, O. 1977. *The Stagecraft of Aeschylus: The Dramatic Use of Exits and Entrances in Greek Tragedy.* Oxford: Clarendon Press.

Thalmann, W. 1980. "Xerxes' Rage: Some Problems in Aeschylus." *AJP* 101: 260–82.

Thomson, G. 1946. *Aeschylus and Athens.* 2d ed. London: Lawrence and Wishart.

Tsagalis, C. 2004. *Epic Grief: Personal Laments in Homer's* Iliad. Berlin: De Gruyter.

Vermeule, E. 1979. *Aspects of Death in Early Greek Art and Poetry.* Berkeley: University of California Press.

Vernant, J.-P. 1991. *Mortals and Immortals.* Princeton: Princeton University Press.

Vernant, J.-P., and P. Vidal-Naquet. 1990. *Myth and Tragedy in Ancient Greece,* trans. J. Lloyd. Revised paperback edition. New York: Zone Books.

Vidal-Naquet, P. 1986. *The Black Hunter: Forms of Thought and Forms of Society in the Greek World,* trans. A. Szegedy-Maszak. Baltimore: Johns Hopkins University Press.

———. 1997. "The Place and Status of Foreigners in Athenian Tragedy." In Pelling 1997a: 110–119.

Vidan, A. 2003. *Embroidered with Gold, Strung with Pearls: The Traditional Ballads of Bosnian Women.* Cambridge, Mass.: Harvard University Press.

Vogt, J. 1975. *Ancient Slavery and the Ideal of Man,* trans. T. Wiedemann. Cambridge, Mass.: Harvard University Press.

Webster, T. B. L. 1970. *The Greek Chorus.* London: Methuen.

Wees, H. van. 1998. "A Brief History of Tears: Gender Differentiation in Archaic Greece." In Foxhall and Salmon 1998b: 10–53.

Weil, S. 1945. "The *Iliad,* or the Poem of Force," trans. M. McCarthy. First published in *Politics* (November 1945). [Reprinted in Miles 1986.]

West, M. L. 1990. *Studies in Aeschylus*. Stuttgart: B. G. Teubner.

———. 1998. *Homeri Ilias* I. Stuttgart: B. G. Teubner.

Westlake, H. 1953. "Euripides' *Troades:* 205–229." *Mnemosyne* 6: 181–91.

White, M., ed. 1952. *Studies in Honor of Gilbert Norwood*. Toronto: University of Toronto Press.

Wiedemann, T., ed. 1981. *Greek and Roman Slavery*. London: Croom Helm.

———, ed. 1987. *Slavery* (*Greece and Rome* 19). Oxford: Clarendon Press.

Winkler, J. 1985. "The Ephebes' Song." *Representations* 11: 26–62 [revised and reprinted in Winkler and Zeitlin 1990].

———. 1990a. *The Constraints of Desire: The Anthropology of Sex and Gender in Ancient Greece*. New York: Routledge.

———. 1990b. "The Ephebes' Song: *Tragoidia* and *Polis*." In Winkler and Zeitlin 1990: 20–62.

Winkler, J., and F. Zeitlin, eds. 1990. *Nothing To Do with Dionysus? Athenian Drama in Its Social Context*. Princeton: Princeton University Press.

Winnington-Ingram, R. 1983. *Studies in Aeschylus*. Cambridge: Cambridge University Press.

Wohl, V. 1998. *Intimate Commerce: Exchange, Gender, and Subjectivity in Greek Tragedy*. Austin: University of Texas Press.

Woodford, S. 2003. *Images of Myths in Classical Antiquity*. Cambridge: Cambridge University Press.

Wycherley, R. E. 1953. "The Painted Stoa." *Phoenix* 7: 20–35.

Zanker, G. 1992. "Sophocles' *Ajax* and the Heroic Values of the *Iliad*." *CQ* 42: 20–25.

Zeitlin, F. 1965. "The Motif of Corrupted Sacrifice in Aeschylus' *Oresteia*." *TAPA* 96: 463–508.

———. 1966. "Postscript to Sacrificial Imagery in the *Oresteia*." *TAPA* 97: 645–53.

———. 1990. "Thebes: Theater of Self and Society in Athenian Drama." In Winkler and Zeitlin 1990: 130–67.

———. 1993. "The Artful Eye: Vision, Ecphrasis, and Spectacle in Euripidean Theatre." In Goldhill and Osborne 1993: 138–96, 295–304.

———. 1995. "Art, Memory, and *Kleos* in Euripides' *Iphigeneia at Aulis*." In Goff 1995: 174–201.

———. 1996. *Playing the Other: Gender and Society in Classical Greek Literature*. Chicago: Chicago University Press.

INDEX